AFRICAN PERFORMANCE ARTS AND POLITICAL ACTS

T0244226

AFRICAN PERSPECTIVES
Kelly Askew and Anne Pitcher
Series Editors

African Performance Arts and Political Acts
Naomi André, Yolanda Covington-Ward, and Jendele Hungbo, Editors

There Used to Be Order:
Life on the Copperbelt after the Privatisation of the
Zambia Consolidated Copper Mines
Patience Mususa

Animated by Uncertainty: Rugby and the
Performance of History in South Africa
Joshua D. Rubin

Filtering Histories: The Photographic Bureaucracy
in Mozambique, 1960 to Recent Times,
by Drew A. Thompson

Aso Ebi: Dress, Fashion, Visual Culture, and
Urban Cosmopolitanism in West Africa,
by Okechukwu Nwafor

Unsettled History: Making South African Public Pasts,
by Leslie Witz, Gary Minkley, and Ciraj Rassool

Seven Plays of Koffi Kwahulé: In and Out of Africa,
translated by Chantal Bilodeau and Judith G. Miller
edited with Introductions by Judith G. Miller

The Rise of the African Novel:
Politics of Language, Identity, and Ownership,
by Mukoma Wa Ngugi

Black Cultural Life in South Africa:
Reception, Apartheid, and Ethics,
by Lily Saint

A complete list of titles in the series can be found at www.press.umich.edu

African Performance Arts
and Political Acts

Naomi André,
Yolanda Covington-Ward,
and Jendele Hungbo, Editors

University of Michigan Press
Ann Arbor

For questions or permissions, please contact um.press.perms@umich.edu

Published in the United States of America by
the University of Michigan Press
Manufactured in the United States of America
Printed on acid-free paper

First published October 2021

A CIP catalog record for this book is available from the British Library.

ISBN 978-0-472-07482-2 (hardcover : alk. paper)

ISBN 978-0-472-05482-4 (paper : alk. paper)

ISBN 978-0-472-12875-4 (ebook)

CONTENTS

Digital materials related to this title can be found on the Fulcrum platform via the following citable URL: https://doi.org/10.3998/mpub.10176359

ACKNOWLEDGMENTS

As with all collaborative projects, this edited volume would not have been possible without the support of numerous people and organizations. First and foremost, we would like to thank the Andrew W. Mellon Foundation, which provided the funding for the 2017 workshop in Johannesburg, South Africa, from which this volume emerged. This workshop on Performance Arts and Political Action in Africa was part of a teaching partnership titled "Joining Theory and Empiricism in the Remaking of the African Humanities" and was jointly supported by the University of Michigan African Studies Center and the University of the Witwatersrand in Johannesburg, South Africa.

We would also like to thank Kelly Askew, the founding director of the African Studies Center at the University of Michigan, as well as J. Henrike Florusbosch, the project coordinator for the African Studies Center, who provided essential logistical support in preparation for the workshop. Donato Somma (University of the Witwatersrand) was also important in the conversations for shaping the workshop. We thank all the participants in the workshop who were able to contribute chapters to the volume. We are also grateful to those who shared their research during the workshop and contributed to the larger discussion around performance and politics in Africa, including Liz Gunner, Ashley Lucas, Kwasi Ampene, Kristina Wirtz, Supriya Nair, and Guarav Desai.

We express our gratitude to the series editors of the African Perspectives series at the University of Michigan Press (Kelly Askew, Laura Fair, and Ann Pitcher) for seeing the value in our volume. We would also like to thank Ellen Bauerle, executive editor at the University of Michigan Press, and Anna Pohlod and Flannery Wise, her editorial associates, for encouraging us to bring this project to fruition and for providing valuable support and guidance from the beginning of this project to its publication. Our volume was considerably strengthened by the comments and feedback of two anonymous peer reviewers. We would like to thank them for their time and attention to each individual chapter. Our volume is greatly improved because of their contributions.

As volume coeditors, we would like to thank our respective institutions for supporting us as we worked on this project: the University of Michigan, the University of Pittsburgh, and Bowen University, Iwo, Nigeria. On behalf of all our contributing authors, we extend our warmest thanks to our families and close friends who have kept us going through the good, as well as the challenging, times. Throughout our working on this volume, all of us have experienced great milestones, including new positions, promotions, marriages, births of children (and our small children growing up!), and retirements. We recognize with deep gratitude the support and understanding of our loved ones and close colleagues as we worked to move this project forward.

Naomi André, Yolanda Covington-Ward, and Jendele Hungbo
April 2021

Introduction

Performance and Politics in Africa: Approaches and Perspectives

NAOMI ANDRÉ, YOLANDA COVINGTON-WARD, AND JENDELE HUNGBO

Performances in Sub-Saharan Africa are rarely cloistered events that occur in isolation, separated from social, political, and broader cultural contexts. In fact, one of the defining elements of performances across African countries is that they are steeped in meaning, drawing on historical legacies, cultural identities, and references to daily life. Interwoven between historical scholarship, contemporary reviews, live performance, and lived experience, performances, whether staged or in daily life, present articulations of changing times. The consciously constructed "work" of performance regularly interfaces with other performed cultural acts, including frequently—and importantly—political action. During (and enduring) political upheaval and oppression, performances provide an opportunity for dialogue, resistance, and political action. In contrapuntal voices, the arts of performance also express continuing and evolving formations of social and national identity and relationships.

Performance and performativity, as we know well, go far beyond the theatrical and spectacular to encompass interactions on many other scales. A dismissive shrug, a new political slogan, the presence or absence of applause, can index vast registers and repertoires of political engagement. Verbal performances, from storytelling and speechmaking to comedy and satire, can produce and sustain ideologies, manage and challenge social positions, and accomplish all manner of social acts. And the performance of religious rites and rhetoric extend communicative interactions to other worldly domains as well as engaging social life in the here and now. These modes of performance appear in diverse genres and wide-ranging media from live venues and face-to-face interactions, to radio, film, television, and social media. Performance is a semiotically rich field: whether performances are mundane or spectacular, they require both conscious and unconscious work and aesthetic choices.

The overall purpose of this volume is to take a multidisciplinary approach to an examination of performance and politics in everyday life in diverse contexts across the African continent. To that end, the volume draws on folklore, theater and performance studies, ethnomusicology, sociolinguistics, cultural anthropology, gender studies, cultural studies, and Africana studies to explore performance and politics in West, Central, South, and East Africa. Our contributors also are based in continental Africa, Europe, and the United States, coming together in this collaborative effort. The chapters emerged from work presented in 2017 as part of the Andrew W. Mellon–funded workshop on Performance Arts and Political Action in Africa, held in Johannesburg, South Africa. This workshop was jointly supported by the University of Michigan African Studies Center and the University of the Witwatersrand in South Africa as part of a teaching partnership titled "Joining Theory and Empiricism in the Remaking of the African Humanities." Over the course of nearly a week, scholars gathered there to discuss many perspectives and approaches on performances, large and small, as they relate to politics at multiple levels in Africa. Included are music, gesture, dance, theater, and spectacle as well as discourse, oral text, and speech acts. Rather than focusing on a specific geographical location or time period, this collection examines how performances, broadly defined, mediate among identity, culture, society, and politics. An act, work, or protest from the past can express new meanings in the changing present. Integral to these themes is the intersectionality between race, ethnicity, and gender as well as other expressions of sexuality, nationhood, economic access, and religious affiliation.

Each chapter takes its own approach to performance, analyzing its meanings and uses in country-specific contexts. Connecting to our volume's consideration of everyday life in addition to performances set apart from everyday life, we find the writings of Leopold-Sédar Senghor, the first president of independent Senegal and a proponent of the Négritude movement, instructive. In his essay on the important role of art in the humanity of Africa and people of African descent, he opined, "in black Africa, art is not a separate activity in itself or for itself: it is a social activity, a technique of living, a handicraft in fact" ([1966] 1995, 51–52). While Négritude is not our primary focus here (though essays by Irvine and Sweet reference Senghor), what is useful is taking this recognition of the importance of art, and by extension performance arts and performance, for the shaping of social relations and everyday life. For our volume, then, bringing such a diverse set of perspectives together enables an expansion of understandings of the operationalization of performance and politics in Africa beyond the most common focus on the state and state-related performance (Castaldi 2006; Straker 2009) to include the banal and the everyday.

The essays in this collection explore how identity, interpersonal relationships, and larger societies are shaped through performance dialogues across Africa. Through various modes of influence the arts of performance retain identifiable characteristics as well as undergo transformation. Such performances are able to demonstrate citizenship and nationhood as well as acts of anticitizenship and paths of migration. Performance acts bespeak social justice and claims making from protesting police brutality, exposing sexual misconduct and violence, to demanding decolonized curricula. Such actions involve linguistic practices that are prescribed and proscribed as well as performance genres that are face-to-face in person and through social media via cyberspace (e.g., #FeesMustFall and #BlackLivesMatter).

PERFORMANCE IN AFRICA

To start, we recognize that performance is an "essentially contested concept" in the sense that there is not one exact agreed-upon definition (Strine, Long, and Hopkins 1990, 183). Drawing upon scholarship and approaches in a variety of disciplines and fields, including theater studies, anthropology, folklore, linguistics, and oral interpretation studies, among others, there are some common elements that appear across different definitions of performance. One such approach regards performance as a special type of communicative behavior, such as folklorist and anthropologist Richard Bauman's understanding of performance as "an aesthetically marked and heightened mode of communication, framed in a special way and put on display for an audience" (1989, 262). Other approaches emphasize the recognition of an audience, such as theater studies scholar Marvin Carlson's statement that "performance is always performance for someone, some audience that recognizes and validates it as performance, even when, as is occasionally the case, that audience is the self" (1996, 6). Similarly, in his work on performance in everyday life, sociologist Erving Goffman expands his definition of performance to include "all activity of a given participant on a given occasion which serves to influence in any way any of the other participants" (1959, 15).

But while the presence of an audience is key, others have pointed toward the importance of consciousness or awareness of the execution of an action in order for action to be considered a performance. "The difference between doing and performing . . . would seem to lie not in the frame of theatre versus real life but in an attitude—we may do actions unthinkingly, but when we think about them, this introduces a consciousness that gives them the quality of performance" (Carlson 1996, 4). Yet another commonly referenced element of a definition of performance is that of restored behavior, a concept introduced by theater studies scholar Richard Schechner to recognize that "all behavior consists of recombining bits of previously behaved behaviors" (2002, 28). All these characteristics—communicative behavior, presence of an audience, heightened awareness or consciousness, reflexivity, and restored behavior—can all be used to define particular actions as performance. And yet, what can performances do in the context of social relationships?

One useful set of ideas related to performance that we can consider is that of *performative* and *performativity*. Linguist J. L. Austin defined performatives as utterances that actually executed an action, when *saying something is doing something* (1962). Judith Butler, a philosopher of gender, applied Austin's idea of performatives to her understanding of how gender is constituted in everyday life through repetitious acts that shape the gendered self (1988). What can be taken from both approaches is a recognition of the critical role of performances in transforming selves and others. Similarly, performativity as concept can be understood in two major ways. On one hand, performativity refers to when something not typically understood as a performance behaves like a performance (such as a piece of writing). On the other hand, when the concept of performativity is used to apply J. L. Austin and Judith Butler's ideas of performatives, it makes possible "a powerful appreciation of the ways that identities are constructed iteratively through complex citational processes" (Parker and Sedgewick 1995, 2).

The concept of performatives are useful here in showing how performances can shape everyday interactions and power relations. In her oft-cited book *Performing the Nation: Swahili Music and Cultural Politics in Tanzania* (2002), Kelly Askew lays out a theory of the politics of performance, based on three points: first, that all those present actively engage in performances in some way; second, that seeing performances as also performative means that they are emergent and not fixed; and third, that performance is related "unambiguously to the active construction of social life" (2002, 23). Her last point especially is critical for our understanding of the significant meanings and uses of performance in multiple contexts throughout various countries across the continent of Africa. The work of renowned authors such as J. H. Kwabena Nketia stress the importance of social context for understanding African music performances in general (1974), while authors such as Christopher Alan Waterman (1990), Johannes Fabian (1990), Veit Erlmann (1996), Lisa Gilman (2009), Tejumola Olaniyan (2004), and David Donkor (2016) illustrate the intersection of performance and politics in works focused on juju popular music in Nigeria, a contentious theater production in the Democratic Republic of Congo, *isicathamiya* music created by Zulu migrant laborers in South Africa, women's political dancing in Malawi, the music of the renowned Nigerian musician Fela Anikulapo-Kuti, and government co-opting of popular performance genres in Ghana.

While all these authors have made great contributions through the examination of performances that are clearly framed and set apart from everyday life, in this volume we examine performance both on stage and in the context of everyday life to explore how performances can shape relationships interpersonally, at the community or institutional level, and even with nation-states. In her oft-cited article "The State of Research on Performance in Africa," anthropologist Margaret Thompson Drewal asserts that "performance is a means by which people reflect on their current conditions, define and/or reinvent themselves and their social world, and either re-enforce, resist, or subvert prevailing social orders" (1991, 2) to highlight the political uses of performance in everyday life. Such an observation connects to the findings of scholars in the growing field of "Black performance studies," which while largely focused on the experiences of African Americans, privileges perspectives that are also useful for studying performance within Africa. Performance Studies scholar E. Patrick Johnson, for instance, notes how "race" comes to be understood and known through performance—"performance facilitates self- and cultural reflexivity—a knowing made manifest by a 'doing'" (2006, 446). Moreover, in their seminal text, Thomas DeFrantz and Anita Gonzalez highlight how Black Performance Theory examines why and how performance, performative, and performativity "matters to Blackness and to contested identities." Black Performance Theory "works to translate and inspire, to politically interrogate and sensually invoke, how realms of performance struggles and troubles illuminate black agency and subjectivity within reimagined spaces of being" (2014, viii). All these scholars demonstrate how performance can be actively used to disrupt social norms, repressive practices, and marginalizing social structures. And while race is often overlooked in discussions of contemporary Africa (Pierre 2012) (often with the exception of Southern Africa), race and other forms of categorization and identity such as class, youth status, ethnicity, and even religion remain salient in the everyday lives of many across the continent.

In this volume, we are intentionally focusing on continental Africa for a number of reasons. We are not making essentialist claims about "Africa"; indeed, as the work of V. Y. Mudimbe shows, much of what the world knows about Africa and Africans was formulated in the European imagination (1988, 1994). Rather, the countries that are included in this volume have a number of shared characteristics: a shared geography in terms of being within Africa as a continent, country membership in the African Union, common histories in terms of experiences of enslavement and European colonization, and a shared geopolitical present in regards to large-scale marginalization within the global political economy and inclusion in the greater Global South. For instance, none of the fifty-four African countries are recognized as high-income countries; moreover, nine of the ten countries with the lowest gross national income per capita in 2017 are in Africa (World Bank). But this is not the entire story; Africa is the only world region where the youth population is increasing (Goalkeepers Report, Bill and Melinda Gates Foundation, 2018), yet the human capital investments are often lacking in many African countries. All these characteristics become salient when performances must be contextualized in their locations, social hierarchies, and histories. For instance, how can students use performance to oppose rising tuition fees? How can migrants pulled to host countries by opportunities that were lacking at home use performance to counter anti-immigrant rhetoric and attitudes? Performances, whether on stage or in everyday life, enable such reflexive challenges to occur.

An examination of recent literature shows that there have been a number of edited volumes on performance more broadly (Santino 2017; Frederik, Marra, and Schuler 2017), yet they do not focus on continental Africa in particular. Over the past few decades there have been some wonderful contributions in advancing the study of performance in Africa. The extensive work of Liz Gunner, especially her special journal issue in the *Journal of Southern African Studies* (1990) and edited volume *Politics and Performance: Theatre, Poetry and Song in Southern Africa* (2001) must be noted. With our volume, we are building upon her efforts by expanding the scope beyond Southern Africa to include West, Central, and East Africa while also considering performance genres beyond theater, poetry, and song in their interaction with politics. Similarly, Karin Barber's *Readings in African Popular Culture* (1997) also broke new ground in the study of performance in Africa, although it was not centered on the concept of performance and did not explicitly engage politics. Frances Harding's *The Performance Arts in Africa: A Reader* (2003) brings together a number of important texts about performance across Africa but does not focus on politics as a central theme. With our volume, our multidisciplinary approach and range of definitions of performance and engagement with performance as a concept, we offer a more recent comparative examination of performances both on stage and in everyday life, providing a set of novel perspectives on the intersection of performance and politics in Africa.

OUTLINE

The book is divided into four thematic sections. The first, "The Play of Social and Political Roles in Everyday Life," brings together three chapters that explore how language and linguistic discourse illustrate a performance of social and political community relationships. Situated along the western coast in Senegal and Nigeria, this collection begins with the performance of language in everyday interactions (e.g., in the marketplace and social exchanges in a village). Such casual communications are juxtaposed with more formal situations: a performed radio play broadcast nationally, a televised political speech, and radio "sterling greetings" that function as a type of personal paid announcement to the general public that involve nuanced codes of adulation and obligation. Within these three chapters, a virtual "call and response" emerges between the messages sent through the verbal fluency of the speakers and the sophisticated literacy of the audiences who are able to interpret the various coded texts.

The opening two chapters present a dialogue between speech and social relationships in Senegal. The first essay provides a set of case studies that include a village chief in his community, a radio play popular with rural communities in 1975, and a formal televised speech by former Senegal president Abdou Diouf in 2010, with attention to his deployment of language within the turns of phrase in spoken French. Through a rubric of joking relationships in markets and households, the next chapter presents the performance of verbal play and how interlocutors recruit audience interaction to construct poetic bridges and patterns of everyday insults and teasing. These stylized interactions happen through *sanakuyaagal*, a Senegalese community cultural practice that allows a space for questioning social hierarchies and relationships between different ethnic groups and structural alliances. In this study, one of these teasing relationships is examined through the last name of a person (frequently the patronym that is passed down along the male ancestral line) and reveals multilayered connections across time, space, and social domains among the participants.

Far from being simple messages that solely convey logistical information, Nigerian public service radio "sterling greetings" also reflect power relationships between different categories of individuals and groups in the community. Broadcast across the nation, with case studies in Ogun State, South-West Nigeria (with its majority Yoruba population), such messages reveal the relationships between different sociopolitical actors in society and the power structures that produce them. A central conduit through which meaning is conveyed is the cultural understanding of gratitude that is mediated through a social experience for the listeners and users.

The second section, "Expressions of Identity, Consciousness, and Migration," brings together three chapters and a play focusing on performance genres that explore themes around immigration and migration, identity, and belonging. Moving through South Africa and Cameroon, these studies reach out to other countries on the African continent, Europe, and the United States. Presented in men's hostels in South Africa as well as on international stages across the world, these theater, dance, and vocal performances enact lived experiences that reflect global anxieties. More than providing entertainment for an evening's outing, these performances shape individual, local, and transnational consciousnesses in significant ways.

The first chapter in this grouping examines the current plight of migrants within their home country by focusing on Zulu male workers from South Africa's rural areas who live in the Wolhunter men's hostel in Jeppestown, Johannesburg, during postapartheid South Africa. The politics of the hostel, mitigated through abject poverty and inner-city violence, are structured through systems of leadership, kinship, and patriarchy. This chapter analyzes how the *isiShameni* dances and music performed by the men living in the hostel provide a microcosm of their everyday relationships and experiences while also embodying an expression of migrant consciousness. The politics of space (explored through dance movement) and place (reflected in migration within South Africa between urban and rural locales as well as the immigration to South Africa from other African countries) aligns the proximity of these men's bodies in dance and contested living environments.

In a cross-cutting analysis of two works that draw on Western classical forms (Clarence Cameron White's opera *Ouanga!* about Haiti, and Reuben Tholakele Caluza's music drama *Moshoeshoe* based on the nineteenth-century Sotho King), the second chapter in this section brings together representations of indigenous peoples in Africa and the Caribbean. Both were composed by Black artists who write into classical music the resilience embodied in indigenous cultural economies coming out of orality-derived performance traditions that tell stories of slavery and colonialism in the northern and southern hemispheres. This analysis leads to a proposed construction of a transnational and pan-Africanist diasporic consciousness. These two musical works from the 1930s are by Black composers who draw from their experiences of colonialism and the legacy of slavery to articulate a new Black Nationalism. Clarence Cameron White, an African American who was shaped by his visit to Haiti, wrote his opera *Ouanga!* (1932) about revolutionary leader Jean-Jacques Dessalines. Rueben Tholakele Caluza, a South African who spent a little time in London and additional time studying in the United States (at the Hampton Institute in Virginia and Columbia University), working with Herbert Isaac Ernst Dhloma's drama, wove together the story of King Moshoeshoe (who was the king of present-day Lesotho) and his rule of his Basotho Kingome during the nineteenth-century wars of Mfecane (isiZulu)/Lifaqane (Sesotho) into *Moshoeshoe* (1939), a musical pageant that combined European musical drama and African oral traditions.

Continuing with the themes associated with the displaced global immigrant in previous chapters, the final chapter of this section follows a one-woman show (*Angalia Ni Mimi!*, by Marthe Djilo Kamga) about the clash between citizenship and the migrant experience for postcolonial subjects who become immigrants across continents in Cameroon, Belgium, and the United States. Presented in French, the playwright/actor Kamga, a lesbian and mother of an autistic child, is an artist whose lived presence is perceived as dangerous and illegal in certain international state contexts. As with other cases in this volume, women's bodies are frequently contested as simultaneously available and "othered" while becoming the sites onto which fear, violence, and displacement are played out. Along with Ekotto's discussion and analysis, we are including the first publication of Marthe Djilo Kamga's *Angalia Ni Mimi!*, the play itself.

The third section, "Gendered Messages of Social Change," brings together two chapters that examine how performances are used to address trenchant social issues across the globe before and during the #MeToo movement. Both drawn on South African performances, these two studies discuss sexual harassment and assault from gendered perspectives. In two solo performances, the first by a woman (*Songs for Khwezi* by Refilwe Nkomo) and the second by a man (*We Are Here* by Antonio Lyons), rape and the feminist project "16 Days of Activism" are presented through differently gendered lenses and highlight these national crises. Both works provide a forum for confronting sexual violence committed against women; the second work offers the unusual perspective of men who are frequently untapped as allies.

The second chapter in this grouping moves across the continent to the eastern coast in Dar es Salaam, Tanzania, and features linguistic play within hip hop. Through everyday references, the socialist past and neoliberal present are articulated in a performance of Ujamaa, a return to "traditional" African values, by hypermasculinist "gangster" rappers. In urban streets, a combination of the local and global are carefully crafted into lyrics that perform the national interests of the public sphere. Connected to the opening section of this collection ("The Play of Social and Political Roles in Everyday Life"), linguistic turns of phrase and the context of social space and place allow these young rappers to participate in new political directions. Though the gangster image can be used to project a hypermasculinity frequently seen in the bling culture of hip hop, these Tanzanian rappers are positioning themselves strategically to legitimize their own voices in the national political discourse.

The final section of this book, "Songs of Protest and Activist Opera," brings together three chapters that focus on vocal genres in South Africa and the Democratic Republic of Congo. These musical sources incorporate Western-derived forms, opera, and Christian missionary hymns, as well as the strategic performance of protest songs. The first chapter analyzes the use of religious songs of protest in the context of religious persecution in colonial-era Belgian Congo, while the second chapter examines the use of European-derived classical music forms such as opera to relate narratives based on Black South African sources and experiences. The third chapter reveals how the power of sung words and music not only brought students from diverse South African universities together to voice their concerns to their institutions during the recent (2015–2017) decolonization of the curriculum movement, but also how these protest songs helped unify the diverse bodies of the students into newly formed allies.

The first chapter in this section moves back in time to the 1920s in the Belgian Congo, where colonial religious interests provided a means to oppress Kongo bodies. Drawing on precolonial embodied practices and Protestant mission Christianity, a MuKongo man called Simon Kimbangu started a prophetic movement (*kingunza*) that colonial administrators and missionaries viewed as a dangerous threat. The chapter examines the role of inspired songs in miraculous healing rituals in the *kingunza* movement and in open public protests against Belgian colonial suppression of the movement and its leaders, such that songs were labeled "seditious." Activities focused around movement and music challenged the power of the church and colonial state and presented an opportunity for the indigenous population in the Lower Congo to transform the local religious and political landscapes.

The second chapter focuses on an adaptation of a beloved Western opera, Puccini's *La Bohème* (1896), into a modern telling set in the township of Khayelitsha as *Breathe Umphefumlo* (2015). The sonic sounding and visual embodiment of Black experience are specific to South Africa, but they have a relevance to new growing global audiences and they create new politics around a genre associated with Western elitism that is redefining itself. Like Mhlambi's discussion of *Ouanga!* and *Moshoeshoe*, André also examines how opera has expanded meanings for expressing Black identity and representations of Black lives with Puccini's young bohemians in Paris transformed into the first generation of born-free Black South African students attending university. As Gonzalez's chapter on gendered violence and sexual assault in works by Nkomo and Lyons demonstrates how theater has a long political tradition in South Africa from the years during the struggle to the present, André reveals how opera has been mobilized to politically engage health pandemics with the tuberculosis crisis in the township of Khayelitsha, just outside of Cape Town.

The final chapter in the collection takes the quintessential form of politicized arts—the protest song—and illustrates how words and music simply set for all voices (as opposed to stylized operatically trained voices) has the power to achieve multiple goals simultaneously. This study includes South African universities that almost exclusively serve Black students from previously disadvantaged backgrounds as well as the esteemed institutions that primarily cater to the affluent students during the #FeesMustFall movement. Rather than the usual racial and socioeconomic level differences that divide these students, protest songs were able to mobilize the students in focusing on their common and separate interests while maintaining a collective solidarity among them.

We are well aware that the scope of this collection is far from exhaustive. In fact, we see this as a strength as the construction and development of performance on the African continent continues to expand and evolve. While it has been critical to our vision to include examples of traditional performances that rely on oral traditions, drama and spoken plays, and *isiShameni* dance, we have also been committed to bringing other types of performance—particularly around linguistic play, spoken word, and hip hop—into the conversation. With the long-term and different mediations of oppression and colonialism, we needed to show how the idea of "authenticity" is flawed and frequently not helpful for reading meaning in performative activities in this new millennium. We wanted to show how Christian missionary hymns could be turned into seditious songs that threatened the colonial regime. The segregated, elitist, all-white genre of opera can be used to express Black Nationalism and raise awareness about tuberculosis in Khayelitsha. Hip hop can draw on Western tropes of violence and materialism, as well as provide a space for young disenfranchised men to express political solidarity with the early goals of nationhood in Tanzania. In this collection we have included discussions of performance as well as the publication of a recent play by Camaroonian born, yet multicontinental traveler, Marthe Djilo Kamga that brings gender, sexuality, maternity, and race all together as she embodies the experiences of being a single mother raising an autistic child in the environment of migration and uncertainty.

Performance is not only an act of presentation; it also encodes experiences for representation. Black peoples and cultures have been subjected to a range of views, assumptions, and misreadings that have not always incorporated firsthand experience. Those of us working on this collection of essays are from countries across the African continent, Europe, the Caribbean, and the United States; all of us have worked in Africa and care deeply about its cultural legacies. Through the collaboration between the coeditors along with the cooperation of the authors in this collection, we have interwoven performance, arts, and political acts together on the African continent in case studies drawn from the early twentieth century up through the beginning of the new millennium.

WORKS CITED

Askew, Kelly M. 2002. *Performing the Nation: Swahili Music and Cultural Politics in Tanzania*. Chicago: Chicago University Press.

Austin, J. L. 1962. *How to Do Things with Words*. Oxford: Clarendon Press.

Barber, Karin, ed. 1997. *Readings in African Popular Culture*. Bloomington: International African Institute in association with Indiana University Press.

Bauman, Richard. 1989. "Performance." In *International Encyclopedia of Communication*, edited by Eric Barnouw, 262–66. Oxford: Oxford University Press.

Bill and Melinda Gates Foundation, 2018. Goalkeepers Report. https://www.gatesfoundation.org/goalkeepers/report. Accessed April 25, 2019.

Butler, Judith. "Performative Acts and Gender Constitution: An Essay in Phenomenology and Feminist Theory." *Theatre Journal* 40, no. 4 (1988): 519–31.

Carlson, Marvin. 1996. *Performance: A Critical Introduction*. New York: Routledge.

Castaldi, Francesca. 2006. *Choreographies of African Identities: Négritude, Dance, and the National Ballet of Senegal*. Urbana: University of Illinois Press.

DeFrantz, Thomas F., and Anita Gonzalez, eds. 2014. *Black Performance Theory*. Durham, NC: Duke University Press.

Donkor, David. 2016. *Spiders of the Market: Ghanaian Trickster Performance in a Web of Neoliberalism*. Bloomington: Indiana University Press.

Drewal, Margaret Thompson. 1991. "The State of Research on Performance in Africa." *African Studies Review* 34, no. 3: 1–64.

Erlmann, Veit. 1996. *Nightsong: Performance, Power, and Practice in South Africa*. Chicago: University of Chicago Press.

Fabian, Johannes. 1990. *Power and Performance: Ethnographic Explorations through Proverbial Wisdom and Theater in Shaba, Zaire*. Madison: University of Wisconsin Press.

Frederik, Laurie, Kim Marra, and Catherine Schuler, eds. 2017. *Showing Off, Showing Up: Studies of Hype, Heightened Performance, and Cultural Power*. Ann Arbor: University of Michigan Press.

Gilman, Lisa. 2009. *The Dance of Politics: Gender, Performance, and Democratization in Malawi*. Philadelphia: Temple University Press.

Goffman, Erving. 1959. *The Presentation of Self in Everyday Life*. Garden City, NY: Doubleday.

Gunner, Liz. 1990. "Introduction: Forms of Popular Culture and the Struggle for Space." Special Issue on Performance and Popular Culture, *Journal of Southern African Studies*.

Gunner, Liz, ed. 2001. *Politics and Performance: Theatre, Poetry and Song in Southern Africa*. Johannesburg, South Africa: Witwatersrand University Press.

Harding, Frances, ed. 2013. *The Performance Arts in Africa: A Reader*. London: Taylor and Francis.

Johnson, E. Patrick. 2006. "Black Performance Studies: Genealogies, Politics, Futures."

In *The Sage Handbook of Performance Studies*, edited by D. Soyini Madison and Judith Hamera, 446–63. Thousand Oaks, CA: Sage Publications Inc.

Mudimbe, V. Y. 1988. *The Invention of Africa*. Bloomington: Indiana University Press.

Mudimbe, V. Y. 1994. *The Idea of Africa*. Bloomington: Indiana University Press.

Nketia, J. H. Kwabena. 1974. *The Music of Africa*. New York: W. W. Norton.

Olaniyan, Tejumola. 2004. *Arrest the Music!: Fela and his Rebel Art and Politics*. Bloomington: Indiana University Press.

Parker, Andrew, and Eve Sedgwick, eds. 1995. *Performativity and Performance*. New York: Routledge.

Pierre, Jemima. 2012. *The Predicament of Blackness: Postcolonial Ghana and the Politics of Race*. Chicago: University of Chicago Press.

Santino, Jack. 2017. *Public Performances: Studies in the Carnivalesque and Ritualesque*. Logan: Utah State University Press.

Senghor, Leopold- Sédar. [1966] 1995. "Négritude: A Humanism of the Twentieth Century." In *I am because we are: Readings in Black Philosophy*, edited by Fred L. Hord and Jordan Scott Lee, 45–54. Amherst: University of Massachusetts Press.

Schechner, Richard. 2002. *Performance Studies: An Introduction*. New York: Routledge.

Straker, Jay. 2009. *Youth, Nationalism, and the Guinean Revolution*. Bloomington: Indiana University Press.

Strine, Mary, Beverly Whitaker Long, and Mary Frances Hopkins. 1990. "Research Trends in Interpretation and Performance Studies: Trends, Issues, Priorities." In *Speech Communication: Essays to Commemorate the Seventy-Fifth Anniversary of the Speech Communication Association*, edited by Gerald Philips and Julia Wood, 181–204. Carbondale: Southern Illinois University Press.

Waterman, Christopher Alan. 1990. *Jùjú: A Social History and Ethnography of an African Popular Music*. Chicago: University of Chicago Press.

World Bank Data Catalog, GNI per capita, Atlas Method (Current US$), https://databank.worldbank.org/data/reports.aspx?source=2&series=NY.GNP.PCAP.CD. Accessed April 25, 2019.

The Play of Social and
Political Roles in Everyday Life

Performing Political Identities

Senegalese Speakers and Their Audiences

JUDITH T. IRVINE

Performances are not only activities of "high culture" performed on a stage or movie set by a cast of thousands. They are also found in everyday life and in the ways people inhabit—and display—social roles and identities. This chapter considers three performances in which Senegalese people enact, for different audiences, social identities having a political valence. I focus especially on the language(s) in which these roles and relationships are displayed. Ranging in locale, time, and scale of circulation, the three performances I discuss are as follows: (1) the speech of a rural town chief and his neighbors in an ordinary social gathering, 1975; (2) a radio play, broadcast nationally in Senegal in a series popular with rural audiences, 1975; and (3) a speech by Abdou Diouf, former president of Senegal and subsequently secretary general of the Organisation Internationale de la Francophonie, on the occasion of the organization's fortieth anniversary, recorded in Paris in 2010.

This chapter has two themes. First, these cases show the varying significance, for Senegalese speakers and their local and global audiences, of verbal fluency in general and the use of spoken French in particular. Linguistic usages reveal much about the speaker: what kind of person she or he might be taken to be—with what personality and in what social position—and what roles the speaker can be seen as appropriately occupying, including political roles. These interpretations depend, in turn, on the audiences who are doing the interpreting.

The second theme is broader and concerns "performance" itself. In illustrating different kinds of performances, from the casual and everyday to the staged and scripted, and from the role taken on by the theater actor to the role of political titleholder, these examples offer an opportunity to consider what we understand by the arts of performance. In particular, the examples will point to the several kinds of role relations and interpretive frameworks in which acts of performance, along with their audiences, are necessarily embedded. Along the way, the discussion will attend to audience uptake and interpretation, since audience participation contributes to creating what a performance is and does. What matters most, however, is that by comparing very different kinds of performances we can grasp the complexity of relations between performers and audiences—relations best understood as layered. The examples suggest that if acts of performance are to be recognized as such—as "performances"—it is not only that they have audiences, but that there are multiple framings, and multiple role relations, that co-occur.

The concept of performance I draw on here comes mainly from the work of Erving Goffman, along with some influences from Richard Bauman and Judith Butler. While "performance" and "performativity" have been defined in different ways and vary by academic discipline, here I consider performance as conduct through which a person, as social actor, becomes socially recognizable as inhabiting a kind of identity and identifiable as taking on— whether successfully or not—some social role. Because performance implies being recognizable, it is mainly relevant to situations when one is observed, or knows oneself to be observable, by others. This applies to everyday life as much as it does to the actor onstage.

It was in regard to this everyday possibility of surveillance by others that Goffman (1963) pointed out the difference between a person's behavior when "in play," that is, orienting to being under observation, and "out of play" or "away," assuming nobody is watching and so, perhaps, staring vacantly or picking their nose. Goffman's extensive use of examples and metaphors from theater and from the biographies of con men has led some scholars to suppose he took all performances to be masks, put on strategically by actors— theatrical or social—who maintain a core persona and set of motives independent of the behavior they perform (see, e.g., Butler 1990, 279). While it is easy to see how some passages in his writings can be read this way, this interpretation misses the reflexivity through which your conduct exudes, and effects, your own assumptions about the self (Goffman 1971, 344). Actually, Goffman questioned the idea that there must be a core persona independent of the social contexts and relationships in which one acts. Conduct is not just a mask to be put on and taken off, even if con men and professional actors can manage to sustain such behavioral fronts for a while. Usually conduct is just what you do when you are engaged in social interaction and you enact the social roles you inhabit. These enactments afford your sense of social identity and self. Your performance provides not only the image others will have of you but also your own self-image; "in the language of Kenneth Burke, doing is being" (Goffman 1961, 88). Accordingly, students of social interaction have written of a person as "doing being [some social role or identity]," meaning performing or enacting the conduct expectable of a person who inhabits that role or identity: a doctor, an educated person, a . . . whatever.[1]

By the same token, we may take the others with whom the social actor interacts as his or her audience, without requiring that the social actor be a stage actor or the performance be on stage or film. Audience uptake, and interlocutors' enactment of complementary roles, show how an actor's performance is being understood. The complementarity and the uptake are crucial to our notion of performance here. Just as one cannot take on the role of leader if there are no followers, so one cannot perform a role without being recognized as doing so, at least by oneself—in some ways and to some extent, one is one's own audience—but ultimately in recognition by others.

1. A VILLAGE EVENING, 1975

My first example comes from a small town in the Kajoor region of Senegal, where I have done ethnographic and linguistic fieldwork, mainly in the 1970s and 1980s. The inhabitants—a population of about 1,250 in 1971[2]—almost all identify ethnically as Wolof and all speak the Wolof language (in addition to whatever else they may be able to speak). It is a warm summer evening, after supper. In the central yard of the town chief's compound, several neighbors are sitting around for casual chitchat with the chief's family. The chief himself has joined the group, which is unusual. (He was often occupied indoors with business affairs, reading, or discussions with people who had come to consult him in his chiefly capacity.) After a while, the sound of a truck is heard in the distance, perhaps delivering supplies to one of the shops in the central plaza of town. The conversation turns to long-distance trucks and their drivers.

In the transcript of this bit of conversation, I have provided the Wolof original, an interlinear word-for-word translation, and a free translation in

English. The Wolof original is presented in order to show some linguistic specifics (I'll get to those), and also to show that there is not a single word of French, not even the names of cities—whose Wolof names differ from those cited on official maps and signage—nor any French loan words. Overlapping talk is shown by large/heavy brackets, while double-slash // represents rapid, almost instantaneous, onset of a new speaker's turn to talk. All speakers in this excerpt are adult men.

Transcript 1³

1 MT: Xamxam   ci   li   nyu xam né, nyoonyu!
          Knowledge about what they know   they (emphatic)
          The knowledge they have, *those* people!

2 MF: E—Tingééj [? Indistinct]
          [name of town, also known as Rufisque]
          Eh—[the ones in] Rufisque. [?]

3 MT: Xamxam,   xamxam   dàll la nyu ko am, ba m'ko doylé
          Knowledge knowledge really they it have till it   suffices
          They *really* have enough *knowledge*

4   Ci diggïnte, diggïnte, aa//
          Between   betwèen
          [to drive] between—ah–

5 Chief: // [indistinguishable] Mariama, yów fi de woon sax.
                                 [JTI]   you here Emph past even
                                 Mariama [JTI], you were *here* then.

6   [pause]   Fekk fu kenn du   nyui   xam   fu—
                     find where anyone neg they-contin know where
                        Turns out nobody knows where—

7 MT: diggïnte   Tingééj   ak   Ndar.
                     between   [town]   and   [town]
                     between Rufisque and Saint-Louis.

8 Chief: li   ca—li nyui   ci— jogé ba xam—[pause]
          what at   what they-cont. about set out till know
          about what—about what they—get to know—[pause]

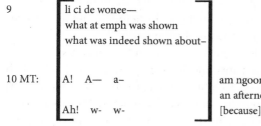

9
li ci de wonee—
what at emph was shown
what was indeed shown about–

10 MT:
A! A— a–

Ah! w- w-

am ngoonent, da   nyu fi musa am
an afternoon expl   they here once have
[because] one afternoon, they once had here

11
benn, benn, benn kii   bu fu—   bu ko musa riix ci
one   one   one *machine* rel. where rel it   once stick in
a, a machine where—that got stuck in

12
genn   kekk.   [pause; then rapid:] kaay topp ko,   topp-topp-topp-topp-
one(aug.) pothole   come push it   push continually
a big *pothole*. [pause; then rapid:] [They] come and push it, pushing pushing

13
topp-topp—mu nyàngg—   mu nyimé   tabasiku!
pushing   it   suddenly active it manage suddenly disengage
pushing—it suddenly moves—it manages to burst out!

14 KN:
A bon   nak-
well   thus
Well then–

15 MT:
Bon nak, bu   nyu jubuló,   demal   ci biir   nger,
well thus when they straighten go-caus. in middle highway
Well then, when they straighten up, they make it go in the middle of the
      highway,

16
kii   bu nyui   law!
machine rel they-cont touch
the machine they were handling!

Why bother with this conversation, in a discussion of performance? Two
kinds of "performance" are on view here. One kind is represented by the
mini-narrative MT offers in explaining his claim about the impressive knowledge of long-distance truck drivers. In a miniature version of the art of the
storyteller, his narrative eventually makes him the center of attention as he
vividly describes an episode in which drivers pushed their truck out of a
pothole. His rapid delivery and repeated *topp-topp-topp* "push-push-push"
illustrate the drivers' efforts. Perhaps I am belaboring the obvious. This kind
of brief narrative is common in Wolof sociable conversation as in our own;

it is a performance in that the performer commands attention for the way he delivers his narration, not just for its content, and whether or not he succeeds in delivering it effectively (as MT does, in this excerpt).[4]

But there is a second kind of "performance," and it concerns the social relationships among the participants and how they are enacted. Although conversational narrative may be a cultural universal, nevertheless there is something specially Wolof about the conversation in the way the dialogue—including the performance of a narrative—displays social identities and relationships. The storyteller is of lower social rank than the other men, whose utterances are brief, or indistinct, or disfluent. Although all these men, including MT, belong to the "high" or "noble" social category (*géer*) that distinguishes them from lower-ranking categories (artisan castes and the descendants of slaves), MT is a junior member of a lineage that has no traditional claim on major political or religious office and is represented in this village only by one household, dependent on the chief's lineage for land and patronage. The contrast here between the relatively low-ranking fluent teller of tales and the relatively high-ranking, less fluent audience recalls—again in miniature—the contrast in speech behavior between broad Wolof social categories. These are the (low-status) griots—professional orators, historians, and artisans of the word—and the high nobility to whom griots direct their most public and elaborate performances. MT is not a griot, and he would never deliver an extended narrative or oration to a larger public, in the daytime (when social "rules" are more strictly observed), or to any group that included actual griots or other persons belonging to the lower social categories. But in this group, in evening chitchat, it is appropriate for him, the lowest-ranking participant, to tell a lively little story.

What about the other speakers represented in the transcript, especially the chief? It is not only that they serve as audience rather than storytellers. Rather, the disfluency that especially characterizes the chief's utterances is itself a convention of high rank. This is a pattern noticeable in the speech of the highest-ranking Wolof nobles, in this village and elsewhere. It is sometimes said to be a sign that their attention is directed to higher things, sometimes said to be a sign of politeness and care for their interlocutors (who would be embarrassed to see the inside of the mouth, and whose well-being might even be endangered by the force of a high-ranking person's breath and utterance), and sometimes said to be simply an innate lack of aptitude for the kind of behavior that is thought to derive, also innately, from low rank. All of these "explanations," which are compatible with one another, account for the fact that the highest-ranking person in an important political position[5] and public context must have a lower-ranking spokesperson, preferably a griot, to represent him (or her) to audiences and to relay his messages. This too is performativity, the socialized behavior appropriate to one's role and even to those social identities that perdure across many contexts. The chief displays his appropriateness for the dynastically grounded position of chief—his identity as a kind of person appropriate for political office—in his disfluent verbal behavior. He is "doing being" a high noble, a chief, in this conversation.

There are additional characteristics, more linguistically specific, that distinguish the styles of speaking that are deemed suited to high nobles and to griots, and to the ways of speaking that replicate those styles in miniature. I have written about those styles and their replication in several publications (e.g., Irvine 1990, 2001); I won't revisit the analysis here, but Table 1 summarizes the way these style contrasts work and the social contrasts they signal.

Notice that these are styles (registers, varieties) within Wolof language. They include no French. In fact, at the time of my fieldwork, command of French was said to be "easier" for persons of low rank, such as griots, or people of Serer ethnicity (all considered low-ranking by these Wolof townspeople), or possibly people of low moral character. Some ambivalence attached, therefore, to the competence in French that was necessary for success within the French colonial system, in the educational system (then exclusively using French language), and in industries managed by French businessmen or technical personnel. In 1975, positions that depended on verbal skills or use of some French were disproportionately occupied by people of low-ranking background in the traditional status system. While Léopold Sédar Senghor, president of Senegal from independence in 1960 to 1981, was an accomplished poet and writer in French—so accomplished that he was named to the French Academy—in rural Wolof eyes it was Senghor's Serer ethnicity, combined with his removal to a French boarding school at an early age, that made it possible. A high-ranking Wolof person mindful of genealogy and tradition, my informants opined, would not speak French so fluently and copiously as Senghor did.[6]

2. "MODERN TIMES": A RADIO PLAY FROM DAKAR, 1975

My second case involves professional actors in a Senegalese radio drama, produced in the capital (Dakar) and broadcast nationally. The drama was part

Table 1. Wolof Style Contrasts and Their Social Correlates

	← Stylistic Continuum →		
	waxu géer	(vs.)	*waxu gewel*
	(high-rank talk)		**(low-rank talk)**
prosody:	Slow		Fast
	Soft		Loud
	Low pitch		High pitch
Style:	Laconic		Verbose
lexis, syntax:	Plain, simple:		Ornate, hyperbolic:
	Lexically condensed		Lexically elaborate
	Little reduplication		Reduplication
	Simple syntax, even disfluency		Complex syntax
	"Mistakes" in noun class morphology		Complex morphology
	Few emphatics		Emphatic and focalized constructions
social distinction:	Senior		Junior
	Higher rank (within caste)		Lower rank (within caste)
	Géer ('nobles')		*Gewel* ('griots')
language stereotype:	Wolof	(vs.)	Pulaar
	Wolof, English		French
		↑	
		Axis of differentiation	

of a regular program, *Jamono Tey* (Modern Times), to which people in my fieldsite avidly listened every week. The program featured dramatizations of contemporary social issues, with a narrator's introduction and commentary about the dilemmas of modernity. In this particular play, the plot hinges on the faithless and irresponsible behavior of a young man in Dakar who neglects his virtuous wife in favor of a dishonest woman who exploits him for his money. Although the play portrayed urban life, in which language use was different from the rural patterns I've shown in the first case, the drama had to engage a Wolof-speaking national audience and be comprehensible to them.

In this case neither the actors nor the characters occupy officially constituted political positions, either local or national. Instead, this example illustrates styles of language use that, though overlapping with those illustrated in case 1, shift some of what the implications of linguistic practices are taken to be. These practices (in case 2) derive from a national politics of language that situates Wolof and French in a contemporary urban setting informed by cosmopolitanism and Senegal's political history as a former French colony. Instead of two Wolof-only linguistic styles associated with social ranking in a hierarchical system that dates back many centuries, the play shows a French-infused Wolof—an urban, "modern" style—contrasting with a "traditional" (or "deep," "pure") Wolof. In the play, personalities and moral valences attach to these styles of language use.

Dakar Wolof, or "Urban Wolof" as it is now often called, incorporates many French loan words and expressions into a Wolof linguistic base. This linguistic mixture is not really new; something like it dates back to the mid-nineteenth century, as McLaughlin (2008) has shown. Nevertheless it has connotations of urban modernity, cosmopolitanism, pro-Western and relatively secular values, and—in some circumstances, and corresponding to the quantity of French in the mix—an abandonment of tradition, including traditional moral precepts. Although the radio play includes no direct commentary on French language or any other aspect of language usage, the utterances of different characters link ways of speaking with personalities, circumstances, and the dilemmas of modern urban life in Senegal. The characters are not political leaders, but their lines are performed in the context of a Senegalese politics of language.

The radio play opens with a narrator who also offers interpretive commentary between scenes. Using almost no French, he announces that the play is about how two people who are courting each other should love each other equally; if they do, they should be able to live in harmony. "So [he announces], we won't delay any more, we are going to eavesdrop on two people. Let's go and hear their conversation." In scene 1, Rama Diop, a young woman in Dakar, chats with a woman friend about her boyfriend, Abou Camara, who has given her a lot of presents. In scene 2, Abou and Rama are courting. Abou has brought Rama some gifts; they declare their love, they talk about their parents' agreement to their marriage, and—as a "modern" couple—they make plans to go out for the evening. Although the vast majority of the dialogue is in Wolof, both characters use a few French expressions, especially about their evening plans. For example:

ABOU: *"On tourne ce soir?"* "Are we going out tonight?"
RAMA: *"Si tu veux."* "If you like."

Scene 3 shows Rama at home talking with her father, who praises her for being an obedient child and asks whether she wants the marriage. The only French expressions he uses are in reference to money: *un million cinq cent mille*: "if he were offering a million five hundred thousand [francs CFA], and you didn't love him, I wouldn't give you to him."[7] The narrator then summarizes the plot so far, approving what the characters have done. So far, they have managed to blend traditional moral precepts (such as respect for parents, who have a say in a marriage because they care about their children) with a modern way of life (in which parents will not force a marriage without each party's consent and in which the partners love each other and enjoy urban activities together).

Fast forward now to a month after the wedding, scene 4, transcribed below. The relationship is going sour. Abou shows his disregard for his wife Rama:

Transcript 2

Speaker	Wolof (French in boldface)	Translation
A[Abou]	Rama	Rama [name]
R[Rama]	Camara	Camara [surname][8]
A	Xanaa yów newu loo woon ci kër gi?	So you weren't in the house?
R	Aa! nijaay dama doon **rañsale**[9] ci gannaaw rek.	Oh! Honey I was just arranging some things in the back.
A	**Même** bu naa ñëwee doo ma nuyyu, **quoi**. Ci waañ wi rek nggai toog, **quoi**. Man daal bokku ma ci kër gi, **quoi**.	When I arrive you don't even greet me! You just sit in the back yard! I don't even belong to the house!
R	Aa! Dama yëgul woon ne ñëw ngga rek, maanggi woon ci gannaaw.	Oh! I didn't realize you had come home, because I was in the back. [yard]
A	Xamu loo waxtu wi mai wàcc?	Don't you know what time I get off [work]?
R	Xam naa ko kay, **mais** xam ngga, defe naa diggënte bi soo ekse rek . . .	Yes indeed I know, but you know, I thought, between that and when you arrive . . .
A	**Bon**, léegi, **midi moins cinq** bu jota-atee ba **midi et demi**, la nggai def mooy nekk ci biir néeg bi di xool ndax maanggi fi.	Okay, now, when it's again 11:55 until 12:30 you should be here inside the house looking to see whether I'm here.

R	Baax na.	Good [=okay].
A	**Sans cela**, doyal naa sa **affaire** aan !	Otherwise, I'm through with you!
R	Muuq!	Never!
A	**Parce que**, fi ku fii ne, da nggai nuyyu, mais looi def ni.	Because if anyone comes here you should greet them; but [instead], this is how you're behaving.
R	Du dara yów tam nijaay !	It's nothing, honey !
A	**Bon parce que** léegi manggai dem.	Good, because now I'm leaving.
R	Aa! Man, jóoba juba manggi waru de. Moom bu ñëwaan, bu ñu tase ci buntu kër gi, daf may foon fi foon fi, yëkkëti, doxante bi ci biir kër gi, ba ngga naan ne ñi mel ni ñaari perantal, te léegi bu ñëwee rek bëgga **commencer** bu ma jamale rek, mu indil ma wax ju dul jeex. Aa! Man de li xaw ma ko.	Oh! Jóoba juba [praise-epithet of her natal clan], I am really surprised! It used to be that when he came, he'd give me kisses, lift me up, we'd run around together in the middle of the house, till you would have said we were a couple of little kids. And now when he comes he just wants to start picking on me, he brings up endless petty words. Oh! I don't know what it's about.

The French loan words and expressions in this transcript are simple. Most of them are peripheral to the main gist of an utterance and would have been widely familiar even to a rural Wolof-speaking audience who might not necessarily have used these expressions themselves. Notice, however, that Abou, the character who is behaving badly, utters the clear majority of them. Meanwhile Rama produces some conspicuously "traditional" utterances: responding to her husband's summons by uttering his surname (clan name) rather than "yes" (*oui* or *naam*) as a Westernized woman might, and, especially, appealing to her own clan ancestors through their praise-epithet.

Scene 5 presents Abou with his wicked girlfriend Yassin, whose demands for gifts and cash threaten to bankrupt him. When Abou leaves her house, she welcomes her real lover Paul—notice the French name—and declares that she is only stringing Abou along for the money. In this scene many French words are inserted into the Wolof utterances: loan words for money and for items of elegant clothing and furniture, as well as French discourse markers (*alors, bon, quoi*, etc.) and various other expressions such as *remarquer, commenter, comprendre, ce soir, régler problème*, and so on. (The discourse marker *quoi*, literally "what," frequent in Abou's speech as well, is an especially salient marker of urban talk.) Finally, with much moralizing by the narrator (all in

Wolof), Abou finds out about Paul, breaks off with Yassin, and returns, much chastened, to Rama and to Wolof.

Of course this dialogue comes from a play, not from real life. We can only see how linguistic usage is represented, not whether it actually conforms to this pattern. But rural listeners evidently took the dialogue as realistic and commented on how untrustworthy "that Abou" was (though exploited, in turn, by the wicked Yassin). Notice that the narrator's virtually unmixed Wolof has a different significance in the play, where it contrasts with the urban characters' usage, from what it might have had if it were natural conversation on the rural scene. The narrator's avoidance of French carries a morally loaded significance only because it contrasts with the French-inserting variety, Dakar Wolof. In the play, the ideological process that constructs French and French insertions as morally corrupt is retrievable through the dialogue's juxtaposition of contrasting voices, that is, the distribution of varieties and of French insertions. In other contexts, the narrator's rapid and fluent speech, with almost no French loan words, might have been construed as an example of "griot talk" as opposed to noble talk, or as rural speech—even the utterances of a "hick" just arrived in town—as opposed to urban. On the radio, where it contrasts with the usage of the characters in the play, it is morally positive but still potentially high-caste and urban.

Bear in mind that this radio play was performed in 1975. It had been only fifteen years since Senegal's independence from France, and French military, commercial, and technical personnel still maintained a strong presence in the country. All public education was in French as was all official business. So French was the language of the "civilizing mission," of education, of political life in high places. Yet public attitudes toward French were ambivalent.

The politics of language in Senegal have changed in recent years. Political speeches and debate in the parliament now are often done in Wolof, to the chagrin of some Pulaar-speaking deputies. Wolof, in roman script, appears in some public signage. And people in Dakar who want to signal how cosmopolitan and "hip" they are tend to sprinkle some American English into their talk, not (or not only) French. In that way they show that they are especially modern, not merely urban. Some such extra signaling is needed since French insertions are so common in Dakar Wolof and are simply taken nowadays to be the ordinary way urban people speak. Meanwhile a countervailing trend among some conservative Muslims is to avoid any French insertions at all. The identities being performed, therefore, by the (gradient) use or nonuse of French vary according to context, religious and political orientation, and historical moment.

3. ABDOU DIOUF: SENEGALESE FRENCH ON THE
INTERNATIONAL SCENE

With all these issues surrounding the use of French by Senegalese speakers, what's an urban-based politician to do? My third case concerns Senegal's second president, Abdou Diouf, and his later career in Paris. Born (1935) in Louga, a mainly Wolof-speaking town, of a Pulaar mother and Serer (at least Serer-origin) father, Diouf grew up speaking Wolof but was educated in French, first in Senegal at a boarding school and then in Paris. After rising through the civil service ranks, he was appointed prime minister by President Senghor, who resigned (1981) in favor of Diouf a couple of years short of the end of his term. Diouf became president for the remainder of Senghor's term and then, in the next election, ran successfully for president as the incumbent. Winning elections in 1983, 1988, and 1993, Diouf lost popularity in the 1990s as Senegal's economy weakened, ethnic violence broke out on the border with Mauritania, and a separatist movement arose in Senegal's southern region of Casamance. By this time Diouf was widely seen as too removed from the people and their problems, a distance manifest (said his critics) in his involvement in French diplomatic circles and his preference for the French language, even in addressing the nation at large.

That Diouf's preference for the French language had become problematic was already evident in 1988, after an election that an opposition party charged was fraudulent. Shortly afterwards, Diouf gave an important televised speech, the annual presidential address celebrating International Workers Day (May 1), but on this occasion also likely directed at calming a restive populace. After giving his address in French, as was usual for official speeches on formal occasions, Diouf switched to Wolof—the language understood by the vast majority of Senegalese—to repeat the address in translation. The switch was highly unusual, both for a formal address and for Diouf himself. But French seemed to remain present in the background of his Wolof version. As Leigh Swigart points out in a detailed discussion of this episode (2000, 94), Diouf began to insert more and more French lexicon into the Wolof version and to produce translations that were too literal, not idiomatic in Wolof. Some listeners heard these expressions as translation errors and serious gaffes. Although there were other Senegalese who praised him for speaking Wolof and thought he sounded sincere, his critics maintained that he was incapable of a fully idiomatic command of the national lingua franca. These kinds of criticisms gained more traction in the 1990s, and in 2000 he lost the election to a longtime opponent. (Afterwards, Diouf was widely lauded, nationally and internationally, for his gracious acceptance of defeat and assuring a peaceful political transition.)

Evidently, the sophisticated command of the French language that had been so crucial within the colonial education system, so important to Senghor's international stature and ability to negotiate favorable relations with France after independence, and a sign of Senegal's leaders' cosmopolitan modernity—a sign initially appreciated by the nation, at least to some extent—was no longer an unquestioned asset if it was not matched by an equal or greater fluency in Wolof. A Senegalese politician with aspirations to the national stage must now be able to perform localness, presenting himself as a Wolof-speaking man of the people. While his Wolof should not be so "pure" as to make him sound like a complete hayseed, it should include fewer French ingredients than some versions of Urban Wolof do if he is to appeal to the nation at large. Subsequent presidents and other politicians have used far more Wolof in their political activities and public communications than Diouf ever did, to say nothing of Senghor.

But this is not the end of Diouf's story. After stepping down from the presidency of Senegal, Diouf largely relocated to Paris. In 2002 he was elected secretary general of the Organisation Internationale de la Francophonie, a post he held until his retirement in 2014. The OIF is an organization promoting the French language and promoting ties between countries in which it has a significant presence, most of which are France's former colonies. In this position, but also before and since he occupied it, Diouf has moved in the highest political circles in France. He is a member of the Honor Committee of the Fondation Chirac (established by former president Jacques Chirac of France).

If we listen closely to Diouf's French, however, it becomes immediately evident that no one in metropolitan France would mistake him for a native French speaker. His French meets the highest standards of grammatical and lexical correctness, but there is a distinctly Senegalese "accent." Transcript 3 is my rendering of a speech Diouf gave in 2010 for the fortieth anniversary of the OIF, recorded on video for an international audience. I don't think you will see any "mistakes" in the written version (if there are any, they are probably from my transcription, not from Diouf's performance):

Transcript 3: *Abdou Diouf: Message on the OIF's 40ᵗʰ anniversary, 2010 (portions).*[10]

1. La francophonie a quarante ans, l'age où l'on devient ce que l'on est, profondément.

"Francophonie" is forty years old, the age when one becomes what one profoundly is.

2. Quarante ans durant lesquels nous avons oeuvré, avec confiance et constance, pour donner corps et substance aux ambitions et aux promesses éclairées de ceux qui signèrent le vingt mars mille neuf cent soixante-dix la convention de Niamey.

Forty years in which we have worked, with confidence and persistence, to give substance to the ambitions and the enlightened promises of those who signed the 1970 Niamey Convention [establishing the organization].

3. Quarante ans durant lesquels nous avons repoussé les frontières de notre espace, élargi notre horizon, gagnant toujours plus de peuples et de nations à notre cause—

Forty years in which we have pushed back the frontiers of our territory, widened our horizon, always gathering more peoples and nations to our cause—

4. —jusqu'à exprimer la diversité constitutive et créative du monde.

So as to represent the diversity, constitutive and creative, of the world.

5–6. . . .

. . .

7. Si la francophonie a pu résister à l'épreuve du temps, si elle a su se régénérer et se reformer, tout en restant elle-même,

If "la francophonie" has been able to withstand the test of time, if it has been able to regenerate and reform itself even while remaining itself,

8. c'est grâce à l'engagement militant de toutes celles et de tous ceux qui l'ont fidèlement servi, et promue, tout au long de ces quarante ans.

It is thanks to the militant commitment of all those [women] and all those [men] who have faithfully served and promoted it—all these forty years.

9. Mais c'est aussi grâce à la langue, et aux valeurs qui nous fédèrent.

But it is also thanks to the language, and the values that unite us [in federation].

10. Car c'est bien la langue française qui confère à notre famille ce supplément d'âme, cette spontanéité dans la solidarité, cette intercompréhension dans le dialogue,

For it is the French language that endows our family with that addition of soul, that spontaneity in solidarity, that mutual comprehension in dialogue,

11. cette conscience aigue de notre ressemblance dans la différence, et de notre communauté de destin par-delà de nos disparités et nos divergences.

That sharp awareness of our similarity within difference, and of our common destiny beyond our disparities and our differences of opinion.

12. C'est bien notre foi partagée en ces valeurs universelles et pérennes, que sont la démocratie, les droits de l'homme, la paix, l'équité, et la durabilité du développement.

It is our shared faith in those universal and perennial values—democracy, the rights of man, peace, equality, and sustainable development.

13. Mais aussi notre foi irréductible en l'homme, tout l'homme, qui nous conduisent à vouloir obstinément que la liberté, l'égalité, le progrès, la prospérité ne soient plus le privilège de quelques-uns, mais un droit pour tous.

But also our irreducible faith in man, every man, which leads us to swear stubbornly that liberty, equality, progress, and prosperity should no longer be the privilege of the few, but the right of all.

14–16. . . .

. . .

17. Que cette journée du vingt mars deux mille dix soit donc, sur tous les continents, la grande fête de la mémoire et de l'espoir.

May this day, March 20, 2010, be, therefore, on every continent, a great celebration of memory and of hope.

Because Diouf's French is grammatically irreproachable, it conforms to the "clarity" and "logic" that proponents of French have claimed for the language since at least as far back as the eighteenth century. These characteristics of French, they assert, together with its role as the language of the 1789 revolution and therefore of liberty, equality, and fraternity, make the language itself a force for civilization. Evidently, Diouf agrees. But his French has a definite Senegalese phonetics, audible in (for example) his syllable-initial stress pattern, his frequent use of an apical [r] rather than velar or uvular, his tendency to substitute [i] for [ü], and other aspects of his prosody and syllabification. The prosodic and syllabic effects are especially noticeable, for instance in the pattern of stress on the initial syllable of a word and in the pause before elisions (e.g., in line 2, *promesse # [z]éclairées*).[11] Table 2 presents my (simplified) analysis of some selected sounds in Diouf's speech as compared with metropolitan French and with the typical phonetics of Senegalese native speakers of Wolof when pronouncing French.[12]

Thus Diouf appears to embody the civilized Francophile African, retaining—to a Parisian ear—signs of African authenticity while displaying faultless grammar and arguing in favor of promoting the French language. Of course he looks the part, as well. The video of his performance was widely circulated, as were other performances—speeches and interviews—he gave during his extended tenure as head of the OIF.

It is interesting to compare the celebrity reception Diouf has had in Paris with the comments, based on experiences from the 1940s, by Frantz Fanon on the difficulties faced by persons of color when they left the colonies for France (Fanon 1967/1952). Speaking the French they had learned under the colonial education system, even speaking it with excellent grammar and lexis, their utterances would be rejected as insufficiently francophone. To render the /r/ in the (northern) French manner, as a uvular or velar sound instead of an api-

Table 2. Wolof "Accent" in French: Some Common Examples

Metropolitan French	Wolof-speaker French	Abdou Diouf
ʁ	řr	mostly řr
œ, ø	ɛ, e	some ɛ
[nasalized V]	[non-nasal V (+n)]	some non-Nasal V
e.g.: ã	a (+ n)	a (+ n)
ü	i	some i
š	s	mostly š
open syllable (mostly)	closed syllable (mostly)	closed syllable; hypercorrect elision
stress final or equal	stress initial	stress initial

cal one, was a particular struggle (1967, 21). Fanon focuses on Antilleans like himself, who experience (he maintains) a special difficulty because they have no language unrelated to French, only a French créole. "Senegalese" meanwhile are dismissed as mere savages (although it is not entirely clear whether he is speaking in his own voice in this passage, 1967, 26),[13] but at least they had their own indigenous languages and works of verbal art, regardless of their competence, or lack of competence, in French.

It is not that race prejudice has disappeared from French life in the years since Fanon's day. But the arenas, the stages (so to speak) on which it is played out have shifted. France's loss of its colonies, among other international developments making public expressions of racism less respectable, are relevant changes. By the twenty-first century, at least in mainstream public circles, a role had become available for a senior African politician—and perhaps other older, well-dressed Africans too—to inhabit and to perform both Africanness and civilized francophone modernity. Still, for ordinary, working-class Africans like the migrants seeking refuge or economic opportunities in Europe, the situation would be different. Attempts they might make to perform "civilized francophone modernity" might not have a much greater chance of uptake from French audiences than Fanon's Antilleans had.

CONCLUSION

At the beginning of this essay I proposed two themes for it. The first theme concerned the linguistic resources Senegalese speakers draw upon in performing social roles and identities, especially political identities. Accordingly, the cases discussed in the essay show that for such performances there have been shifts in the uses of the Wolof and French languages, including varieties of each language. The shifts depend on the historical moment, setting (and personnel), and audiences. Even though "Urban Wolof" is not a new phenomenon, demographic changes have vastly increased the population of urban centers in Senegal, both in absolute numbers and in relation to rural areas—so that today, the difference between urban and rural ways of speaking may well tend to drown out the caste-related stylistic differences within Wolof that I identified, in a rural context, in the 1970s.[14] Meanwhile, the social acceptability of a Senegalese "accent" in French is probably greater in Paris today than it was some decades ago, as long as other aspects of French language are standard and the speaker's dress and comportment conform to relevant Parisian norms. Still, it is likely that the acceptability illustrated in Abdou Diouf's case rests heavily on his personal biography: his history as an African president who accepted the results of an election that went against him; and his role as ambassador for the OIF (la Francophonie) and for African participation in it. He is known to be an internationally recognized and respected political figure.

As for the second theme, "performance" itself, to call all these ways of speaking "performances" calls attention to the fact that they are all contingent, relational, variable, and require, to greater or lesser degree, appropriate socialization and skills. The role-related performances such as the Senegalese chief's disfluent talk are not inevitable expressions of a person's essence, although some ideologized views—Senegalese or European/American—see them as innate, somehow caused by a person's culture, language, race, or caste rank. Instead, these ways of speaking depend on settings and audiences; speakers vary their language use accordingly. While some social identities and roles are inhabited for longer in one's life than others, they are still embedded in social relations and constituted through "concrete and historically mediated acts of individuals" and through "the legacy of sedimented acts rather than a predetermined or foreclosed structure, essence or fact" (Butler 1990, 274).

Notice that the concept of "performance" drawn upon here does not require all aspects of the role-appropriate behavior to be undertaken consciously. It doesn't even require that there should be a core self, separate from the role, that manipulates it strategically. Only the actors in case 2 can be supposed to have a persona that is fully separate from the roles they assume in the play, a persona that would be revealed in later discourse after the actors have left the stage. We cannot know, however, whether the actors were aware of the specifics of their linguistic practice, even of how much French they used. Nothing explicit was said about this, and there are always questions about how aware an actor is of the detailed behaviors through which she or he conveys a character. What is important is that audiences found the portrayal of characters convincing and talked about them afterwards almost as if they had been real people.

Meanwhile there can be little doubt that politicians like Diouf, speaking in their political capacity, can be seen as performing for an audience. Diouf's performance not only spoke to the merits of the organization whose anniversary he was celebrating, but it also displayed his own qualities that made him an appropriate incumbent of his political position. Likewise, the speech of the rural town chief in case 1 displayed his appropriateness as incumbent of the chiefship. The role of chief was not locally understood as achieved through individual effort, or elected, or term-limited, even though there might be more than one candidate to succeed a chief who dies or steps down. Instead, it was thought to be a matter of genealogy and of qualities of character—of personal essence—that are acquired from ancestors and from the experiences that shape one's being, physical and psychological. Locally, the chief's conduct would be understood to reveal that essence, and not at all to represent a face he could take on or discard at will. He displayed the identity and personality that qualified him to occupy his role. Although a Wolof chief could be deposed if his conduct was incompatible with his position, the reasons for removing him would have to focus on his ancestry and physical being as much as on his conduct. In other words, they must be cast in terms of inherent essence as well as in terms of his deeds. In short, even when an identity is conceived as inherent and permanent, identities must be performed if they are to be maintained.

What about the concept of "performance" itself? I have cited Butler, but she writes not so much about "performance" as "performativity." In so doing, she attaches her work to that of the philosophers Austin and, especially, John Searle, who have written on performative expressions in language (such as "I hereby dub thee Sir Lancelot") and what became known as the theory of "speech acts." Although linguistic performatives are interesting, Searle has taken this line of work in directions that emphasize the individual mind rather than on social relationality and the ways an interlocutor's uptake can recast what an utterance counts as.[15] Goffman, meanwhile, uncovers much about the patterns of ordinary social interaction, yet genre conventions, linguistic forms, and discourse histories beyond the single face-to-face interaction do not get much attention in his work. For genre considerations we can look to Bauman (2004), although his "performances" tend to be special, set apart from ordinary conversation. Mini-performances like MT's narrative in case 1 are indeed set off, in their small way, from the rest of the conversation, but the chief is performing too, in his way.

Those dimensions of social life in talk—genre conventions, linguistic forms, and discourse histories—are the places, I believe, to explore in order to see "performance" in the necessary ways: as sufficiently capacious to include the enactment of social roles in everyday life, yet not obscuring the features that make staged performances distinctive. What the different kinds of performances in the three cases suggest is that we think of performance as layered. Staged performances add a framework of interpretation and participation without subtracting the frameworks that go with other kinds of role-inhabitance, even the reflexivity through which speakers listen to themselves.

NOTES

The fieldwork discussed here was supported by the National Institutes of Mental Health, the National Science Foundation, and the Volkswagen Foundation. Thanks are also due to the many Senegalese people I have worked with over the years.

1. Hence such expressions as "black is as black does," emphasizing conduct as the basis of social identity rather than some inherent bodily essence. See also Butler 1990.

2. By 2006, the last time I visited, the population was approaching four thousand. It is now larger still.

3. This transcript was previously published in Irvine 1990.

4. In many relevant papers on the performance of folklore genres, Richard Bauman has discussed "performance" as invoking a special interpretive frame, a kind of staging, with focus on the manner of delivery. See Bauman 2004.

5. Or an important religious position; see McLaughlin and Villalón 2011. The spokesperson might or might not be a griot in that case, but must be lower-ranking.

6. If such a person did speak fluent and copious French, his or her claim to high rank and moral status would be questioned, especially if any other aspects of behavior failed to coincide with traditional norms. Thus it was rumored that a local schoolteacher who not only spoke French but was said also to drink large amounts of beer and consort with low-caste women could not really be of high rank. It is not clear which of these factors was most important; I only observed the linguistic one. His reputation improved after some changes in his domestic arrangements, but before long he left town. Whether his departure was simply a normal administrative transfer or something else, I do not know.

7. Notice a parallel here with Jane Hill's (1995) analysis of a narrative in an indigenous Mexican language, Mexicano (=Nahuatl). The speaker uses Spanish expressions when referring to money and politics in an externally derived capitalist world.

8. Traditionally, a Wolof-speaking wife responds to a summons by uttering the husband's surname, no matter who summons her. This utterance marks Rama as conforming to traditional notions of wifely comportment.

9. From French *ranger*. The French stem has been incorporated into Wolof grammatical morphology. A Wolof speaker might not recognize this as a loan.

10. The video can be viewed through the OIF; Diouf 2010.

11. In Wolof, a word cannot begin with a vowel. One effect on Wolof-speaker French is to render an elision as the next word's initial consonant, as Diouf does here.

12. For more systematic treatments of Wolof "interference" in French, see Calvet 1965 and Boutin et al. 2012. These phonetic effects are sociolinguistically variable (Boutin, Gess, and Guèye 2012, Boula de Mereüil and Boutin 2011, Thiam 1998).

13. Fanon's "Senegalese" were not necessarily from Senegal at all. Probably he refers to the soldiers in the *tirailleurs sénégalais*—African regiments in the French colonial army—soldiers who came from any of the African colonies, perhaps mainly from Mali and Côte d'Ivoire.

14. It is not clear to me that there has been any substantial recent change in caste-related stylistic differences in Wolof in rural areas. I did not see much change when I was last in rural Senegal in 2006. There seemed to be some other differences in ways of speaking, but I was not there long enough to track them closely.

15. See, e.g., Searle 1998.

WORKS CITED

Bauman, Richard. 2004. *A World of Others' Words: Cross-Cultural Perspectives on Intertextuality*. Malden, MA: Blackwell.

Boula de Mereüil, Philippe, and Béatrice Boutin. 2011. "Évaluation et identification perceptives d'accents ouest-africains en français." *Journal of French Language Studies* 21, no. 3: 361–79.

Boutin, Béatrice A., Randall Gess, and Gabriel Marie Guèye. 2012. "French in Senegal After Three Centuries: A Phonological Study of Wolof Speakers' French." In *Phonological Variation in French: Illustrations from Three Continents*, edited by R. Gess, C. Lyche, and T. Meisenburg. 45–71. Amsterdam: John Benjamins.

Butler, Judith. 1990. "Performative Acts and Gender Constitution: An Essay in Phenomenology and Feminist Theory." In *Performing Feminisms: Feminist Critical Theory and Theatre*, edited by Sue-Ellen Case, 270–82. Baltimore: Johns Hopkins University Press.

Calvet, Maurice. 1965. *Le français parlé: Étude phonetique, interférences du phonetisme wolof*. Dakar: Centre de Linguistique Appliquée de Dakar.

Diouf, Abdou. 2010. *Préparer la francophonie de demain*. https://www.francophonie. préparer-la-francophonie-de-demain.html.

Fanon, Frantz. 1967/1952. *Black Skin, White Masks.* Translated by Charles Markmann. New York: Grove Press.

Goffman, Erving. 1961. *Encounters.* Indianapolis, IN: Bobbs-Merrill.

Goffman, Erving. 1963. *Behavior in Public Places.* New York: Free Press.

Goffman, Erving. 1971. *Relations in Public.* New York: Basic Books.

Hill, Jane. 1995. "The Voices of Don Gabriel." In *The Dialogic Emergence of Culture*, edited by Dennis Tedlock and Bruce Mannheim, 97–147. Urbana: University of Illinois Press.

Irvine, Judith T. 1990. "Registering Affect: Heteroglossia in the Linguistic Expression of Emotion." In *Language and the Politics of Emotion*, edited by Catherine Lutz and Lila Abu-Lughod, 126–61. Cambridge: Cambridge University Press.

Irvine, Judith T. 2001. "'Style' as Distinctiveness: The Culture and Ideology of Linguistic Differentiation." In *Style and Sociolinguistic Variation*, edited by Penelope Eckert and John Rickford, 21–43. Cambridge: Cambridge University Press.

McLaughlin, Fiona. 2008. "On the Origins of Urban Wolof: Evidence from Louis Descemet's 1864 Phrasebook." *Language in Society* 37, no. 3: 713–35.

McLaughlin, Fiona, and Leonardo Villalón. 2011. "Mettre en scène la légitimité: Un discours de feu Xalifa Abdoul Aziz sy et de son jottalikat." In *Communication wolof et société sénégalaise*, edited by Anna Maria Diagne, Sascha Kesseler, and Christian Meyer, 323–44. Paris: L'Harmattan.

Searle, John. 1998. *Mind, Language and Society.* New York: Basic Books.

Swigart, Leigh. 2000. "The Limits of Legitimacy: Language Ideology and Shift in Contemporary Senegal." *Journal of Linguistic Anthropology* 10, no 1: 90–130.

Thiam, Ndiassé. 1998. "Catégorisations de locuteurs et représentations sur le mélange wolof-français à Dakar." In *Imaginaires linguistiques en Afrique*, edited by Cécile Canut, 91–108. Paris: L'Harmattan.

The Socio-poetics of Sanakuyaagal

Performing Joking Relationships in West Africa

NIKOLAS SWEET

INTRODUCTION

Veering from one side of the road to the other as it dodged the pothole-pocked asphalt, an old Renault bus reclaimed from years of hard service lurched past several towns on the outskirts of Kedougou City. An increasingly denser patchwork of small thatch huts announced our arrival to this border town of twenty thousand inhabitants in southeastern Senegal, nestled between the Fouta Djallon mountains of Guinea and the gold-rich lands bordering Mali. The bus made one final stop at a police outpost, where an officer jumped up from a chair underneath a small shade structure. Dressed in shades of blue, the officer jumped up the front entrance of the bus and bellowed out a greeting to the weary travelers as he squared his shoulders with the rows of seated passengers.

Speaking in Wolof, a language of coastal Senegal, the man asked, in a forcefulness that shattered the early morning calm, whether we were are all too tired to say hello. A passenger replied that we had had a *panne*, a breakdown on the difficult journey. "Panne c'est prévu," ("Breakdowns are to be expected") answered the officer curtly. One woman behind me finally replied to his initial question by muttering a polite response. The officer then rotated his head from one side of the bus to the next while asking in French "Est-ce qu'il y a des Peuls[1] ici?" ("Are there any Peuls here?"). Encountering silence, he scanned down the line and asked several passengers, "Vous êtes Peul?" Then the officer planted himself in the center aisle and bellowed out in French:

"Je vais vous couper la tête tous.
Vous êtes venu dans notre pays habiter.
Je vais vous tous chasser."

"I will cut off your heads, all of you.
You all have come to live in our country.
I will chase you all away."

The weary passengers sat in place, seemingly unfazed by these ostensible threats that echoed into the back of the bus. After a short pause, the officer looked up and down the aisle and pointed to two young men, "toi et toi avec les verres!" ("you and you with the glasses!"). The two young men reluctantly checked themselves for identification papers. Unsatisfied with what they produced, the policeman beckoned one of the young men off of the bus and led him outside into a small building obscured from the rest of the passengers. "Les deux-là c'est des Peuls," ("The two there are Peuls") a friend suggested to me in a whisper.

In this chapter, I examine routines of *sanakuyaagal*,[2] forms of institutionalized teasing in West Africa often viewed more broadly as joking relationships in anthropological scholarship. Routines range from light-hearted teasing between friends to moments of ambiguous insults or threats in the meeting of strangers like the one I just described. Central to local understandings of *sanakuyaagal* routines was the sense that interlocutors were not to become upset or take seriously confrontations with their *sanaku* joking partners. The *sanakuyaagal* joking routines I examine here draw primarily on correspondences between ethnic groups and last names (most often patronyms, which are passed down along the male line), and they provide speakers with frames for placing and recognizing others in social interaction.

Across Senegal and neighboring countries in the Sahel, *sanakuyaagal* routines are hard to avoid. Passionately drawn upon and discussed by my interlocutors, these routines provided an idiom through which researchers and guests such as myself were drawn into conversation by those recruiting us into their patronym and ethnic associations. Although *sanakuyaagal* teasing often drew on patronyms (e.g., Diallo-Ba or Ndiaye-Diop) and ethnic groups (e.g., Serer-Pullo), they also implicated relational oppositions within the family unit, such as privileged relationships between grandparent and grandchild, cross-cousins, or junior and senior in-laws. These relationships have often been described as entailing mutual obligation (e.g., funeral responsibilities), economic exchange (e.g., gifts to partners), and hierarchical distance (e.g., a "slave-master" idiom). While I focus primarily on interactions drawing on ethnic and patronymic play in this chapter, I do not wish to sharply define *sanakuyaagal* in these terms, and instead I demonstrate how interlocutors apply creative principles of equation and analogy in practice.

Examining these routines as performances shows how interlocutors may draw on poetic principles and social idioms in interaction to navigate different relationships among one another, thereby linking particular speakers to posited social types. While much of the literature insists on the obligations and systematicity of joking relationships as a social logic or structure, a performative perspective allows for an examination of the ways these relational routines are creatively mobilized by interlocutors. Instead of looking to structural alliances afforded by any ostensible system of ethnic and patronymic correspondences, I argue that we must look to the emergent poetics of interaction to account for how they affect social relations. I begin this chapter by presenting *sanakuyaagal* routines and placing them within a literature in anthropology that has emphasized structural alliances. I continue with three examples of *sanakuyaagal* routines in interaction that show how creative uses emerge through a verbal creativity that posited novel equivalencies, socio-poetic principles of equation and reformulation that allow interlocutors to reformulate patronymic or ethnic *sanakuyaagal* correspondences. I conclude this chapter with an example showing how members of an autochthonous ethnic group that had not traditionally figured into joking correspondences managed to enter the game of *sanakuyaagal* by creating poetic bridges based on poetic similarities.

The perspective of performance shows that joking correspondences—established links between patronyms (for instance Ba-Diallo), ethnic groups (Serer-Peul), and generations (grandparent-grandchild)—are not merely automatic, but rather entail a creative deployment of relational grounds such that these interactions constitute relatively open systems of social recognition. Joking routines varied from quick comments embedded in greetings to longer narratives that drew on shared narrative structures, themes, and characters through which interlocutors teased one another. Routines of *sanaku* teasing within a frame of play often featured story plots, particular character traits, and settings that drew on histories of contact between ethnic groups and of problematized relationships in an idiom of gluttony, theft, and hierarchy. In so doing, interlocutors were able to voice socially recognizable characters and to play with relationships between individuals and social types by embedding joking partners within larger social imaginaries. Potentially drawing on a Serer-Peul relation in the opening encounter, for instance, the police officer employed the idiom of *sanakuyaagal* to constitute groups as protagonists and place them in a national sphere that had been invaded by outsider Peuls ("You all have come to live in our country."). Although he did not identify himself as Serer in the interaction, it is telling that many passengers assumed him to be, partly because of his teasing of Peuls.

Scholars have attributed to joking relationships considerable prominence on the West African social landscape: as a foundation of pan-Africanism (Ndiaye 1993), a framework for peaceful ethnic relations within the Senegalese nation-state (examined for instance by Smith 2006), or instead as a subversive anti-rite that chips away at social normativity (Douglas 1975). Rather than reifying the connections established during *sanakuyaagal* routines, I draw on encounters of face-to-face interaction to track how this joking is deployed and reinterpreted by linguistic actors. In so doing, I highlight creativity in joking relationship routines partly to compensate for assumptions about African social life that are relegated to rigid, parochial views of kinship and affinity. While other scholars have examined ways in which discourses about joking relationships mediate ideologies of nation-statehood and peaceful ethnic relations (Smith 2004, 2006), this chapter adopts an interactional perspective and draws on systematic observations and audio recordings.[3]

REFRAMING JOKING RELATIONSHIPS

Amid a large literature that spans the fields of anthropology, folklore, history, and political science (Radcliffe-Brown 1940; Brant 1948; Radcliffe-Brown 1949; Mauss 2013; Christensen 1963; Johnson and Freedman 1978; Sharman 1969; Rigby 1968), the example of joking relationships has previously served to buttress static, structural views of human societies as systems that require mechanisms for mediating relations among its constituent groups. West Africa has provided a prominent locus for the elaboration of this structural model of kinship (Fortes and Evans-Pritchard 1940). As the conceptual home for descent theory in the study of kinship, West Africa has offered an image of insular ethnic and linguistic islands (Amselle 1985). This chapter shows that even seemingly structured practices such as *sanakuyaagal* provide flexible resources for furthering new mobilities and conceptualizing the self and others in plural ways.

Rather than a tight system of social structure, African histories of contact, migration, and exchange have contributed to flexible networks of relational play that extend connections based on affinity, namesake relationships, and flexible interpretations of relatedness. Far from village archipelagoes, the existence of more or less shared norms for *sanakuyaagal* routines across swaths of Sahelian West Africa provides evidence of a broad linguistic and cultural diffusion. This is not surprising given important histories of Sahelian migration and trade (Brooks 1993) and, among linguists, the recognition of strong areal features in the form of the Sudanic belt (Güldemann 2008). Studying routines of joking relationships in interaction contributes to an understanding of how West Africans manage increasingly dispersed social networks by drawing on routines of verbal art to place one another in the idiom of caste, kin, affinity, or friendship.

Looking at joking relationships as the performance of political action means eschewing a reified "map" of categorical correspondences and equivalencies, one that obscures the agency of individuals who invoke and deploy relationships. In practice, interlocutors employ these routines in creative ways: to bring people into interaction or to constitute relationships among imagined groups in interaction. Previously, for instance, joking relationships have been divided between kin-based and non-kin-based relationships, and between categorical vs. noncategorical joking relationships (Apte 1985). Many anthropological perspectives have tended to reify joking relationships as a distinct genre and have overlooked how *sanakuyaagal* routines are related to other performance genres like praise oratory, storytelling, and teasing.

Joking relationships provided an early object of anthropological investigation that emerged from a study of kinship systems (see for example Labouret 1929; Lowie 1912). Robert Lowie, like his mentor Franz Boas, stressed the particularity of human societies rather than broad comparative theories. Radcliffe-Brown combined ethnography from fieldworkers like Lowie with his own work on mother's brothers in South Africa to provide a comparative theory of joking relationships (Radcliffe-Brown 1924, 1940, 1949). Placing these kinds of case studies in a comparative perspective, Radcliffe-Brown viewed joking relationships as a ritual of license that functioned to mediate social relations between kin or affines through the forces of conjunction and disjunction: "The theory that is here put forward, therefore, is that both the joking relationship which constitutes an alliance between clans or tribes, and that between relatives by marriage, are modes of organizing a definite and stable system of social behavior in which conjunctive and disjunctive components, as I have called them, are maintained and combined" (Radcliffe-Brown 1940, 200).

Approaches to joking relationships in the tradition of Radcliffe-Brown, however, have tended to read social structure into joking relationship routines partly by presupposing the groups brought into interaction. Still very much an active project, joking relationships continue to provide fertile terrain for projects of social imagining. These approaches locate understandings of patronymic, occupational, and ethnic correspondences within national, regional, or universalist frames to imagine social entity. For instance, joking relationships projected onto national boundaries have provided a frame for conceptualizing peaceful ethnic relations within the Senegalese nation (Smith 2006; Canut and Smith 2006), while other approaches have conceptualized joking relationship correspondences as the scaffold for a pan-African identity (Ndiaye 1993).

Based on Radcliffe-Brown's comparative approach, one can compare *sanakuyaagal* with similar categorical relations of teasing, for instance in North America (Berens and Hallowell 2009; Lowie 1912) and across Africa (Rigby 1968; Hagberg 2006; Sharman 1969; Christensen 1963). In East Africa, similar joking relationships known as *utani* are activated between particular ethnic groups (Beidelman 1964). Past approaches to *utani* have noted how these joking relationships can be viewed more as total social facts, phenomena that structure generational, lineage-based, and affinal relationships and encompass the reciprocity of gift giving or ritual responsibilities at funerals. Perspectives from this chapter can be applied to the East African context insofar as *utani*, like *sanakuyaagal* in West Africa, both offer interactional frames that individuals may inhabit through shared understandings of teasing.

Even in the Sahel, joking relationships were not a unitary practice. Differing conventions in interaction means that this genre was not a monolithic practice but rather a heterogeneous set of overlapping interpretive practices (characterized as a syncretic practice, for instance [Galvan 2006]). The existence of entextualized correspondences and equivalencies nevertheless provided a well-worn model of relational play that allows West Africans to posit connections between themselves and present or imagined actors by drawing on patronymic, occupational, ethnic, or other idioms. But instead of positing the social scale of joking relationships beforehand in the frame of the nation-state or a pan-African identity, the perspective of performance allows us to trace that the social work participants are performing in interaction.

PATRONYMIC PLAY

Sanakuyaagal routines in West Africa were interwoven with broader performances of conversational verbal art that drew on socially meaningful names, in particular patronyms. Patronyms[4] (*yettore*) provided a highly salient medium of social identification in southeastern Senegal and across West Africa. In a context where uttering first names (*innde*) was often read as casual or even disrespectful toward parents or elders (a broad trend noted by Fleming and Slotta 2015), interlocutors often began interactions by addressing others by their patronyms, or asking for them directly (e.g., "yettore maa?" "what is your last name?"). Many routines featured standard teases, often embedded in the greetings when individuals first recognized one another or asked of other's patronyms: "Yee, yette Ba moyɏaa, ɓe wujjay" ("Whoa! Bas are no good, they steal"). Patronymic as well as certain ethnic correspondences thus provided a staple of performed joking connections, and I provide a list of certain attested correspondences in table 1 below. Although this provides an overview of name-based correspondences that have provided grounds for *sanakuyaagal* routines, interlocutors could often creatively reinterpret the relational grounds (i.e., the correspondences between patronyms or ethnic groups). For this and other reasons it is not possible to offer a definitive list of *sanakuyaagal* correspondences. Later in this chapter, I detail ways in which interlocutors shaped them through socio-poetic creativity.

While patronyms often provided clues to an individual's ethnic membership, caste, or provenance, this could be ambiguous in practice (e.g., "Yette Souare ko Pullo?" ("Is a Souare a Peul?"). Pular patronyms in particular did not always map neatly onto stable ethnic or lineage-based group membership, and therefore they could be interpreted to propose other connections between interlocutors.[5] Individuals found to be sharing the same last name could use this as grounds to indicate some other association in the idiom of kin, in-law, or benefactor. For example, patronyms could be used to draw kinship connections in conversation, as *mussiɓe*: "oo ɗoo ko Diallo, ko mussiɓe meŋ" ("This guy is a Diallo, he is our kin"), a kola nut seller once said about a nonrelated client with whom he shared a patronym, Diallo. But although patronymic and ethnic correspondences might give the impression of a stable web of alliances, in practice interlocutors readapted connections in performed routines. While in many cases surnames carry ethnic and other social indexicalities, the possibility of changing names (permanently, as part of healing routines or momentarily during interactional renamings), the heterogeneity of alternate forms and equivalencies, and an indeterminate relationship between ethnicity and patronyms meant that reading identities from patronyms was in practice ambiguous. In table 2, I give an idea of the kinds of ethnic associations certain patronyms carried in the region of Kedougou. Likewise, table 3 provides a snapshot of certain patronyms that fall within the social associations of southeastern Senegal.

The existence of any purported patronymic correspondence (see table 1 above, e.g., Diallo—Kante), however, did not necessarily mean that a *sanaku* connection would be established. In a first instance, those who sit in a joking relationship with one another do not necessarily invoke their relationship at all times, and while certain individuals might invoke a joking relationship, a partner might not necessarily reciprocate (Launay 2006). Examining joking

Table 1. Some Attested *Sanakuyaagal* Correspondences

Patronymic Correspondences

Diallo	Ba
Barry	Sow
Keita	Kanté
Ndiaye	Diop
Camara	Dramé
Camara	Cissokho
Diaby	Danfakha
Diaby	Cissokho
Diallo	Kanté
Keita	Diaby
Diallo	Bindia
Ba	Boubane
Souaré	Keita
Souaré	Camara
Cisse	Dramé
Kante	Fofana
Diakhite	Diallo
Sidibé	Barry
Mballo	Diao

Ethnic Correspondences

Pullo	Serer
Serer	Diola

Table 2. Patronyms with Multiple Ethnic Associations

Patronym	Ethnic Associations in Kedougou Region
Sangaré	Pular, Bambara
Bakayoko	Pular, Bambara
Toure	Pular, Diakhanke
Coulibaly	Pular, Bambara
Kanouté	Pular, Diakhanké, Bambara
Cissokho	Pular, Bambara, Diakhanké
Kante	Pular, Bambara, Diakhanké
Sidibé	Pular, Bambara
Samoura	Pular, Bédik, Bambara, Diakhanké
Keita	Pular, Bédik, Bambara, Diakhanké
Souaré	Pular, Malinke
Ndiaye	Toucouleur, Wolof
Sadiakhou	Jallunke, Diakhanké
Camara	Jallunke, Diakhanké
Ly	Pular, Toucouleur
Sall	Pular, Toucouleur
Ndiaye	Pular, Toucouleur
Deme	Pular, Toucouleur
Sakho	Diakhanke, Bambara

relationships as a performance is to recognize that correspondences mobilized and ratified in interaction constitute an achievement. Name-based or ethnic correspondences do not necessarily constitute an ever-present relational context, but must be invoked and deployed by West African social actors. More broadly, previous scholarship in social interaction has shown that any particular identity cannot necessarily be used to predict configurations of stance alignments in interaction (Du Bois 2007; Lempert 2008). In the first place, joking relationships are only one possible categorical relation among many and are often deployed alongside a range of coexisting relational idioms such as namesake, blood relation, neighbor, or in-law. Furthermore, no two social actors necessarily have exactly the same conception of correspondences or equivalencies, particularly given the regional breadth of overlapping conceptions of *sanakuyaagal* across the Sahel. Finally, *sanakuyaagal* constitutes a historical genre in the sense that new and competing correspondences can be constructed in interaction that readapt socio-poetic connections. In what follows, I draw on three examples of *sanakuyaagal* talk to demonstrate the negotiation of joking relations in social interaction.

Table 3. Some Ethnic Associations

Ethnic Identification	Patronyms/Surnames in Kedougou Region
Pular	Ba, Barry, Diallo, Diakhité, Dia, Diao, Baldé, Camara, Ka, Sow, Sao, Ly
Malinké	Danfakha, Dansokho, Kouyaté, Kanouté
Sarakholé	Diawara, Doucoure, Gassama, Fadiga
Bambara	Coulibaly, Traoré, Diarrah, Bakayako, Kanté, Sangaré
Diakhanké	Danfakha (male), Damba (female), Dansokho, Diaby, Dembelé, Cissokho, Guirassy, Tandjigora, Diakhaby, Sakho, Soumaré
Bassari	Bindia, Boubane, Bianquinch, Bonang, Bandiar

PERFORMANCES OF *SANAKUYAAGAL* IN FACE-TO-FACE INTERACTION

Example One: The Father of Them All

Joking relationship routines afforded one possible interactional frame within which interlocutors embodied characters and navigated relationships in their daily greetings and practices. This first example demonstrates how such interactional routines of *sanakuyaagal* provide shared settings, plots, and problematics through which teasing interlocutors could place one another. While routines could draw on highly particular histories of interaction or "inside jokes," they also drew on broadly shared narrative settings and on characters that played upon themes of gluttony, patronage, hierarchy, and idiocy. This first example features Guinean and Senegalese traders in southeastern Senegal's largest border town, Kedougou City, who frequently teased one another based on a widely invoked correspondence between Fulɓe (sg. Pullo) and Serers.

In the busy downtown market of Kedougou City transformed in recent years by a gold rush and an expanding highway system, these daily exchanges provided ways of recognizing and accounting for colleagues or strangers. Here interlocutors made subtle inferences about one another based on names, bearing, or language, invoking a number of possible social frames for interpreting one another as kin, junior, or joking partner. Drawing on a commonly cited correspondence of Serer-Pullo, Diallo, a Guinean Pular merchant selling clothes and small electronic devices, regularly exchanged teases with a nearby hardware merchant, Mar. Diallo and other Fulɓe market sellers

Table 4. "The Father of Them All"

Diallo: late twenties male Guinean Pular merchant
Mar: early thirties male Serer merchant

(In Pular)

#	Speaker	Speech
1	Diallo	Ko miŋ woni baaba maɓɓe fow! Ko miŋ soodani mo kafe Touba o yari mo.
2	Mar	Serer no waawi nangugol jungo Pullo o yeeya mo.
3	Diallo	Ooɓ! Mi jaabataa ɗuŋ! Ko miŋ woni baaba Serer fop!

English:

#	Speaker	English Gloss
1	Diallo	I am the father of all of them! I'm the one who bought him Touba-style coffee and he drank it.
2	Mar	A Serer can grab a Pullo by the hand and sell him.
3	Diallo	No way! I'm not down with that. I'm the father of all Serers!

had made quick work of his patronym by twisting it into the Pular word for rice, "maaro." These charges of gluttony played upon local practices of hospitality in which guests are often welcomed and encouraged to share in meals with the hosts. In this context, the configuration of guest and host offered a scene and a cast of characters that market sellers and arriving clients could inhabit throughout the day.

Along with witchcraft, theft, and in this case gluttony, tropes of patronage in an idiom of hierarchical relations underlay many such routines. Here, for instance, Diallo claims to be the father (*baaba*) of Serers (line 3), one who procures the coffee. Claims of superiority, and indeed slavery (*maccuɓe* or *haaɓe*) were common (here on line 2, "A Serer can grab a Pullo by the hand and sell him"). This made reference to historical relations between certain occupational groups or castes, which were often characterized by hierarchies of social and bodily difference (see for instance Tamari 1991; Irvine 1973; Hoffman 2000). While often described as just play by interlocutors, these themes thus hinted at historical relations between populations, in this case being "slave" or "serf" status in what continues to provide many West Africans with a casted identity. Rather than trying to read idioms of *sanakuyaagal* teases directly against the social history of southeastern Senegal, however, interlocutors often productively deployed such characterizations. Not a static practice or merely an interactional instantiation of past political alliances, *sanakuyaagal* routines provided opportunities to creatively embed and refashion associations of social types.

Yet these ostensibly adversarial acts of teasing and insult were predicated on a close interactional collaboration.[6] Viewed in this way, even an argument or the exchange of insults necessitates a level of interactional cooperation through which interlocutors manage turns, timing, or agreement on the nature of their conversation as "a verbal duel" in the first place. Interlocutors were thus socialized into the conversational genre of *sanakuyaagal*. Teasing with charges of patronage, gluttony (or hospitality), hierarchy, and idiocy, conversationalists played with themes that I describe here as chronotopes, configurations of time, space, and narrative that make legible certain characters, kinds of actions, and plots (Lemon 2009; Bakhtin 1981). Drawing on Bakhtin, Lemon notes that "chronotope is not simply a point or a plane in space-time, not merely a scenic backdrop or surround of period and place. It shapes the logic by which events unfurl, their syntax, the rhythmic quality of plausible actions and counter-actions" (Lemon 2009, 839). Socialization into these narrative chronotopes thus makes legible certain kinds of plots and allows interlocutors to narrate stories dialogically. Once deployed, routines provided publicly available frameworks for constructing dialogic narratives in interaction, thereby making public particular legible scenes that others might enter into in order to animate characters and relationships.

Example Two: Stance and Epistemic Authority

In the following example I show how interlocutors construct a narrative together in the idiom of *sanakuyaagal*, managing their interactional stance through the dialogic narration of this story. Here the concept of stance helps to analyze an evolving relationship among interlocutors in terms of how they align themselves with respect to a position or object of evaluation (Du Bois 2007; Lempert 2008; Irvine 2009). This encounter features two primary interlocutors who ostensibly sit as *sanaku* and have teased one another on these grounds before (Mamadou as a Pullo and Faye as a Serer). Rather than simply tease one another in an idiom of a Serer-Pullo rivalry, however, the two interlocutors cede knowledge of the narrated event (i.e., epistemic rights) to one another, which ultimately leads to a collaborative narrative construction.

As this conversation unfolds, I am sharing a pot of tea at the home of Mamadou Diallo, who is chatting with several of his neighbors and with Faye, a Serer man from coastal Senegal who works as a local teacher. At one point in the conversation, some of Mamadou's neighbors begin to make statements about a strong Pular work ethic, statements that lead to some lighthearted exchanges. Pular work ethic was often linked to associations of Fulɓe as wily and self-interested individuals who live in closed communities defined by byzantine kin relations. This correspondence between Pullo and Serer was widely acknowledged one, animating heated volleys of teasing exchanges in the region of Kedougou, a place where Serer merchants stood out in a region populated significantly by Fulɓe. As the neighbors attend to themselves in conversation, Faye begins to tell Mamadou a story.

After "Peuls" become the topic of conversation, Faye thus proposes the story of "un petit Peul" ("a little Peul"), who, as he insinuates, stole something in the night. The nighttime constitutes a common ludic chronotope, a site of mischievous acts of theft and misrecognition between joking partners. Rather than counter Faye with insults by continuing along a Peul-Serer axis,

Table 5. "They Caught Some Little Peuls Here"

Setting: courtyard of Mamadou's house in Kedougou City, with other family members and neighbors present

Speakers

Mamadou: identifies here as Pullo, resident of Kedougou, mid-thirties
Faye: Man identifying as Serer from coastal Senegal, teaches in a local school, mid-thirties
Relational correspondences employed: (Peul—Serer); (Diallo—Ba)

#	Speaker	Speech	Translation
1	Faye	il paraît qu'on a attrap-	apparently they caught-
2	Faye	eh on avait attrapé des petits Peuls ici	eh that they caught some little Peuls here
3		haha ((group laughter))	haha ((group laughter))
4	Faye	hier nuit mais je ne s-	last night but I don't kn-
5	Faye	je n'étais pas au courent quoi	I didn't know what was going on
6	Mamadou	na alors c'est les Bas	or it's the Bas then
7	Mamadou	hier il y avait des idées ( ) ici	yesterday there were ideas (unintelligible) here
8	Faye	moi je	me I
9	Faye	en ce moment je dormais certainement	at that moment, I was surely asleep
10	Faye	ce sont les yette Ba quoi	it's the Bas then
11	Mamadou	ce sont les Ba	it's the Bas
12	Faye	oui	yes

however, Mamadou invokes Bas as a type, a Pular patronym that is widely held to be the joking partners of his own patronym, Diallo (line 6, "or it's the Bas then"). Looking ahead to lines 10 and 11, Faye and Mamadou ultimately fall into agreement about the culpability of these nonpresent Bas and align their stances in this regard. Eschewing the logic of a Fulɓe-Serer rivalry in this way and shifting to a Diallo-Ba opposition allows the two *sanaku* partners to find common ground among those considered to be "arch rivals" in the region of Kedougou. In this way, the affordance of patronymic or ethnic correspondences does not determine stance alignments in face-to-face interaction. Rather, interlocutors can draw on or posit linked correspondences to transpose connections to posited, nonpresent characters.

This interactional result is not accidental, however, but emerges out of a particular interactional matrix in which Mamadou and Faye negotiate epistemic authority, namely, how they evaluate one another's knowledge of events and, through it, their rights and responsibilities to contribute in conversation. This configuration is first initiated by Faye, who, on line 5 epistemically defers to Mamadou in the narrative of the story itself by claiming that he was not entirely informed, "je n'étais pas au courent quoi" ("I didn't know what was going on"). It is after this moment that Mamadou is able to propose the figure of the Bas, "na alors c'est les Bas" ("or it's the Bas then") on line 6. Further insisting on Mamadou's epistemic expertise, Faye states on line 9, "en ce moment je dormais certainement" ("at that moment, I was surely asleep"). In so doing, Faye deftly embeds his epistemic deference toward Mamadou in the reported narrative event itself. Faye uses the nighttime setting of the inchoate encounter between Fulɓe and Serer as a rhetorical cover to explain away his ignorance, thereby allowing Mamadou to present an alternative character, the Bas, as a foil.

As a performance of social connectivity, this example demonstrates how the adoption of different scalar perspectives can alter status alignment in social encounters. Mamadou and Faye's interactional alignment is partly achieved by playing upon *sanakuyaagal* correspondences that cut across different levels, in this case between ethnic groups (Serer-Fulɓe) and within Fulɓe (i.e., Peul) as a group (Diallo-Ba).

As with the previous encounter, this kind of dialogic storytelling is achieved through socialization into the genre of *sanakuyaagal*, which nevertheless has entailing effects for social types at the same time that it presupposes certain characteristics and connections. This interaction does not simply import social models into interactions but constitutes relevant groups and

Table 6. The Negotiation of Epistemic Authority

#	Speaker	Translation	Epistemic Authority
1	Faye	apparently they caught-	use of "apparently" ("il paraît") to mark story as purported
2	Faye	eh that they caught some little Peuls here	
3		haha	
4	Faye	last night but I don't kn-	insists that he did not know
5	Faye	I didn't know what was going on	insists on his ignorance
6	Mamadou	or it's the Bas then	Mamadou is able to cite a new participant
7	Mamadou	yesterday there were (unintelligible) here	
8	Faye	me I	
9	Faye	at that moment, I was surely asleep	narration of his past involvement cedes epistemic rights to Mamadou
10	Faye	it's the Bas then	Faye ratifies Mamadou's assertion
11	Mamadou	it's the Bas	
12	Faye	yes	

embeds them in particular configurations. In this case, the patronyms Diallo and Ba were recursively imagined within larger ethnic spheres by drawing upon the construction of "les Bas" as a social type. These dialogic joking routines thus feature emergent practices of typification through which particular characteristics (patronymic, ethnic, kinship, etc.) were referenced and linked up to social types, for example, Bas as buffoons, Diallos as wily thieves, or Serer as untrustworthy companions.

But *sanakuyaagal* constituted only one part of a rich performance tradition rich in verbal play through which interlocutors recognized one another; others included nicknaming, interactional renaming, and the creative employment of address terms. While certain ritual practices such as naming ceremonies and state-mandated identity cards might appear to provide fixity to naming, one could not rely on assumptions of stability. As with nicknames, patronyms, saint names, namesakes, taboo names, and adoptive names, names were not merely tags to refer to individuals but were used as significant social resources that indexed past relationships, constituted social persons, and diversified social actors' capacities for social interaction.[7] In

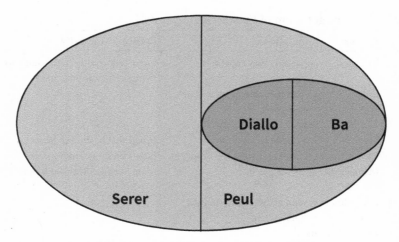

Embedding Correspondences in a *Sanakuyaagal* Encounter

face-to-face interactions, individuals could be momentarily rebaptized as in interactional renaming such as "hande aŋ ko Ba" ("today you're a Ba"). This itself a common strategy in joking routines that, once established, could be drawn upon by other interlocutors. The negotiation of names constituted an important strategy for building connections among transnational migrants from across West Africa in a boom town region where building expansive social networks was paramount.

Example 3—*Sanakuyaagal* and performing hospitality

The previous examples examined the performativity of *sanakuyaagal* routines in which actors inhabit different social roles, navigating relationships in a way that cannot necessarily be predicted by the existence of certain ethnic or patronymic correspondences. In so doing, interlocutors engaged in processes of typification and social identification through which they placed one another and also constituted and imagined social groups in interaction. In the following example, I show how *sanakuyaagal* routines constituted a performance of hospitality and recognizing others in the rural borderlands of Senegal and Guinea.

Sanakuyaagal routines were often embedded into greetings between hosts and guests, used to investigate the provenance of travelers approaching weekly markets in villages and in similar contexts where peripatetic groups converged. In the village of Taabe, a village of around three hundred individuals southwest of Kedougou City in the foothills of the Fouta Djallon mountains, *sanakuyaagal* routines offered interactional frames for articulating hospitality in the welcoming of guests. Like many of its neighboring villages on top of the plateau, Taabe has historically been a zone where populations could seek refuge at the interstices of secular and religious states.

As the dominant patronym in Taabe, Diallos considered themselves owners of the land and traced their lineage back to original founders earlier in the twentieth century. As joking partners of the Diallos, those with the last name Ba were often made to stand out. For example, one woman who bore the patronym Ba lived just down the road from the village chief. When men from the village walked by, they would often call out to her that she was an interloper, threatening to change her name to Diallo. When things went wrong, Bas were often blamed as quintessential scapegoats. Quick comments about Bas could be detected in the mutterings and murmurings after everyday spills and mistakes: "yette Ba ko ɓe boni koŋ" ("Bas are the worst"). When children (or even adults) made absent-minded mistakes like reaching for two spoons at the same time during dinner or wearing shorts inside out, residents would often invoke the character of a Ba as a witness, exclaiming what they might do if they were present ("If a Ba were here to see you . . ."). Invoked in this way, Bas constituted imagined witnesses and interlocutors, who offered relational foils for conceptualizing excuses and articulating norms. In this capacity they also provided imagined interlocutors through which residents could voice desires or articulate responsibilities to children. *Sanakuyaagal* talk was not dependent solely on the presence of one's joking partners, but rather offered a framework for constituting imagined interlocutors.

To visit Taabe and the plateau villages as a Ba was to be surrounded by one's joking partners and to inhabit a marked category that required a constant cultivation of verbal repartees. But it was in many ways a position of honor as well. To be revealed as a Ba was to be put on stage and to be an interlocutor whose interaction as performance was more highly scrutinized. For instance, when I first arrived in the village of Taabe many years ago with several other companions, we climbed up the steep mountain path to the entry of the village, where we met a man looking after some cattle. During our quick greetings, he asked for our last names. The affect of our interlocutor changed instantly as one of my travel companions admitted that her last name was Balde, which was often considered equivalent to the patronym Ba. "Yeee aŋ ko Ba, mi hummay maa jooni," I remember hearing, as the man built upon a correspondence between his name Diallo. ("Whoa you're a Ba,

I'm going to tie you up [with the cows]"). While Barry was a patronym more common in the region of Kolda to the west, the Taabe resident interpreted this in local terms, identifying an equivalence between Ba and Barry.

In this way, joking relationships routines often appeared as stark break-throughs into performance (Hymes 1973), available during the course of a wide variety of other social situations. When strangers did arrive in Taabe, *sanakuyaagal* routines provided one frame through which Taabe residents and incomers evaluated one another. For instance, at an NGO meeting to discuss the community's response to the region's 2014 Ebola epidemic just across the border in Guinea, *sanaku* talk broke through sober discussions of preventive initiatives. Similarly, when a group of educators arrived to test Taabe's cohort of primary school students hoping to pass their qualifying exams, the guests' patronyms were quickly assessed for potential connections. As Taabe hosts and professors learned of each other's patronyms, a flurry of insults and teases, interspersed with laughter, accompanied these moments of recognition. As the entire delegation first met with Taabe's notables, the official agenda was punctuated by storytelling between joking partners. In the embodied theater of joking relationships, performances could come at almost any time, thereby providing interlocutors with narratives and characters to inhabit for episodes of teasing and storytelling.

In the following example, *sanakuyaagal* routines emerge as an idiom for recognizing others in the context of hospitality among increasingly mobile populations within a region undergoing social and economic change. These routines constituted an emerging site of social typification and discovery. In the village of Taabe, many adults had spent time away during periods of cyclical migration before eventually settling back down in the village. In so doing, they had encountered and built relationships with individuals from across Senegal and West Africa. One day, Taabe's village chief was delighted to tell me that a man he had befriended while working as a baker in western Mali would be spending a few weeks with us as a guest. Alpha Ba was a consummate traveler who had business interests and family all across Mali, Senegal, and Guinea. As an avid storyteller, he regaled us with perilous tales from the gold mines, stories from a time when he and the chief had lived together in Mali. Bearing the last name of Ba, however, situated Alpha as a prime target for teasing. Indeed, hearing of a Ba in their midst, many villagers visited him on his first day, and *sanakuyaagal* routines often animated these first meetings. Much of the next days were spent exchanging stories and catching up on news in front of a boiling kettle of tea.

As a routine that drew emphasis upon one's interactional responsibilities to attend to interlocutors, *sanakuyaagal* could be deployed to maintain and renew a communicative channel. Viewed in this way, language is not merely a system of reference for picking out things in the world, and *sanaku* routines could offer a resource for rekindling contact with interlocutors after conversations had lulled. In the following interaction, Taabe's chief (Chief) and another Taabe elder (Diallo), both bearing the patronym Diallo, sit with Souare (Souare), another household head from a nearby hamlet, and chief's dear friend, Alpha Ba (Ba). After several minutes of listening to Arabic prayers together, Taabe's village chief breaks the silence by teasing his *sanaku*, exclaiming "elder witch!" (mawɗo ñanne) in a deep voice. He soon continues, exclaiming "They fly around at night!" ("kanɓe ɓe wiiray jemma de") on line 15. The chief and another local elder lay down charges of witchcraft upon Bas, until Souare, an elder from a nearby village, comes to Ba's defense on line 27, exclaiming "Hold on now. . . . Bas are our in-laws."

Important to note from the outset is that Bas as a collective group do not constitute any stable in-law group with respect to Bas or indeed the Souares. This is to say that Ba, Diallo, or Souare, and Pullo patronyms in particular do not share a sense of clan-based affinity as a marriage group in general. This underdetermination, however, opens the possibility for locally salient, contextually specific relationships to be woven into joking correspondences. In this way, *sanakuyaagal* routines present a possible idiom of social identification that could be interwoven with other idioms of affinity, kinship, neighborliness, or even universality in the name of religion.

As shared routines for social play, teasing Ba by launching charges of witchcraft initiates a frame for other participants to enter into this performance. On line 16, Souare enters the fray and identifies Bas as his *esiraaɓe*, respected elder in-laws who are owed deference and respect. He draws on this fact to justify his defense of them in the context of an invoked correspondence between Diallo and Ba. Echoing Souare's typification on lines 17 and 22, Alpha Ba soon confirms this affinal relationship from his perspective and aligns with Souare, exclaiming "us and the Souareeɓe, they are our in-laws." By drawing the focus away from the Ba-Diallo axis, Souare invokes a joking relationship between Souare, his own patronym, and Camaras. This move ends up providing a kind of resolution, since no Camaras are present to contest their tongue-in-cheek belittlement.

Rather than automatically falling into position along the axes of joking correspondences as structural operators, this example shows how *sanaku*

Table 7. "The Souares Are Our In-Laws"

Speakers

Chief: elder male, village chief of Taabe
Diallo: elder male, Taabe resident
Souare: elder male, from a nearby hamlet
Ba: elder male, lifetime friend and guest of the Taabe's village chief

#	Speaker	Pular	Free Translation
1		((silence for many minutes))	
2	Chief	mawɗo ñanne	elder witch
3	Diallo	mm	mm
4	Chief	kanɓe ɓe wiiray jemma de	them, they fly at night
5	Diallo	mm mm	mm mm
6	Diallo	yette Ba ɓen	the Bas
7	AB	[ñanne (hiɓe) toŋ	witches (are) over there
8	Chief	[yette Ba ɓen	the Bas
9	Diallo	alaa ɗun kay	none of that
10	Souare	heh heh he: [hah hah	heheheehehe
11	Diallo	[ko ( )	that's (unintelligible)
12	Chief	yette Ba ɓeŋ kay	the Ba's indeed
13	Souare	he ha ha ha	he hahaha
14	Diallo	ɓe suuɗoray yahugol jemma ngol	they hide their nighttime business
15	Chief	laaɓi [poy	that's right
16	Souare	[eh: accee de meneŋ yette Ba ɓeŋ ko esiraaɓe ameŋ	hee hold on now. For us, Bas are our in-laws
17	AB	eeyo: (-no)	ye:ah uh
18	Souare	[accee	hold on
19	AB	[meneŋ kay (.) ɗuŋ waɗèŋ ( )	us then (.) that let's do it (unintelligible)
20	Souare	eeyo accee yette Ba ɓeŋ tawaaka	yeah hold there on with the Bas
21	Chief	naaneŋ [( ) attaya wi'uɗaa honduŋ ((aside))	hear me ( ) tea you said what ((aside))
22	AB	[hay meneŋ e yette Soua-reeɓe beŋ ko meŋ esiraaɓe	us and the Souares they are our in-laws
23	Souare	eeyo meneŋ	yup us
24	Souare	si eŋ haalay ko yette Camara ɓeŋ	if we're talking, it's the Camaras
25	AB	mm hmm	mm hmmm
26	Souare	yette Camara ɓeŋ kay mom	those Camaras indeed

performances emerge in relation to other social idioms like affinity. As in the previous example, these kinds of calculations provide opportunities for constituting and imagining social groups, in this case by typifying individuals as members of a categorical group (e.g., Souares as collective in-laws). This scenario demonstrates that joking relationship encounters do not merely draw on pre-established groups with fixed alignments, but rather that individuals are able to constitute relevant groups and frames of evaluation over the course of interactions (e.g., Bas as an in-law group). Rather than a closed encounter between speakers and hearers, *sanakuyaagal* routines provide initial interactional matrices that an audience can break into and transform. Viewed in this way, processes of typification (e.g., the Souares as in-laws) stand as a performative achievement.

NEGOTIATING EQUIVALENCIES

Within *sanakuyaagal* routines, a further principle of flexible play arose when interlocutors drew equivalencies between certain patronyms in such a way that two different names were understood to be equivalent. In many cases equivalencies were motivated on the basis of a shared occupational niche, a perceived ethnic link, as well as certain formal poetic resemblances between terms. This historical and poetic logic of equivalencies meant that certain patronyms within and across ethnic groups could count as the same, for instance that Diallo among Guinean Fulɓe, and Kane or Ka among northern Senegalese Fulɓe, count as the same name. In the previous example, I showed how Balde and Ba were construed as equivalent terms based on their poetic similarity. Even outside teasing routines, interlocutors, often debated these equivalencies, stating for instance that "Ka et Diallo, fow ko gootuŋ" ("Ka and Diallo are the same thing"). In the case of Guinea, for instance, southern Mande names often carried correspondences with northern Mande names (McGovern 2013). These equivalencies, which provide the grounds of performed *sanaku* relations, thereby demonstrate the futility of establishing any exhaustive list of joking partners. The following table provides some attested equivalencies deployed in the region of Kedougou.

Looking across cases, however, it was possible to identify certain principles that motivated these equivalencies. These include occupational distinctions between farmers and blacksmiths grounded in notions of occupational interdependence, noble and casted groups grounded in hierarchy, or Islamic converter and converted animist grounded in domination. For instance, certain blacksmithing patronyms such as Cissokho and Kante were often used interchangeably and—for the purposes of *sanakuyaagal*—could be deployed against names associated with farming. Moreover, many Guinean Fulɓe merchants in the downtown Kedougou markets whose ancestors brought Islam to the indigenous populations of Kedougou identified their *sanaku* partners as those individuals whose ancestors had been converted (Diallo 2001). Given this transformational logic of ethnic groups and patronymics, it was possible to envision an encompassing system of social connectivity across the social landscape of Sahelian West Africa (Ndiaye 1993).

Certain patronymic correspondences were legible across great distances. Indeed, links between Diallo and Ba were enshrined in stories from the settlement of the Fouta Djallon. Other correspondences such as Kante and Keita figure in the historical battle between Sumanguru Kante and Sundjata Keita that figures in the *Sundjata Epic*, a foundational piece of oral history that chronicles the founding of the empire of Mali (Niane 1965). While some correspondences were thus enshrined in widely disseminated histories, other correspondences on the other hand had narrower ranges or might only have succeeded over the course of a single interaction.

In the region of Kedougou, for instance, I often heard conflicting accounts of whether Fulɓe sit in a joking relationship with Jaxanké or Malinké. Given that there is no universal list of *sanaku* partners and that these connections are sustained and regulated in interaction, a certain level of ambiguity permeates any *sanaku* relationship constructed in interaction (Launay 2006). In

Table 8. Some Patronymic Equivalencies Attested in the Region of Kedougou (to be read across)

Patronymic Equivalencies			
⇒ Diallo	Kane	Ka	
⇒ Ba	Baldé	Diakhité	Mballo
⇒ Sow	Sidibe		
⇒ Cissokho (male)	Sakiliba (female)	Doumbia	Kanté
⇒ Danfakha (male)	Damba (female)		
⇒ Keita (male)	Soukho (female)		
⇒ Diaby	Diaoune		

Note: Such that Barry and Ba could count for the same name. Some such as Danfakha and Mamadou refer to names in which men are given the male version of the name, while women bear the female version.

the face of these ambiguities, newly minted or contested correspondences that are strongly motivated in an interaction could possibly succeed. Furthermore, the entextualized performance of patronymic correspondences in the first place provides a frame for other links to be created that might not have a life beyond these passing interactions. Therefore, rather than searching for an exhaustive list, the perspective of performance can capture how interlocutors monitor and motivate particular name-based connections in interaction.[8] As shown by the examples in this chapter, this approach draws greater attention to the broader participation framework and contingent processes of ratification by copresent participants rather than limiting analyses to *sanakuyaagal* talk between merely two interlocutors.

POETIC AS POLITICAL: CONSTRUCTING BASSARI JOKING CORRESPONDENCES

I began by arguing that processes of equation and relational play captured through the perspective of performance reveal emergent stance configurations and social imaginaries by West African social bricoleurs. While most patronyms common in southeastern Senegal—particular those of Mande, Pular, Wolof, Serer, and Diola origin—were broadly understood to be implicated in systems of correspondences, there were those names that, at first glance, did not appear to figure into this Sahelian relational chronotope. I conclude this chapter by briefly discussing verbal creativity that has allowed some to construct novel poetic associations into routines of *sanakuyaagal.*

Among these, the historically matrilineal Bassari,[9] commonly identified as the autochthonous inhabitants of Kedougou, did not ostensibly figure into the logics of joking relationships that largely encompassed Sahelian populations. Working primarily as broad-spectrum hunters, gatherers, and seasonal horticulturalists, raiding and conflict with incoming Fulɓe populations had forced "animist" Bassari from what were once extensive territories to more inaccessible and therefore more defensible locations. Today, Bassari villages are located in the most mountainous parts of Kedougou. Even to this day, some Bassari and Fulɓe often admit a mutual uneasiness that continues to be animated by histories of confrontation.

Nevertheless, alongside increased movement and contact among Bassari and other populations in southeastern Senegal, over time many Bassari have managed to construct poetic links between their last names and Pular names based on formal parallelisms. While Bassari surnames including Bijar, Bou-bane, Bindia, Biesse, and Biankesh have been traditionally figured in matri-lineal terms, in contrast with a dominant logic of patrilineality in the area, in recent decades many are also traced patrilineally. Drawing on poetic par-allelisms, many of these common Bassari names are now regularly linked to Pular names in the region of Kedougou. As was related to me by both Bassari and Pular sources, Boubane has come to be understood as equivalent to the Pular patronym Ba, such that Diallo-Boubane has been motivated as a joking correspondence (based on the equivalence <u>Ba</u> = Bou<u>bane</u> and the correspon-dence Diallo-Ba). Similarly, the common Bassari name Bindia has in many cases been made to stand as equivalent to Diallo (<u>Dia</u>llo = Bin<u>dia</u>) based on the sharing of the sound [dʒa] (often written in French orthography as "dia"). These forms of poetic bricolage have meant that Bassari in the region of Kedougou can—with a bit of poetic finesse—selectively sub themselves into the game of joking relationships.[10]

While other less common Bassari names did not to my knowledge figure as readily into the system of correspondences, it was striking how flexible urban Bassari had become in adopting and motivating name-based connec-tions. While Bassari communities in principle followed matrilineal logics, some who anticipated a default assumption of patronymy would offer their father's last names in moments of self-presentation. Many Bassari were thus interactionally flexible in offering last names to their neighbors who might understand one's surname to be the name of one's father, here *yettore* (in Pular), *nom de famille* (in French), or *jaamu* (in Malinke). Bassari of Kedou-gou City, in fact, often entertained a wealth of naming systems including birth-order names and Catholic "Saint" names, in addition to secret names acquired during initiation ceremonies. Some Bassari youth I met also went by Muslim given names. This social flexibility enabled by the many different ways of calling and addressing provided tools for creating connections with one's consociates. Considering the relational opportunities that names may offer to their bearers, it is not surprising that individuals would maximize potentially invokable links to a range of possible patronyms and nicknames. At the same time, however, when it was not interactionally advantageous to do so, these same connections could be denied.

The example of the Bassari furthermore demonstrates how groups draw equivalencies through the construction of poetic bridges across genres and practices and not only across names. Many Bassari I talked to conceived of their own *classe d'âge* (age grade) system as akin to or indeed part of

Table 9. Bassari-Fulɓe Poetic Bridges

Bassari Given Name	Equivalent Pular Patronym	Sound Image
Bou**ba**ne	**Ba**	[ba]
Bin**dia**	**Dia**llo	[dʒa]

sanakuyaagal. Among the Bassari, girls and boys are initiated into a *classe d'âge* ranging from one to six that defines their social roles and responsibilities for much of their adult lives.[11] These *classes d'âge* correspond to six years, after which point one enters the next *classe d'âge*. One's *classe d'âge* defines the kinds of activities one can engage in and provides a set of norms for engaging with individuals from another *classe d'âge*. One significant aspect of the system is that any two *classes d'âge* separated by a year are understood to have a system of mutual teasing and license. In this way, ranks one and three, or four and six, are understood to stand in a joking relationship with one another. These examples demonstrate the porousness of joking relationships in performance and thereby offer further evidence of anything but a monolithic practice. In short, the case of Bassari equivalencies shows that interlocutors can manage to insert themselves into routines of *saakuyaagal* through socio-poetic performances of verbal creativity.

CONCLUSION

This chapter has drawn on examples of face-to-face interaction through the perspective of performance in order to argue that *sanakuyaagal* correspondences do not predetermine stances or interactions. They constitute an achievement rather than an automatic function of categorical belonging. Interlocutors draw on multiple relational idioms, poetic devices, and shared chronotopic narratives that are open to reformulation. Not only a dyadic relationship between two joking partners, these joking performances are, so to speak, played upon an open stage that overhearers may join or comment on based on their shared knowledge of this narrative chronotopes. These examples provide evidence of a rich, creative, and ever-changing practices of social interpretation by West African bricoleurs.

As demonstrated through three extended examples from *sanakuyaagal* routines in southeastern Senegal, routines of *sanakuyaagal* constitute emergent performances that reformulate relational premises. Not only a map of virtual connections, these correspondences are built and reformulated by speakers in interaction in such a way that they depend on audience and interlocutor for ratification. They provide shared tools through which individuals inhabit certain social personae and ways of speaking, as guests, hosts, or in-laws (see Irvine, chapter 1 in this volume). They furthermore demonstrate the usefulness of considering interlocutors not as unitary persons with fixed identities, but as multilayered actors whose practices of self-presentation emerge in relation to one another and through interactional genres such as *sanakuyaagal*. Everyday acts of teasing develop widely shared narrative chronotopes in West Africa, thereby animating imagined characters and scenes with idioms of theft, gluttony, and hierarchy through which interlocutors reinterpret histories of social contact in the frame of play. Teasing routines allow interlocutors a platform for making connections across time and space, for typifying certain groups (e.g., "the Diallos") and for providing scenes in which corporate bodies (of in-laws for instance) may be imagined. Finally, joking routines demonstrate the power of poetics to drive connections across social domains, as demonstrated by certain Bassari who have inserted themselves in the game of *sanakuyaagal* through socio-poetic logics. While *sanakuyaagal* relationships do not neatly map on to political alliances between lineages, ethnic groups, or speakers, they do provide West Africans with meaningful relational tools for placing and evaluating one another in social interaction.

Transcription Conventions

[	overlapping
(.4)	pauses of .4 seconds
(.)	pauses of less than .2 seconds
(( ))	transcriber comments
( )	unintelligible
-	indicates speech that is broken off
:	an extended vowel (ye:)
=	equal signs indicate latching, utterances following one another with no perceivable pause

Special Symbols

This chapter employs several commonly employed special symbols to write local languages that are adapted from the IPA alphabet.

Ŋŋ	voiced velar nasal
Ɓɓ	voiced bilabial implosive
Ɗɗ	voiced alveolar implosive
Ƴƴ	liquid velar implosive
Ññ	palatal nasal
Xx	voiceless velar fricative

NOTES

1. Peuls, an ethnic group from the region, often draw on an ethnic-based correspondence to establish a teasing relationship with Serers, of which the gendarme was inferred to be a member. Although they are called Peuls in French, they refer to themselves as Fulɓe (pl.) or Pullo (sg.) in their language, Pular.

2. In this chapter, I employ the local term commonly employed in southeastern Senegal, *sanakuyaagal* in Pular (or *sanaku*, one's joking "partner"), which has Mande origins and hints at its broad diffusion across the linguistic and cultural landscape of West Africa. *Sanakuyaagal* is often considered quintessentially Mande, first enacted after the Empire of Mali's founding in the thirteenth century. Studying *sanaku* joking routines at the periphery of its ostensible range, however, allows for a glimpse of how it is extended, adapted, and disseminated more broadly.

3. Most of the data I draw on were collected while conducting anthropological field work in southeastern Senegal from 2014 to 2016.

4. I refer to most of these last names or surnames as patronyms, since in this part of West Africa they are most often passed down along the father's side. Women who married into families, however, typically retain their own last name, and these are often drawn on in forms of debate. While youth and those in familiar relationships do often refer to each other by their first names or nicknames, the most common form of respectful address is through last names. Most names listed here are properly patronyms passed on patrilineality, with the exception of Bassari names such as Bindia, Boubane, etc., which I address in the conclusion.

5. Many thanks to Mike McGovern for reminding me that Mande patronyms do in many cases follow along clan affiliations.

6. Not only confrontations, joking in the idiom of Pular and Serer were also expressed as originating from a historical relationship between two ancestors, a Serer for instance who helped out his fellow hunting partner in a time of hunger by offering him a piece of his own leg, an act of kindness that resulted in a privileged relationship.

7. Among elite Yemeni women, for instance, the adoption of "male names" allowed adult women to interact publicly with men who were not part of their intimate family circle, thereby affording increased possibilities for social interaction (Vom Bruck 2006).

8. In this light, the tables of correspondences that I included in this chapter provide a record of *sanakuyaagal* in interaction and should not be viewed as an exhaustive list.

9. Bassari refer to themselves as 'Bëliyan, and they speak Oniyan, which is known to outsiders as Bassari. They are often linked with "Tenda," or Bedik populations, and misidentified as Tenda.

10. It is telling that even among those who had not previously heard about equivalencies between Bassari and Pular often immediately accepted their legitimacy based on poetic parallelisms. On one particular occasion, I asked a Pullo friend if he knew about these particular correspondences between Bassari and Pular names. He replied initially that he did not; however, he was instantly persuaded by the poetic parallels between Ba-Boubane and Diallo-Bindia. This episode hints at underlying strategies in which residents of the Kedougou region interpret *sanaku* correspondences and partnerships not through a fixed "rule book" of correspondences, but through principles of association that draw on poetic correspondences.

11. See Gabail 2012 for a discussion of Bassari initiations. For more on Bassari in the region of Kedougou, refer to Gessain 2003; 1979; Nolan 1977; N'Dong 2010.

WORKS CITED

Amselle, Jean-Loup. 1985. *Au Cœur de l'ethnie: Ethnies, Tribalisme et État En Afrique.* Textes à l'appui. Série Anthropologie. Paris: Éditions La Découverte.

Apte, Mahadev L. 1985. *Humor and Laughter: An Anthropological Approach.* Ithaca, NY: Cornell University Press.

Bakhtin, M. M. 1981. *The Dialogic Imagination: Four Essays.* Translated by Michael Holquist. Austin: University of Texas Press.

Beidelman, Thomas O. 1964. "Intertribal Insult and Opprobrium in an East African Chiefdom (Ukaguru)." *Anthropological Quarterly* 37, no. 2: 33–52.

Berens, William, and A. Irving Hallowell. 2009. *Memories, Myths, and Dreams of an Ojibwe Leader.* Edited by Jennifer S. H. Brown and Susan Elaine Gray. Montreal; Kingston; Ithaca: McGill-Queen's University Press.

Brant, Charles S. 1948. "On Joking Relationships." *American Anthropologist* 50, no. 1: 160–62.

Brooks, George. 1993. *Landlords and Strangers: Ecology, Society and Trade in Western Africa. 1000–1630.* Boulder, CO: Westview Press.

Canut, Cécile, and Etienne Smith. 2006. "Pactes, Alliances et Plaisanteries." *Cahiers d'études Africaines* 184, no. 4: 687–754.

Christensen, James Boyd. 1963. "Utani: Joking, Sexual License and Social Obligations Among the Luguru." *American Anthropologist* 65, no. 6: 1314–27.

Diallo, El Hadj Maladho. 2001. *Histoire Du Fouta Djallon.* Paris: L'Harmattan.

Douglas, Mary. 1975. *Implicit Meanings: Essays in Anthropology.* London: Routledge & Paul.

Du Bois, John W. 2007. "The Stance Triangle." In *Stancetaking in Discourse: Subjectivity, Evaluation*, 139–82. Amsterdam: John Benjamins Publishing Company.

Fleming, Luke, and James Slotta. 2015. "Named Relations: A Universal in the Pragmatics of Reference within the Kin Group." *Proceedings of the Chicago Linguistics Society* 51: 165–79.

Fortes, Meyer, and E. E. Evans-Pritchard, eds. 1940. *African Political Systems*. London: Published for the International African Institute by the Oxford University Press.

Gabail, Laurent. 2012. "Performing Opacity: Initiation and Ritual Interactions across the Ages among the Bassari of Guinea." *HAU: Journal of Ethnographic Theory* 2, no. 2: 138–62.

Galvan, Dennis. 2006. "Joking Kinship as a Syncretic Institution." *Cahiers d'études Africaines* 184, no. 4: 809–34.

Gessain, M. 1979. "Implications Anthropologiques de l'évolution Des Bassari Du Sénégal Oriental Depuis 1900." *Bulletins et Mémoires de La Société d'anthropologie de Paris* 6, no. 4: 389–97.

Gessain, M. 2003. *Bassari: Guinée et Sénégal, 1927–2002*. Saint-Maur: Editions Sépia.

Güldemann, Tom. 2008. "'Macro-Sudan Belt': Towards Identifying a Linguistic Area in Northern Sub-Saharan Africa." In *A Linguistic Geography of Africa*, edited by Derek Nurse and Bernd Heine, 151–85. Cambridge: Cambridge University Press.

Hagberg, Sten. 2006. "The Politics of Joking Relationships in Burkina Faso." *Zeitschrift für Ethnologie* 131, no. 2: 197–214.

Hoffman, Barbara G. 2000. *Griots at War: Conflict, Conciliation, and Caste in Mande*. Bloomington: Indiana University Press.

Hymes, Dell. 1973. *Breakthrough into Performance*. Urbino, Italy: Centro internazionale di semiotica e di linguistica.

Irvine, Judith. 1973. "Caste and Communication in a Wolof Village." PhD dissertation, University of Pennsylvania.

Irvine, Judith. 2009. "Stance in a Colonial Encounter: How Mr. Taylor Lost His Footing." In *Stance*, edited by Alexandra Jaffe, 53–72. Oxford: Oxford University Press.

Johnson, Ragnar, and Jim Freedman. 1978. "Joking Relationships." *Man* 13, no. 1: 130–33.

Labouret, Henri. 1929. "La Parenté à Plaisanteries En Afrique Occidentale." *Africa: Journal of the International African Institute*, 2, no. 3 :244–254.

Launay, Robert. 2006. "Practical Joking." *Cahiers d'études Africaines* 184, no. 4: 795–808.

Lemon, Alaina. 2009. "Sympathy for the Weary State?: Cold War Chronotopes and Moscow Others." *Comparative Studies in Society and History* 51, no. 4: 832.

Lempert, Michael. 2008. "The Poetics of Stance: Text-Metricality, Epistemicity, Interaction." *Language in Society* 37, no. 4: 569–92.

Lowie, Robert Harry. 1912. *Social Life of the Crow Indians*. New York: The Trustees.

Mauss, M. 2013. "Joking Relations." Edited by Jane I. Guyer. *HAU: Journal of Ethnographic Theory* 3, no. 2: 317–34.

McGovern, Mike. 2013. *Unmasking the State: Making Guinea Modern*. Chicago: University of Chicago Press.

Ndiaye, Raphael. 1993. "Ethno-Patronymic Correspondences and Jocular Kinship." *African Environment* 8, nos. 3–4: 93–124.

N'Dong, Babacar. 2010. *Les Bassari Du Sénégal à Tambacounda: Une Communauté Traditionnelle En Milieu Urbain*. Minorités & Sociétés. Paris: L'Harmattan.

Niane, Djibril Tamsir. 1965. *Sundiata: An Epic of Old Mali*. London: Longmans.

Nolan, Riall W. 1977. "L'histoire des migrations bassari, influences et perspectives." *Journal des africanistes* 47, no. 2: 81–101.

Radcliffe-Brown, A. R. 1924. "The Mother's Brother in South Africa." *South African Journal of Science* 21 (December): 542–55.

Radcliffe-Brown, A. R. 1940. "On Joking Relationships." *Africa: Journal of the International African Institute* 13, no. 3: 195–210.

Radcliffe-Brown, A. R. 1949. "A Further Note on Joking Relationships." *Africa: Journal of the International African Institute*, 19, no. 2:133–140.

Rigby, Peter. 1968. "Joking Relationships, Kin Categories, and Clanship among the Gogo." *Africa* 38, no. 2: 133–55.

Sharman, Anne. 1969. "'Joking' in Padhola: Categorical Relationships, Choice and Social Control." *Man* 4, no. 1: 103–17.

Smith, Etienne. 2004. "Les cousinages de plaisanterie en Afrique de l'Ouest, entre particularismes et universalismes." *Raisons politiques* 13, no. 1: 157.

Smith, Etienne. 2006. "La Nation «par Le Côté»." *Cahiers d'études Africaines* 184, no. 4: 907–965.

Tamari, Tal. 1991. "The Development of Caste Systems in West Africa." *Journal of African History* 32, no. 2: 221.

Vom Bruck, Gabriele. 2006. "Names as Bodily Signs." In *The Anthropology of Names and Naming*, 225–50. Cambridge: Cambridge University Press.

Participation beyond Gratitude

'Sterling Greetings' and the Mediation
of Social Ties on Nigerian Radio

JENDELE HUNGBO

INTRODUCTION

A few years ago, when election campaigns were on in Nigeria, a top politician vying to return to office as a state governor accused a caller on a live radio show of ingratitude. In the reckoning of the politician who held the office he was seeking again, his constituents were expected to first of all show gratitude to him for things he had done previously to "change their lives" and for the growth of their communities before confronting him with a list of demands and things they expect from him should he secure their mandate for another term. In ending his response to the "ungrateful" caller, the politician called attention to a Yoruba saying: *yin'ni yin'ni k'eni o se mii*, which loosely translates to "gratitude begets additional goodwill."[1]

This kind of scenario, which played out on live radio between the politician and the caller, is symptomatic of the accepted atmosphere where gratitude is an expected and necessary act in return for good deeds (real or imagined), magnanimity, and acts of philanthropy performed by individuals acting on their own (or on behalf of the government) in Nigerian society. It is against this background that this chapter traces the development of the mediation, through radio, of the expression of gratitude as a way of life among listeners and users of two radio stations in Ogun State, in the southwest of Nigeria, where the population is mostly Yoruba. In addition, I argue that the ways in which messages are crafted in "Sterling Greetings" (a subcategory of

69

personal paid announcements) point to a kind of performativity at the core of such greetings, which aim to make their subjects assume a position of power and create a sense of loyalty. My deeper inquiry is: What sense can we make of Sterling Greetings beyond the public displays of affection, reverence, and overwhelming respect portrayed on radio?

GRATITUDE IN THE CONSTRUCTION OF STERLING GREETINGS

The rich body of work dealing with the concept of gratitude (Carr 2015; Froh, Bono, and Emons 2010; Jackson 2016; Lambert, Graham, and Fincham 2009; Merçon-Vargas, Poelker, and Tudge 2018) explores how gratitude is a form of appreciation expressed by an individual or group believed to be at the receiving end of what is perceived to be a good gesture. It is "a positive response to receiving a benefit" (Froh, Bono, and Emons 2010, 144) and can be further classified as part of what Chouliaraki conceives as "traditionally marginal practices" (2010, 228), which are significant in the understanding of self-mediation and identity politics. Gratitude can then be seen as a moral affect and prosocial behaviour through which the value of social harmony and interpersonal relationships can be strengthened. This value is further captured in the contention that "gratitude is a psychologically and socially beneficial human quality of some moral significance" (Carr 2015, 1475). In the course of appreciating what is valuable or meaningful to one person in a gesture expressed by another, a social rapport develops that may lead to other forms of conviviality and connection. Proposing a prototypical classification of gratitude, Lambert, Graham, and Fincham (2009) argue that lay conceptions of the term are much more productive than the ones framed by research. For the purpose of this research, it will be important to take into account both scholarly and lay perspectives of gratitude in order to have a more nuanced understanding of the phenomenon. Regarding Sterling Greetings, it is important to mention that the lay understanding of gratitude can also be argued to stem from the orality and spontaneity of radio and messages disseminated through its medium. The quick improvisatory nature of verbal exchange over the radio shapes how Sterling Greetings create meanings for the diverse listening audiences.

As a moral virtue, gratitude signposts power relations between individuals and groups in society. The power position of the perceived giver in an act of kindness is often elevated beyond that of the receiver, who is expected to show gratitude. Such relations of power may be defined by different factors, such as age, financial means, or political power. There is also nothing sacrosanct about the direction in which gratitude may proceed. In the case of age as a determining factor, for instance, an older person may be grateful to a younger individual when that older person receives a gesture of goodwill from the younger one. In light of this, gratitude can then be seen as a pervasive principle in the polity. This pervasiveness often extends to the arena of politics, whereby it is given expression through various forms of media.

This study focuses on two radio stations in southwest Nigeria where the majority population is Yoruba and gratitude is an extremely important moral concept. This region is made up of six states including Lagos, the commercial nerve center of the country. For the Yoruba and other ethnic groups residing in the area, gratitude is a way of life; hence the common saying *Eni t'aa se loore ti ko dupe, bi olosa ko ni l'eru lo ni* (an ingrate is worse than an armed robber). In other words, there are the general expectations of gratitude as a necessary act in return for good deeds and magnanimity (expressed as acts of philanthropy) performed by both individuals and the government.

THEORETICAL AND METHODOLOGICAL CONSIDERATIONS

This chapter adopts a cultural approach to critical discourse analysis (Blommeart 2005; Janks 1997; Macdonald 2003; Scollo 2011; Wodak 2004) as a way of making sense of the multiple embedded modes of the display of power playing out in the composition and transmission of Sterling Greetings announcements on OGBC 2 FM and Paramount FM.[2] This approach is a form of "a critical approach to discourse, with more of a cultural bent" (Scollo 2011, 3). In this chapter, I look at discourse beyond the question of language. I adopt a more holistic approach by viewing discourse as "meaningful symbolic behaviour" (Blommaert, 2005, 2), in which case I position the radio as a medium "that extend(s) cultural practices, symbols, and narratives to millions of people simultaneously across great distances" (Hayes 2000, xiii). This ability to reach a multitude across distances also reflects the significance of "radio broadcasting as an ideal means of mediating and moderating the vibrant force of popular culture" (ibid., xiv). Apart from combining elements of theory and method, a cultural approach to discourse "endeavours to create and advocate new or alternative discourses that are inclusive, non-hegemonic and collaborative with regard to cultural 'others'" (Shi-xu 2005, 68). In addition, a study of Sterling Greetings on radio implies a form of audience participation by ordinary members of the public who are also involved in the dissemination of messages through radio. This kind of participation produces discourses that "focus on the articulation of audience participation through . . . practices" (Carpentier and De Cleen 2007, 265). In terms of methodological approach, this chapter provides an ethnographic evaluation of radio content. In this study I make use of Sterling Greetings announcement scripts collected from the two radio stations over a period of two weeks within the months of May and June 2014. The scripts collected are the ones that were actually transmitted by the stations. OGBC 2 FM and Paramount FM were purposely chosen for their track record in maintaining an archive of their broadcast material as well as the similarity in their market and clientele. While they are both in Abeokuta, the capital city of Ogun State, they also source their clients from similar organizations and community associations. The contiguity of their location also makes them likely to air similar advertisements and Sterling Greetings addressing the same events around the same time.

STERLING GREETINGS

Sterling Greetings appeared on the Nigerian broadcast media scene as a sub-category of public service announcements. The term was coined by radio stations in Nigeria to reference those kinds of personal paid announcements that sound like ordinary greetings that occur in everyday life situations. Approaching public service announcements from the perspectives of affect and persuasion, James Price Dillard and Eugenia Peck contend that those who use this kind of communication often seek to "evoke an emotional response in the audience" (2000, 461). It is pertinent to note that though elements of the Yoruba praise chant, popularly called *oriki*, may be incorporated into Sterling Greetings (especially when composed for the evocation of emotional appeal), it is nonetheless a distinct cultural form that serves its own specific purpose. Different radio and television stations have dedicated time slots during which such announcements are aired. On some stations, including the two being considered in this chapter, public service announcement slots are called personal paid announcements (PPA). The reason for such redesignation is not far removed from the fact that such services are produced for a fee by radio and television stations in the country, a practice that negates the original principle of free service in the public interest. During these time slots, short, scripted announcements ranging from government directives on policy and sundry matters, to information about forthcoming public, community, and personal events are aired to sensitize the audience. For instance, it is common during such time slots to hear about a monthly "environmental sanitation" exercise; an upcoming visit by a politician to a community; a religious activity like a vigil, Christian prayer session, or Islamic lecture; or local festivals. While public service announcements "traditionally relied on donated rather than paid advertising media" (Murry, Stam, and Lastovicka 1996, 1), Sterling Greetings, like most forms of personal paid announcements, are financed by the clients who seek to use the media platform for the dissemination of particular messages. These can be classified into social, political, community, and faith-based types of greetings. In other words, the events for which Sterling Greetings slots are procured from radio stations are usually diverse. They could be private or personal celebrations, community events, or even government programs and official celebrations involving individuals and groups across different classification divides. It is also worthy of note that Sterling Greetings may come before an event (pre-event Sterling Greetings), during an event or after (post-event Sterling Greetings).

The redesignation of public service announcements as personal paid announcements and the further creation of a subcategory known as "Sterling Greetings" reinforces the significance of radio as a medium that continually mediates the lived experiences of its audience in unique ways. As Andrew Dubber argues, this connection to the lived experience of the audience runs much deeper than the creation of different time slots to take care of peculiar interests. Rather it "performs and shapes it through the features, spoken word, routines, music choices and regular segments that make up its content" (2013, 47). It is in this regard that in addition to the signature tunes for the slots, each type of script or event may also attract the use of carefully selected music that complements the event or the mood of a particular script. An Islamic song for instance, plays in the background for Sterling Greetings promoting a Muslim event or a Muslim personality, while a Christian song will accompany a Christian celebration.

As a new radio genre, Sterling Greetings offers an opportunity for us to make sense of the medium as an enabler of public performance. Reiff and Bawarshi argue that "the materiality of public performances can provide a critical framework for studying processes of public engagement and can contribute to our understanding of public performances" (2016, 5); the implication of such frameworks can be teased out for questions of performance and participatory media (see Chouliaraki 2010). While Sterling Greetings allow for the voices of the less powerful individuals in society to be heard through radio, it also offers us a chance to see appreciation performed by people who have received gestures of goodwill. In the next section of this chapter, I present a few illustrations of the ways in which social ties are mediated on OGBC 2 and Paramount FM through Sterling Greetings.

MEDIATING SOCIAL TIES ON RADIO

The greetings reproduced in this section are generic scripts with which the different forms of greetings were performed on the two radio stations. In each case, the script could be a joint production of the station's marketing department and the client or even his, her, or their representative. The name of the individual or group is simply inserted in the ellipsis when the script is read on air. The first script falls under the category of political Sterling Greetings.

> I . . . welcome our special guest of honour, the executive Governor of Ogun State, Senator Ibikunle Amosun (FCA) to his administration's 3rd anniversary golf tournament which tees off at 8:00am, Saturday 7th June, 2014 at the club House.
>
> ANNOUNCER: . . . (SOURCE: OGBC 2, SATURDAY, JUNE 7, 2014; PARAMOUNT FM, FRIDAY, JUNE 6, 2014).

The above script addressed to a state governor and presupposing that the addressee listens at the time it is rendered on air constitutes a form of performance of affection without necessarily giving consideration to any other form of negative relations that may exist between addresser and addressee. It is common to see marketers from radio stations go around to politicians and their followers with this kind of prescripted announcements before, during, or after special events. Such events could be religious festivals, anniversaries, or even personal celebrations by people in positions of authority. Frequently, people buy into this kind of Sterling Greeting as a way of affirming their loyalty to political leaders or colleagues. In affirming this loyalty, the politician or powerful government official often occupies a subject position powerful enough to command the loyalty of the other individual or group in question.

In some cases, though, the performance of loyalty may also be an attempt to curry some kind of favour from the powerful individual. Consider the next Sterling Greetings sample.

I . . . congratulate our amiable leader, the executive Governor of Ogun State, His Excellency Senator Ibikunle Amosun (FCA) on the occasion of his administration's 3rd anniversary in office. We appreciate you for all the good things you have brought to our dear state in the past three years in your commitment to your agenda of the Mission to Rebuild Ogun State.

ANNOUNCER: . . . (SOURCE: OGBC 2, WEDNESDAY, MAY 28, 2014).

In the script above the pre-event Sterling Greeting is full of praises for the state governor for his perceived "good deeds." He is also described as an "amiable leader" to make him feel loved by the sponsors of the greetings. The underlying political undertone also seems to place the "celebrant" above his predecessors as he is said to be on a mission to "rebuild."

A faith-based Sterling Greeting often comes from adherents or promoters of religious beliefs and principles. The three samples below are drawn from two different faith-based organizations whose adherents made use of Sterling Greetings to show appreciation to those who joined them in celebrating an event.

I . . . On behalf of my family congratulate the Living Perfect Master and the World Teacher Satguru Maharaji, on the occasion of Maharaji being bestowed with the award of the Global Pillar of Yoruba tradition and culture by Ile Asa Yoruba Atewonro Park Enuwa Ile-Ife Osun State on Saturday 7th June 2014. Your divine presence in Nigeria since 1980, 34 years ago and the spiritual proclamation all along have awakened our tradition and culture among our people. *A dupe fun akitiyan Maharaji fun irapada alawodudu kuro lowo amunisin oko eru ati itanje emi fun idagbasoke to peye* [We appreciate Maharaji's efforts at redeeming the black race from slavery and spiritual deceit for genuine development].

ANNOUNCER: . . . (SOURCE: OGBC 2, JUNE 7, 2014)

In this instance, we find a combination of both a congratulatory message and gratitude. In addition, the script can be said to harbour numerous social discourses touching on history, memory, and faith. While the reference to slavery and colonialism speaks to a metaphoric representation of conflict and power relations among different groups or class structures in the southwestern part of Nigeria, where both Satguru Maharaji as well as the audiences of the two radio stations are based, the reference to the spiritual implicates faith, which has also become a site for the distribution of power in contemporary

African society. The reference to the redemption of the Black race speaks to the historical tensions generated by different kinds of beliefs and preferences in the quest for the ultimate salvation in African societies, where the colonial experience and globalisation are complicit in the rootedness of both Christianity and Islam.

The list of announcers attached to the script in this instance is spread across different states of the country. They include names of individuals from Kaduna in northern Nigeria, Bayelsa in the south-south geopolitical zone, and the Igbo-speaking eastern part of the country. While such diversity attempts to expand the presence of the subject of this announcement beyond the southwest zone where he is based, it also seeks to lay claim to an interethnic relevance that has the potential of positioning him as a spiritual leader with a large following or acceptance. The code switching that occurs towards the end of the script further attempts to universalize the subject as an iconic "Black Messiah," whose sphere of influence cuts across various boundaries.

Assalamu alaikum wa rahmatullahi wa barakatuh[3], awon omo egbe FOM-WAN, Federation of Muslim Women Association of Nigeria n ki baba wa, Surajudeen Ishola Adekunbi, speaker Ogun State House of Assembly ati gbogbo awon alejo wa kaabo si ibi yinyan omo igbimo titun ti egbe FOM-WAN ti ipinle Ogun, ti yio waye ni ojo kejo osu kefa odun yii ni ojo Aiku (Sunday) ni dede agogo mewa owuro, ni mosalasi awon osise ijoba ti o wa ni Oke-Ilewo Abeokuta. A tun fi asiko yi ki awon imam wa to n bo ati gbogbo omo egbe patapata ku ayeye. A gbaa ladura pe Olorun yio mu ojo ro. Amin. Maasalaam.

OLUKEDE: . . .

[Assalamu alaikum wa rahmatullahi wa barakatuh, members of FOMWAN, Federation of Muslim Women Association of Nigeria welcome our father, Surajudeen Ishola Adekunbi, speaker Ogun State House of Assembly and all our invited guests to the election of a new executive council for FOMWAN in Ogun State coming up on Sunday 8th June 2014 by 10 am at the Civil Service Secretariat Mosque, Oke-Ilewo Abeokuta. We also welcome our imams and all our members to the event. We pray that God grants us the grace to witness the day. Amin. Maasalam].

ANNOUNCER: . . . (SOURCE: OGBC 2, SATURDAY, JUNE 7, 2014, SUNDAY, JUNE 8, 2014; PARAMOUNT FM, SATURDAY, JUNE 7, 2014, SUNDAY, JUNE 8, 2014).

In the following Christian Sterling Greeting, the main subject matter is a church vigil. Scripted as a welcome message, the greeting also promotes the vigil by creating an awareness that serves as an invitation to the public.

> . . . . N ki Olori ijo African Church, His Eminence Emmanuel Udofia, awon bishop, awon alufa agba ati awon eni owo pelu omo ijo The African Church kaabo si akanse iso oru solution nite ti yoo waye lojo Friday otunla laago mewa ale ni The African Church, Solution Camp Sam Ewang Estate, Abeokuta. Bakan naa la tun ki Ven. Jeremiah Okunlola Baba Orioke ku igbalejo. Olorun Orioke Yiyanju yoo yanju oro gbogbo wa. Amin.
>
> OLUKINI. . . .

> [. . . *welcome the Primate of the African Church, His Eminence Emmanuel Udofia, archbishops, bishops, venerables, and congregrants of The African Church to the special night vigil tagged Solution Nite coming up this Friday by 10 pm at The African Church, Solution Camp, Sam Ewang Estate, Abeokuta. We also congratulate the Chief Host Ven. Jeremiah Okunlola Baba Orioke on the occasion of the special vigil. May the God of Solution provide succour for all our needs.*]
>
> ANNOUNCER: . . . (SOURCE: PARAMOUNT FM, WEDNESDAY, JUNE 11, 2014).

When Sterling Greetings attempt to mediate social ties in a community, discourses around communality, the quest for development, cooperation, and the like come to the fore.

> The co-ordinator, Olori Yetunde Gbadebo, President, Elder M A Olonade, on behalf of Obantoko Community Stakeholders Association express our profound gratitude to the Commissioner for Community Development, Honourable Duro Ayedogbon, Chairman Odeda Local Government, Sulaiman Bankole, Honourable members, Senator Gbenga Obadara, Honourable Oludaisi Elemide, the Oba of Obantoko, Oba Adesanu II, Police PRO Omoba Muyiwa Adejobi, PRO V.S.O. Prince Soji Ganzalo, NSCDC Commandant Mr Aboluwoye, all our donors, the press, Fajol Hotel, [and] all those who worked for the success of our seminar on security challenges held at Fajol Hotel Obantoko on Thursday 5th June 2014. May God bless, protect and prosper you all. Thank you
>
> ANNOUNCER: OBANTOKO COMMUNITY STAKEHOLDERS ASSOCIATION(SOURCE: OGBC 2, SATURDAY, JUNE 7, 2014)

A key point to note is the question of ambivalence, which arises when we deal with the authorship of Sterling Greetings. While some of the scripts might be written by the clients (and this happens on rare occasions), radio stations themselves more often than not prepare scripts in line with the associated events. In certain cases, the already prepared script becomes a marketing tool with which clients are convinced to "send messages of appreciation" or recognition during the staging of such events. Wherever the authorship of the script lies, its effectiveness still depends to a considerable extent on the delivery capacity of the reader, who provides another level of mediation in the entire process. While a good announcer might do justice to a Sterling Greetings script, another might through the sloppiness of presentation render the message itself uninspiring. On the other hand, an overdramatization of a script either during composition or rendering may also alter the mood of the message (see Rodero 2012). Such form of dramatization is sensed in the examples given above, especially in the Guru Maharaj case.

Mediated discourse, as Ron Scollon argues, is "a form of social interaction" (1999, 151) that bears witness to relationships between the producers of messages and the people at whom such messages are targeted. While most of the announcements or greetings are enacted through a general "one type fits all," for scripts composed by an individual member of an organization or an agency (such as a script writer, an editor, or a salesperson at the radio station), the individual whose name appears as an "announcer"—the originator of the greeting—is credited with a form of participation where his, her, or their voice features merely performatively. In other words, a "*crisis* of voice, across political, economic and cultural domains" (Couldry 2010, 1) defines the participatory opportunity in an event this kind of programme offers. Following in this line with Couldry, Jan Blommaert also points out the significance of voice in the understanding of discourse. For Blommaert, "an analysis of voice is an analysis of power effect" (2005, 4). The question of distribution of power and the effect it may have on the value of participation for both the audience and users of sterling greetings become obvious in the protocols of execution that govern them. With a similar script written by one person, the "greetings" become unified in content and form, thereby discounting the possibility of different people displaying varying dispositions towards the same individual or event. The implication of this is, in the words of Couldry, "the loss of the connecting narratives that would help us to grasp many specific breakdowns as dimensions of the same problem" (2010, 1).

Radio messages, like most other forms of mass communication, often provide peculiar narratives. Such narratives become stronger and more effective when people are allowed to give account of themselves. The nature of power and its distribution is, however, one major hindrance to the realization of these peculiar narratives on radio. Blommeart argues succinctly that "power, its actors, its victims, and its mechanisms are often the talk of the town, and our everyday conversations, our mass media, our creative arts gladly use power as themes and motifs in discourses on society at large" (2005, 1).

CONCLUSION

Positive comments become building blocks in the edifice of the public presentation of identity; negative assessments carry the potential of a reading in a bad light. In other words, the positive implications of gratitude can signal the effects of power and become a scale of measure for the acceptance, or rejection, of the personality at whom it is directed. Nonetheless, this does not rule out the negative tendencies of sycophantic gratitude, another possibility in situations where power inequities are combined with the lack of a direct freedom of expression.

The flamboyance and flowery use of language embedded in the structure of most Sterling Greetings scripts suggests an attempt to impress both the individual at whom the message is directed as well as the audience. With such a dramatic use of language, an attempt to massage the ego of the subjects of Sterling Greetings, the performative nature of such greetings is further borne out by the fact that the same script may serve a multitude of announcers. An announcement script is written by a designated scriptwriter at the radio station and limits the individualized sincerity from the announcer to the individual whose name features on the announcement.

Through Sterling Greetings, gratitude is celebrated as a cultural asset. Its circulation through radio is a form of historicization, which offers further understanding of power relations in a way likely to be regarded by stakeholders as participatory citizenship. But the structures of presentation, especially of scripted Sterling Greetings, seem to alienate the principle of voice as a process. The kind of inclusion that Sterling Greetings offer on Nigerian radio falls short of the full potential radio provides, with its nuanced mediation and social experience for the listeners and users. Highlighting the value of participation on Nigerian radio will depend on how more programs like Sterling Greetings provide for the mediation of experience in a more "socially grounded" manner.

NOTES

1. This translation and subsequent ones are provided by the author.

2. While OGBC 2 FM is owned by the Ogun State government, Paramount FM is one of the local channels recently established by the federal-government-controlled Federal Radio Corporation of Nigeria (FRCN).

3. Standard greeting in Islam translated as "may the peace, mercy, and blessings of Allah be with you."

WORKS CITED

Blommaert, Jan. 2005. *Discourse: A Critical Introduction*. Cambridge: Cambridge University Press.

Carpentier, Nico, and Benjamin De Cleen. 2007. "Bringing Discourse Theory into Media Studies: The Applicability of Discourse Theoretical Analysis (DTA) for the Study of Media Practices and Discourses." *Journal of Language and Politics* 6, no. 2: 265–93.

Carr, David. 2015. "Is Gratitude a Moral Virtue? *Philosophical Studies* 172, no. 6: 1475–84.

Chouliaraki, Lille. 2010. "Self-Mediation: New Media and Citizenship." *Critical Discourse Studies* 7, no. 4: 227–32.

Couldry, Nick. 2010. *Why Voice Matters: Culture and Politics after Neoliberalism*. London: Sage.

Dillard, James, and Eugenia Peck. 2000. "Affect and Persuasion: Emotional Response to Public Service Announcements." *Communication Research* 27, no. 4, 461–95.

Dubber, Andrew. 2013. *Radio in the Digital Age*. Cambridge: Polity.

Froh, Jeffrey, Giacomo Bono, and Robert Emons. 2010. "Being Grateful Is beyond Good Manners: Gratitude and Motivation to Contribute to Society among Early Adolescents." *Motivation and Emotion* 34, no. 2: 144–57.

Hayes, Joy. 2000. *Radio Nation: Communication, Popular Culture and Nationalism in Mexico, 1920–1950*. Tucson: University of Arizona Press.

Jackson, Liz. 2016. "Why Should I Be Grateful? The Morality of Gratitude in Contexts Marked By Injustice" *Journal of Moral Education* 45, no. 3: 276–90.

Janks, Hilary. 1997. "Critical Discourse Analysis as a Research Tool." *Discourse: Studies in the Cultural Politics of Education* 18, no. 3: 329–42.

Lambert, Nathaniel, Steven Graham, and Frank Fincham. 2009. A Prototype Analysis of Gratitude: Varieties of Gratitude Experiences." *Personality and Social Psychology Bulletin* 35, no. 9: 1193–1207.

Macdonald, Myra. 2003. *Exploring Media Discourse*. London: Sage.

Merçon-Vargas, Elisa, Katelyn Poelker, and Jonathan Tudge. 2018. "The Development of the Virtue of Gratitude: Theoretical Foundations and Cross-Cultural Issues." *Cross-Cultural Research* 52, no. 1: 1–18.

Murry, John, Antonie Stam, and John Lastovicka. 1996. "Paid-Versus Donated—Media Strategies for Public Service Announcement Campaigns." *Public Opinion Quarterly* 60, no. 1: 1–29.

Reiff, Mary, and Anis Bawarshi. 2016. "From Genre Turn to Public Turn Navigating the Intersections of Public Sphere Theory, Genre Theory, and the Performance of Publics." In *Genre and the Performance of Publics*, edited by Mary Reiff and Anis Bawarshi, 3–32. Boulder: University Press of Colorado.

Rodero, Emma. 2012. "Stimulating the Imagination in a Radio Story: The Role of Presentation Structure and the Degree of Involvement of the Listener." *Journal of Radio and Audio Media* 19, no. 1, 45-60

Scollo, Michelle. 2011. "Cultural Approaches to Discourse Analysis: A Theoretical and Methodological Conversation with Special Focus on Donal Carbaugh's Cultural Discourse Theory." *Journal of Multicultural Discourses* 6, no. 1: 1–32.

Scollon, Ron. 1999. "Mediated Discourse and Social Interaction." *Research on Language and Social Interaction* 32, no. 1–2: 149–54.

Shi-xu. 2005. *A Cultural Approach to Discourse*. New York: Palgrave Macmillan.

Wodak, Ruth. 2004. "What CDA Is About." In *Methods of Critical Discourse Analysis*, edited by Ruth Wodak and Michael Meyer. London: Sage.

Expressions of Identity, Consciousness, and Migration

The Phenomenology of Collapsing Worlds

isiShameni Dance and the Politics of Proximity in Jeppestown, Johannesburg

THOMAS M. POOLEY

Dance is an art of proximity. Dance embodies ways of being in the world and modes of action that articulate the experience of proximities simultaneously personal, interpersonal, and communal. This chapter explores the politics of proximity in the performances of abaThembu migrants from Msinga in the province of KwaZulu-Natal who live at the Wolhuter men's hostel in Jeppestown, Johannesburg. The hostel's location has fashioned its name: 'Jeppe.' For more than a century, tens of thousands of men have trekked to Jeppe in search of a better life. Generations have danced *ingoma* in its precincts in contests of space, place, and identity. *Ingoma* is read here as a technology of mediation and peace making that has gradually lost its potency in the postapartheid era. The changing spatial dynamics of the city are no longer dominated by the kinds of intraethnic conflict for which *ingoma* was effective. Increasingly, it is conflicts between citizens and non-citizens that have turned violent with no clear channel of communication. The media labels attacks on African nationals as xenophobia, while the state insists there is no hate; it is mere criminality. Hostel residents at Jeppe are reportedly perpetrators of this violence. To understand better the conditions that give rise to it, this chapter explores how hostel dwellers experience the politics of space in Jeppestown, and how this is expressed in dance. The spatial dynamics of the hostel and city are interpreted here through the prism of performance. *isiShameni*, a genre of *ingoma*, is prevalent at Jeppe. *isiShameni* dance teams are cohesive social units that give cogent expression to the politics of the hostel as a frontier in the city. Negotiating hostel life is about defining spaces and establishing normative relations within and across them. Dancers figure these spaces with familiar symbols, and in so doing establish strong bonds of community and allegiance. How does *isishameni* articulate a politics of proximity in the African city? What does *isishameni* tell us about the phenomenology of space and about the projection of consciousness through movement?

Space may be imagined in several dimensions. For Maurice Merleau-Ponty, space is not an ordered "setting" but an agential mode. Space is "the means whereby the position of things become possible. This means that instead of imagining it as a sort of ether in which all things float, or conceiving it abstractly as a characteristic that they have in common, we must think of it as the universal power enabling them to be connected."[1]

The situation of a person in space enables, constrains, and affords action. Paul Stoller writes that "[i]n the phenomenological approach to spatial patterns, observers and/or social actors are no longer *in* space, but constitute it through the dynamic actions of their consciousness."[2] Space is "a constituted conceptual force" used politically.[3] The territorialization of space by migrants in the inner city shows how competition over impoverished spaces may lead to violence and to expressions of hatred. The management of these spaces is an enduring challenge when the norms governing communities are degraded, or rendered obsolete, and where radically new ways must be found to contend with difference. *isiShameni* dance offers a window to the dynamics of a society shaped by these competing forces. This chapter explores the agency of dancers in constituting space as an extension of their social and political imaginaries inside and outside the hostel.

JEPPE (2013)

A white Toyota bakkie stops on Main Street. The Dladla brothers emerge and I am bundled in between them. Four of us are cramped into the front seat as we drive through the dilapidated grey warehousing and shuttered shops of Jeppestown to park opposite the iconic green gate of the hostel on Wolhuter Street (fig. 1). The lettering is a relic: "Wolhuter Men's Native Hostel/ ____ Mans Koshuis Wolhuter." The lettering "Native" has been effaced, but the imprint remains. The Afrikaans word has been gouged out. Hostel security guards want to know what this *umlungu*, this white man, is doing here. The Dladla brothers, whom I know from Msinga, give a brief explanation

The entrance to "Jeppe" on Wolhuter Street in Jeppestown, Johannesburg (Photo: Thomas Pooley)

before leading me through the steel turnstiles. They are members of the abaThembu tribe and I have been invited to film their annual dances. Inside the hostel I sense the excitement of the day brewing in the long shadows. Hundreds of men are milling about in the high-walled courtyard between the brown-bricked blocks that enclose Jeppe's residences. Green Telkom telephone booths hang silent in the morning sun. Washing lines suspend over rank open drains coursing with black sludge. Tuckshops, cellphone shacks, *shisa nyamas*, and laundries fill the inner sanctum. The air hums to the heavy beat of *umaskandi* music. To my astonishment there are children wandering about who stare up at me. "We are happy here," shouts a drunk. "There are no women!"[4]

Block 2 is our destination. We climb the stairs. The immediacy of the darkness disorients me. My head is spinning. There is no light. Ndididi's brother Sakhile guides my feet using the tiny luminous cellphone screen on his Nokia. I follow, bent double, trusting in each next step. The Dladlas' room is to the right of the landing on the second floor. It is dark in the corridor leading to their room; there is no functional lighting. A doorway to the right leads to a small room, roughly four meters by six. We sit sharing three beds and a bench. Two men are asleep, oblivious, on thin strips of foam set atop the one-meter-wide concrete slabs; they are working the night shift. I am handed a desk chair with semiattached back rest. Most of the chairs have been decapitated and assembled amidst a selection of tube televisions. The antique glass globes add to the anachronism of this insular chamber. Newspaper cuttings line the walls with soccer results, betting. Ndididi studies these intently. He'd have won R6,850 had Poland not drawn with England in the World Cup qualifier last night. "Who is my team?" he asks me cheerfully in his black and gold Amakhosi shirt. "Sundowns." "Oh yes, Patrice's team." Patrice Motsepe is the billionaire businessman who owns the richest club in South Africa. "But I also support Wits. I studied there." "Oh, the Clever Boys." A pause. "Ah, so you're Pule!" laughs Ndididi, referring to the former Chiefs legend Jabu Pule, whose surname is pronounced similarly to mine. I ask about Mashunka and the men's families back home. "How often do you get to see them?" "It's not like it used to be," says Ndididi. "Now men go back not just twice a year but sometimes monthly. It's R170 to Msinga direct from Jeppe, one way. But we must bring stuff, Danono, meat, nappies, otherwise there will be trouble from our wives!" So the cost is more like R700 to R1000. That's a lot of money when all you can get is "piece jobs."

A single glass globe hangs in the Dladlas' room. There are live electrical wires protruding out in bunches, connections sprouting into the passage. We walk past the kitchen-dining room toward a distant emergency exit. I catch a glimpse of the smoke-black stovetops, men preparing luncheons in the half-light. Beside them a putrid mass of garbage is climbing to the ceiling. The corridor is seeping effluent. The door to the showers has been padlocked. There is no hot water. "It used to cost R27 a month to stay here, but now nobody pays, or maybe 4 out of 100," says Ndididi. "Things have changed a lot. There's no maintenance any more. It is the ANC's fault. They're always making promises." The posters pinned to Jeppe's walls feature only the face of Prince Mangosuthu Buthelezi, the leader of the Inkatha Freedom Party. Ndididi had plans to run as a councilor for the IFP in his ward at Mashunka. We inspected election results outside the courthouse at Mathintha back in 2012. The stakes are high. The difference between winning and losing an election is a contest: employment versus unemployment. It is time to go. We're heading for an exit like the end of a mine shaft.

The white-blue sky of a summer's day sings a gentle breeze. It is time for the dancing. Hundreds of spectators are arriving on the lawns of Jeppe Park on Jules Street. Clumps of men deliberate their *stokvels*. But some of the young dancers are already rearing to go. A large semicircle is forming in straggles. The tribal elders sit on stools directly opposite the dancers. They are fronted with bottles and boxes of alcohol, untouched. Soon a strong chorus is clapping and singing. It is a steady clap, clap, clap-clap, clap. No drums, no instruments, just voices and hands. The men dance singly and in pairs, presenting themselves in mock aggression, hands raised above their heads, feet falling to the beat and in syncopation against it. *isiShameni* dancers gather power in their thighs with legs lifted high in anticipation and release. The individual "one-one" dances are short and demonstrate speed and agility. *Mbadadas* are worn to cushion the blows. These special-purpose rubber-soled dancing shoes protect feet from the colossal impact of *ingoma* stamping. The thud of dancing feet mimics the heavy crushing of grains.

The afternoon begins with the younger, less-experienced men who have yet to master the advanced, complex dance routines. One or two steps, stamp, and then the characteristic leap backward into the chorus of singers behind them. The more experienced dancers shimmy, adding nuanced and sometimes humorous gestures. A favorite is to adopt a series of poses, out of time to the beat, and in so doing to extract the mirth and approval of the crowd. The dancing in troupes is different. Coordination is precise, exact, fine-tuned, and military. But the carefully practiced routines also build inevitably to the series of high leg lifts, and the almighty stamp and leap backward into a feigned death. The large, open, grassed lawns in front of the dancers are hardly utilized. Instead, they keep close together, often bumping against each other and leaping over one another. The *isishameni* pose is static and vertical. Timing is essential. Those who flounder are rooted out by the *igoso*, who leads the troupe with his singing and gesticulations. He commands the dancers, instills discipline and respect, and enforces the law.

Sukelwa's posture is balanced, confident, and composed. He dances with men from the Nomoya district. Their uniform consists of white vests marked with red-crossed bands, dark trousers rolled up and tied with tasseled skins at the knee, orange armbands, and white *mbadadas*. This attire identifies them. I first filmed Sukelwa and his troupe dancing at Mashunka, Msinga, in the midlands. Here on the lawns of Jeppestown the audience is different. Men from neighboring districts sing and clap along to the songs known to all, standing as an *impi* (army) flanking the *amasoja*. They share the bonds of tribe and custom, of histories intertwined, rivalries made and unmade; and increasingly these men recognize kinship and friendship across divides.

They dance together, and they identify with a common set of gestures and norms. Dances are measured to a common consciousness, and so too the merits of a troupe's choreography. When Sukelwa rises from his last dance, he does so as an *isoja*, as one who carries the determination of his fellows, as one who embodies the identity of a shared heritage by constituting space in their image.

THE POLITICS OF VIOLENCE

Jeppe is a world in flux. Home to more than ten thousand migrant men living out of 3,200 rooms, Jeppe is one of the largest and most overcrowded migrant hostels in South Africa. Men sleep in shifts and share quarters on floors. In recent years the hostel has attracted media attention for criminal activities associated with its residents. Most outsiders despair at its violence. But hostel dwellers know differently. They express frustration, anger, and resentment at the politics of neglect that characterizes the administration of the hostels. Their narratives turn to violent crime and joblessness, to speculation on the slow, grinding macroeconomics that is beyond their control, indifferent to their needs. At the heart of Jeppe's struggle is the decades-long decay of social norms and values that accompanies chronic unemployment. The normative experience of migrancy in twentieth-century South Africa rested on systems of support premised on employment among kin and on systems of order and discipline imposed through customary law and the social stratifications governing home and family life in rural country districts.[5] These foundations have been eroded to such a degree that men find it difficult to orient themselves to recognized norms. The bonds between generations have been loosed, the idea of the nuclear family dismantled. Factors external to the hostel have gradually eaten away at the integrity of life within its walls. The hostel space was designed to enclose. But this enclosure pushes back against its alienation, alienating those who would threaten its sovereignty.

The state of the hostels and the patterns of habitation that characterize them are the product of a complex history characterized by enforced alienation.[6] Successive colonial and apartheid governments imposed on Black South Africans a life of migrancy from rural homesteads to rapidly industrializing towns and cities.[7] This was accomplished through a series of dispossessions and enslavements that began in the seventeenth century. But the more immediate roots of the current landlessness and segregation is to be found in the legislative agenda of the Union government established between the British and the Boers in 1910. Land was stolen en masse from indigenous South Africans with the passing of the Native Land Act of 1913. Black families were forced off the arable land to make way for white farmers, for mining, and for the general exploitation of natural resources.[8] This was but the culmination of centuries of colonial subjugation, and it only reinforced the racist agenda that white South Africa had guaranteed by excluding nonwhites from full participation in government. The acquisition of South Africa's natural resources and the enslavement of Black labor had drastic consequences for the livelihoods and social dynamics of rural communities. Taxation of land, beasts, huts, and homes forced men, and later women, to work in the mines and in urban settings to earn wages. And so began patterns of migrancy that persist today in the dynamics of joblessness, hopelessness, landlessness, and poverty experienced by a large cross-section of South Africa's population. While millions of South Africans consider themselves urbanites, there are still millions more whose lives integrate the distant yet intimately connected spaces of metropolis and rural village. These migrants have imagined new forms of music, dance, and art that intersect and make sense of these realities, as has been widely documented for *isicathamiya*,[9] *umaskandi*,[10] *ingoma*,[11] aurality,[12] and many other genres and expressive forms.[13]

VIOLENCE IN JEPPESTOWN

A culture of violence persists in Jeppestown. The factors informing this violence are deeply rooted in the history of the community. During apartheid, the migration of rural disputes to the urban hostels fomented intraethnic tensions that were sustained by apartheid security forces, who provided weapons and ammunition to warring factions.[14] Tensions were exacerbated by the removal of Black South Africans from their ancestral lands and resettlement in confined spaces. Conflicts over land and resources resulted in bloody battles between neighboring communities. Stock theft and assassinations were commonplace in rural *izigodi*, and this violence spread to the homeboy networks in and around Johannesburg, Durban, and other industrial areas. A cycle of reprisals destabilized areas that had formerly been ordered by respected modes of governance and justice. The plight of these displaced communities was desperate: fighting for jobs, fighting for a place to live, fighting for ancestral land.

Party political violence was stirred in the 1980s and became more intense through the transition period between 1990 and the first democratic elections in 1994, when it reached devastating levels in clashes between the African National Congress (ANC) and Inkatha Freedom Party (IFP), and the Azanian People's Organization (AZAPO). GG Alcock worked in the Johannesburg hostels and in the rural country districts at the time. "KZN was a complete warzone," says Alcock. "The violence was in essence tribal. [. . .] The scale of it was unbelievable. When I arrived in Joburg [in the late 1980s] it was when they had this hectic fighting in KZN and it spread to the hostels."[15] The hostels became fortresses that were barricaded to the outside world, inhabitable only by relations and friends. Men did not interact with local communities for fear of death, and so the hostels became increasingly isolated even from their immediate surroundings. Jilly Kelly has described the scale of violence in KwaZulu-Natal, and its extensions elsewhere, as civil war.[16] She argues that this war was facilitated by the apartheid government arming Inkatha against the ANC and using its "total strategy" to effect "an international proxy war" that lasted until as late as 1996.[17]

With the advent of democracy, tensions gradually subsided. In the late 1990s and 2000s, the IFP lost considerable ground to the ANC. The rise to power of President Jacob Zuma (the T-shirts read "100% Zulu Boy") was itself a performance that shifted the dynamics in the predominantly Zulu-speaking regions and in the hostels.[18] The violence did not disappear, but it was less deadly. At the same time, other new forces began to emerge in the postapartheid political economy that undermined the social structures governing hostel life. In the early 2000s, riots and looting in the Gauteng townships and hostels were labeled xenophobia by the media.[19] An influx of refugees and immigrants from Zimbabwe, Nigeria, Malawi, Mozambique, Sudan, Ethiopia, Congo, and elsewhere engulfed Jeppestown. Foreigners set up shop in dilapidated and abandoned buildings and created viable businesses. Hostel dwellers perceived these immigrants as competitors for jobs, and some resorted to looting and intimidation to force them out. There were reports of assault and murder.[20]

The state has done little to address the resultant crisis. When I visited Jeppe in 2013 the communal lighting was nearly all out. There was no hot water. Raw sewage seeped in open drains. "The suspension of basic services is an attempt by government to shut down the hostel because of the crime and violence associated with hostels," wrote journalist Mbali Phala. One of the residents, Mr. Mngomezulu, complained that the media "portrays us as angry mobsters that are about violence."[21] This reputation is recognized by crime journalists. Nomsa Maseko wrote that "the hostels have always been dangerous places to visit, even for the police. As a crime reporter in the late 2000s, on at least four occasions I was present when officers who entered hostels were killed. Following the xenophobic attacks—in which seven people died—the police and army jointly raided some of these hostels. The Jeppestown Wolhuter men's hostel in Johannesburg was the first to be searched for weapons in April."[22] For some current and former hostel dwellers from Msinga, crime ranks third on the list of potential "employment" options at Jeppe. Renowned dancer Sakephi Mbatha left for this very reason, saying that with so few opportunities for work he did not want to be tempted into a life of crime.[23]

Induna Manyathela Mvelase is the headman for Jeppe hostel responsible for the welfare of its residents. Interviewed in 2017 about the violence and xenophobia in hostels, he said, "Police are discriminating against hostel dwellers; they keep saying criminals live here, but the truth is criminals live all over the country. We didn't start the violence." On the charge that hostel dwellers loot foreign-owned shops, Mvelase replies: "It's only because they're hungry; many are unemployed." The perception is that foreigners, or outsiders, are being favored for jobs. They undercut South Africans by working for a lower wage and out of desperation are prepared to accept unfavorable conditions. "They must just go back to their countries, because they're taking our jobs," says Sibangani Langa.[24] "Residents of the Jeppe men's hostel have repeatedly demonstrated against foreigners who own car workshops and spaza shops in the area, accusing foreigners of committing crimes such as drug dealing and prostitution."[25] A similar narrative is told to me by Jeppe residents. "Protestors point to issues such as struggles with employment and housing, but ostensibly their claim is that police have failed their neighborhoods and they need, as a community, to take up the fight against drugs and prostitution. Nigerians have been a key target and a number of homes have been torched and foreigners, from various African backgrounds, forced to flee."[26]

The mayor of Johannesburg, Herman Mashaba of the Democratic Alliance, claimed that "undocumented migrants" were responsible for the crime epidemic in Johannesburg. According to official statistics there were eighty-eight murders committed in Jeppestown in 2016. In May 2017 the Member of the Executive Council [MEC] for safety and security in the Gauteng province, Sizakele Nkosi-Malobane, described the policing challenges in Jeppestown as "horrific." "The Gauteng Department of Community Safety has attributed

Manyathela Mnandi Mvelase, Jeppe Induna (Photo: Thomas Pooley)

the high levels of crime in Joburg's eastern suburbs to a lack of personnel and patrolling vehicles. Jeppe is considered to be the worst affected police station as it is short of 7 vehicles and 44 personnel, while also experiencing high levels of contact crime, including murder, assault and robbery."[27] To make sense of all this, I talked to Induna Manyathela Mvelase (IM), and other hostel dwellers to get their side of the story. I knew Fezela Zwane (FZ) from Mashunka. He used to live at Jeppe and accompanied me as translator in a 2017 visit.[28]

IM: Eish, even when I open my Bible, I don't know where to open it to. We had jobs when there were white people leading the country. They closed the borders with other countries. The South Africans, even those who are not educated, they would be working if there were not so many people coming from outside the country. They are competing with the South Africans, they are taking everything from South Africans. Not Zimbabwe, all over.

TP: And they work for less?

IM: Yes, they take everything. And then the South Africans get nothing.

TP: So the government needs to be stricter with the borders?

FZ: It did not used to be so easy for outsiders to get in. This means the law was stricter. You came for a reason. Same applies to us. If you go somewhere you must go for a reason.

IM: Firstly, can I ask you a question? [directed at TP] Are you here in South Africa as a South African?

TP: Yes.

IM: Were you aware that in those days [i.e., during apartheid] women's body parts were cut up and sold? [pause] No, but now they are.

FZ: You hear it on each and every radio station.

IM: Secondly, since you are a South African. The body parts of cars that are at panel beaters. Are you aware of this?

FZ: What he means is that if you walk out and see these factories you will see that most of them are full of car parts. Where are those cars coming from? People are stealing them. Foreigners. But during those times [during apartheid] there were not these problems. Even for body parts.

TP: Are there foreigners living here in Jeppestown?

IM: [Laughing.] All over. We don't even know where the accidents for these cars happen. It goes back to the borders.

TP: And the police are not doing anything?

IM: [Laughing. Coughing.] Yes, there are police, but they are confused about what to do.

TP: They told me that here in Jeppe there are more murders here than in Hillbrow. How is the crime here?

IM: It is confused because, here, the crime of hijacking is high but you never know where it came from. Foreigners are involved, as well as South Africans.

TP: What about drugs, is that a problem?

IM: The drugs issue that you can't promote and say that it is a problem here. You can see there is drugs but you can't point exactly where it is. Myself I am a father. If I see children standing on the street selling prostitutes—it hurts me deeply. If you see a child you want to see it do good things, not bad things. All this points to government, it is their responsibility. Prostitutes, drugs, car hijackings, jobs.

Msukelwa Mvelase, the induna's son, has lived in block 2 for nearly twenty years, and is a dancer for *noMoya isigodi*. I ask him, too, about living conditions in Jeppe.[29]

MM: We are not sleeping here. But it is the people outside.

FZ: They are shooting.

MM: If someone goes out and gets shot we go out and check if it's our friends and family. But it is safe inside.

FZ: There is security at the gate.

MM: The problem is that these criminals do things outside then run here and hide from the police. This gives us a bad reputation.

FZ: There used to be a big problem with hijacking. Now the induna doesn't allow any cars inside Jeppe. I got special permission for you to park next to his place. They used to hijack cars and drive them into the hostel, and the police were too scared to come inside.

JEPPE (2017)

Fezela carries my bag and belongings through block 2 of the hostel. I must not be seen walking through Jeppe concealing anything. A stumbling man in green grabs hold of me. "R10, *umlungu*, give me R10." I say, "No, I'm not carrying money," but he persists in wrenching my wrist, pressing against me. I try to remain calm; he's drunk. Msukelwa and Fezela move quickly, urging him off without using force. He relents, grudgingly, chuckling under his breath. I'm hurried through the turnstiles and out onto the street, one man on either side of me, guns concealed. "Don't worry," says Fezela, "everyone knows me. You will be safe." Sure enough, I hear men calling from the hostel above. "Hawu, Fezela, kunjani baba?" [Hey, Fezela, how are you sir?] We walk briskly to a side street. We are close to the park now, still within sight of the hostel. On the pavement we approach a car on a hoist, wheels removed. Men are sitting around drinking beer from green bottles. Some stare blankly at me. We are being conscientiously ignored. Chickens run. For sale signs stand inside the adjacent warehouse. Its appearance is dilapidated and anonymous. In Jeppestown there are many such buildings. Most were factories or workshops that have been taken over by migrants seeking work or shelter, or by the families of men living in the hostel.

The stench of sulfur is overpowering. I hold my breath and stoop through the makeshift doorway. Tiny wooden rooms line the darkness, padlocked and windowless. These places they call "emkhukhuwini," chicken shacks. Sizakele Zwane is a woman in her mid-forties from Nambithi in KwaZulu-Natal. She moved here in 1996 with her two children, looking for work. The government had promised family housing for the men of Jeppe that year. The result was a surge of hopeful arrivals. "I have six children that I am looking after," says Sizakele.[30] "When their father passed away I moved here looking for work to support them." More than twenty years later she still lives in the single room she started with. There's no running water, no toilet, nothing besides a bed, cabinet, side table, and some photos on the wall. The unit is neat and tidy, clean. "The problem here," she says, "is the criminals. Guns. There are too many." "What about support from the municipality?" I hesitate to ask, feeling numb. "There are no services here. But I do have child grants for two of my kids." Sizakele's husband arrives. He's from Jeppe and sings *isicathamiya* with a group called "Es'killer." They practice in the basement of block 2 during the night. Sometimes they compete elsewhere when they can afford it. I am struggling to make sense of the place, of the rationale for the lives lived here. Why, why here? "I sell beer to support my children," explains Sizakele. "My friend sells chickens, and she kills them for the guys in Jeppe." Everyone is afraid of the dark, and of what happens at night with the guns and the drugs and the prostitutes and the police and the hijacking. And of all those people outside, those foreigners, what are they doing?

The collapse of the abaThembu worlds at Jeppe is evident from the large number of men leaving the hostels, the reduction in elders, and the death of so many men from tuberculosis and AIDS. I ask Induna Mvelase what has changed at Jeppe since he arrived forty years ago, in 1977, and he is studied in his answer:

Yabonake, kushintshile kakhulu. Kushintshe uinhlonipho, kushintshe umthetho.
You see, it has changed a lot. Respect has changed, law has changed.

"Do you mean respect for elders," I ask? "Firstly," he says, emphasizing his point in English, "the elder people are still there, but they don't have respect from the younger generation. Secondly, the law was there, used by the elder people, but now there is no more of that law." The young men just will not take instruction. They no longer respect their elders and do as they please without consequence. The decline in the performance culture at Jeppe, which includes *isicathamiya*, *isishameni*, and *umaskandi*, is ascribed to financial constraints. Men cannot afford to travel between hostels, to competitions, and back home. GG Alcock suggests other reasons, pointing to a new, "urban" generation. "Everyone's got a cellphone, they're more likely to listen to house music than *maskandi*. They're still into that, but it's not as big. I think there's a kind of cultural erosion, in a sense. You also have less and less big community events, even in December." Fewer communal ceremonies take place because these are expensive to organize. The opportunities for dancing and singing have dwindled. "Weddings are very rare because people can't afford *lobola*. People are *lobaling* for years. So people live apart, or they do 'vat en sit' which is living together illegally. So the youth are exposed to less and less big events. If you go to an event even at Msinga, you see all the young school-age kids watching the dancing, in the past they would have been dancing. They're not even singing along because they don't know the words."[31]

Sakephi Mbatha is a renowned dancer who lived at Jeppe for years. I asked him why he returned home to Msinga after living at Jeppe and Nance-field hostels. "It was very, very difficult," he says, "because I didn't find piece jobs, and nobody was going to look after me. I was scared that maybe I will be tempted into criminality, so maybe I must just go back. [. . .] Since the elders went home it became difficult for us. The youngsters can't take care of each other. Most of the elders have come back [to Msinga], many of them passed away. The youngsters are left there."[32] The decline has negatively impacted the homeboy networks and the practices of music and dance that sustained them.

Induna Mvelase tells a similar story. "*iZingili* was finished long ago," he says. "And *isicathamiya* is going down slowly. Before, in those times, people who were working they were coming from the hall in the basement. They used to compete here, they put money for the winners. The judges decide number 1, 2, 3. All of that goes down with the value of money." But why do they need money for music?

> People are not working. They need money for competition, for traveling. Because those people performing there are living in Daveyton, Boxburg, deep Soweto, West Rand, and come together to make a group of song. Those things are now no longer there. Secondly, in *isicathamiya*, it cost because they wear same suits, same trousers, same tire, same shoes. Was expensive because they wear two-piece. [. . .] Some other *ingoma*, like *zingili* and *ishameni*, there was that for happiness *ingoma*, not for competition, just to enjoy. But even that comes lower because there is no money to get that happiness any more whereby, because of that time, dancing together they were drinking and each other to be happy. It goes back to traveling issues.[33]

The wider social and economic malaise in Jeppestown is registered in performance. The stories told by Induna Mvelase, Dladla, Zwane, and Mbatha embody the fundamental changes that have accompanied South Africa's transition from apartheid state to liberal democracy. But they also figure broader geopolitical shifts that are continental in scope and consequence. It is at least in part the mass movement of migrants across Africa that has given rise to the contested spatial dynamics of South Africa's cities. The xenophobic incidents of the late 2000s and after demonstrate serious and violent enmity between migrants. In the context of these violent interactions, ethnic affiliations are affirmed. The practice of dance may once have been a means to quell such violence. But this was only possible when *ingoma* was itself a lingua franca.

UMGANGELA, STICK FIGHTING

In the 1970s, *isishameni* came to replace stick fighting contests known as *umgangela* that had been used in the past to resolve violent conflicts between *izigodi*. The homeboy networks in the hostels who danced together in private and at community events came to function as fighting units.[34] Tensions over land tenure and skirmishes between families were defused through the practice of *umgangela* during the summer months when men returned to their rural homesteads. Stick-fighting contests were an important check on tensions and were regulated by strict rules overseen by the *izinduna* and tribal elders. Jonathan Clegg describes how *umgangela* was "a means of expressing, actually being violent, but at the same time containing district opposition. You have these very strict rules—you may not hit a man when he's down, if he says 'Kumu' or 'Manutshe' you have to stop beating him."[35] The abaThembu call stick fighting of this nature *uphenge*. The practice of *uphenge* and its role in conflict was corrupted by various social factors, including competition over access to land and jobs on farms. By the 1980s it had taken on a negative connotation.

> People now just want to win, to enforce their domination over other districts, and the ritual aspect of the *uphenge*, this inter-district stick fight, loses its cohesion. You have people being killed, hacked, people going to *uphenge* carrying *pangas*, choppers and spears. Fighting sticks are weapons of playing. Men play with these things. If I hit a man and he dies it's a mistake. These are not weapons of war. In *umgangela* to this day if you hit a man and he dies, there is no court case.[36]

When *uphenge* began to exacerbate violence and could no longer contain turmoil between districts in a peaceful fashion, an alternative was sought in team dancing.[37] A culture of *ingoma* developed with sanctioned rules that restricted and controlled the performance of aggressive or threatening acts. This practice is still evident at Jeppe and at performances back at Msinga. "The *isishameni* they are doing like they were fighting—but they were not fighting, they were dancing,"[38] says Induna Mvelase. This aggressive dancing is carefully monitored by women. At weddings they use *intelezi* [herbal medicines] to calm the dancers. It is also the role of the *igoso* to restrain his dancers and to ensure that things do not get out of control. Sakephi Mbatha explains that the *igoso* must have special vocal qualities and must "enforce the law." He need not be a talented dancer. It is the qualities of leadership and creativity that are most prized.

> The *igoso* must have a nice voice. That's the main factor. He can make all these people come together and sing nicely. It is the main role. The *igoso* organizes the people. After you have been elected you must pass your law. Then you say every weekend you must come here at about 8 o'clock. It's all from the *igoso*, the *igoso* must pass the law. They are doing the rules in hostels. They just look for a big room in the hostels to practice.[39]

The principle of *umthetho* is a feature of the social structure of hostel life that *isishameni* embodies. Most of the dancers in a troupe will share a place of origin in KwaZulu-Natal or a direct family connection. They dance as a team practicing on weeknights and weekends.[40] On Sundays men gather to discuss business, to consult on their *stokvel* investments, to drink and dance. The dancing is a form of entertainment, but it also solidifies the bond between men by affirming rank and identity. At the end of the year the dancers perform in an all-day display of interdistrict dancing. These hostel dances serve as practice for the weddings, *umemulos* (coming-of-age ceremonies) and *imisebenzi* (return of the spirit ceremonies) that will take place over the Christmas holidays back in KwaZulu-Natal. The social structure of dance teams is homologous to that of the *izigodi*. Each *isishameni* dance team is coordinated by a leader called an *igoso* and an *iphini* (second in command). Their role is to schedule practice sessions, choose songs, and train the youngsters in the correct steps and gestures. Most teams consist of thirty to forty dancers called *amasoja* (soldiers). The rank-and-file dancers are generally young men under the age of thirty. A similar hierarchy and regimentation are observed in other Zulu dance forms like *umzansi*.[41]

isiShameni is characterized by the alternation of two phases. One involves coordinated dancing in groups. This is contrasted with the alternation or sometimes simultaneous dancing of two individuals in competition, a practice termed "one-one." The texts of the songs may be about skirmishes in the home districts, love forsaken and love begotten, or even about hostel gossip, an opportunity to spill the beans. Tensions between individuals are expressed, aired for all to hear, and are sometimes left unresolved. Once you have had your turn you must step aside, as it were. Tensions between groups are resolved in part through interactions with the audience who are interlocutors in the performances, responding to the gestures and feats of the dancers.

The stylistic features of *isishameni* are distinct from other forms of *ingoma* danced across much of southeast Africa.[42] In *umzansi*, a style common across the southern parts of KwaZulu-Natal, lines of men march in step and range around the dance arena, often in a militaristic fashion. When men dance individually or in unison they move forward and back, using the space in a linear fashion. *isiShameni* is distinct in gesture and structure with its emphasis on the vertical.[43] A characteristic feature is the relatively static use of the dance space. Dancers initially use minimal lateral movement emphasizing upward gestures with their arms with a vertical stamping motion. As the routine nears its end there is dynamic movement but still within the confines of a relatively small compass of no more than two to three meters in diameter.

The audiences at performances play a role in defining this space. Often the encroachment of the audience restricts the dancers to an even narrower circle. Sukelwa's dancing offers a case in point. He summons massive power from his thighs, holding his body firmly in place with arms raised above a position on his haunches. It is the strength of his core that enables him to reach upward to the heavens, one foot firmly planted, with the stability needed to deliver a powerful stamp from directly above his head. The gestural lines of *isishameni* emphasize this vertical trajectory. The politics of proximity in *isishameni* is marked by spatial constraint. The individual expression of this constraint relies on terrific bodily strength to dance an aesthetics of alignment. The balanced bodily axis is definitive of the *isishameni* dance ideal. When the dance ends with a characteristic leap backward, it is a leap immune to the bodily pain of landing. In this final act, the spatial limits of the dance floor are severed. The dancer exits the sanctioned space having expressed his spiritual being and belonging.

THE PHENOMENOLOGY OF COLLAPSING WORLDS

When homeboys dance *isishameni* today, it reinforces ties of identity and belonging that feel more urgent than ever. The spatial and social dynamics of dance point to the complex social imaginary out of which Zulu migrants fashion their worlds on the urban frontier while drawing on strategies of kinship and tradition rooted in their places of rural origin. Dancers enact their realizations of space through play. Dance as play is used to territorialize space, to mark its boundaries, to condition its fields of interaction, and to assert ownership over its domains. But as social praxis it does more than this. It constitutes a structure for living a disciplined life in the city within a close network of kith and kin governed by *umthetho* and *inhlonipho*. The voices in this narrative speak of the collapse of the dance world, and of its laws and customs. This collapse is evident in the behavior of thousands of hostel dwellers who raided downtown Johannesburg in August 2019.[44] Ignoring IFP leader Mangosuthu Buthelezi's call for peace and tolerance in the face of xenophobic violence, they fired salvos in the air with their guns before marching to nearby Maboneng, where they allegedly ransacked shops and assaulted African nationals. This show of force by a generation asserting its independence from the traditional Zulu leadership offers the clearest indication yet of the collapse of custom and of the fraught politics of proximity that now obtains in one of Johannesburg's most contested urban spaces.

NOTES

1. Maurice Merleau-Ponty, *Phenomenology of Perception* (New York: Routledge, 1945 [Transl. 1962]), 284.

2. Paul Stoller, *The Taste of Ethnographic Things: The Senses in Anthropology* (Philadelphia: University of Pennsylvania Press, 1989).

3. Stoller, *The Taste of Ethnographic Things*, 67.

4. This section is based on ethnographic research at Jeppe and on the author's interviews with Ndididi Dladla and Sakhile Dladla at Jeppe Hostel, Johannesburg, on December 1, 2013.

5. Judith Temkin Irvine and Liz Gunner, "With Respect to Zulu: Revisiting ukuHlonipha," *Anthropological Quarterly* 9, no. 1 (2018): 173–207.

6. Penwell Dlamini, "Renovation of Johannesburg Hostels to Start Soon," accessed online on July 31, 2017, at https://www.timeslive.co.za/news/south-africa/2017-07-31-re novation-of-johannesburg-hostels-to-start-soon/.

7. William Beinart, *Twentieth Century South Africa* (New York: Oxford University Press, 2000).

8. Harold Wolpe, "Capitalism and Cheap Labor-Power in South Africa: From Segregation to Apartheid," *Economy and Society* 1, no. 43 (1972): 425–56; Cherryl Walker and Ben Cousins, "Introduction," in *Land Divided, Land Restored: Land Reform in South Africa for the 21st Century*, ed. Cherryl Walker and Ben Cousins (Johannesburg: Jacana, 2015), 1–23.

9. Veit Erlmann, *Nightsong: Performance, Power and Practice in South Africa* (Chicago: University of Chicago Press, 1996); Liz Gunner, "Zulu Choral Music—Performing Identities in a New State," *Research in African Literatures* 37, no. 2 (2006): 84–97.

10. Kathryn Olsen, *Music and Social Change in South Africa: Maskanda Past and Present* (Philadelphia: Temple University Press, 2014); Carol Muller, *Focus: Music of South Africa*, 2nd ed. (New York: Routledge, 2008).

11. Veit Erlmann, *African Stars: Studies in Black South African Performance* (Chicago: University of Chicago Press, 1991).

12. David Coplan, *In the Time of Cannibals: The Word Music of South Africa's Basotho Migrants* (Chicago: University of Chicago Press, 1994).

13. David Coplan, *In Township Tonight: South Africa's Black City Music and Theatre*, 2nd ed. (Chicago: University of Chicago Press, 2007).

14. Philip Bonner and Vusi Ndima, "The Roots of Violence on the East Rand, 1980–1990," seminar paper presented to the Wits Institute for Advanced Social Research, No. 450 (October 18, 1999).

15. GG Alcock, interview with the author, eHlathini, Johannesburg, June 2, 2017.

16. "South Africa's transition from apartheid to democracy is often heralded as a miracle, both bloodless and peaceful. But as Nelson Mandela walked proudly out of Victor Verster prison in 1990 after twenty-seven years in jail, civil war wracked the nation's townships and countryside. Over twenty thousand South Africans died in this conflict

(1985–1996), more than in any other period of the struggle to overthrow apartheid. Conservative estimates suggest that the war displaced some two hundred thousand people. The world watched with bewilderment as civil war ravaged South Africa, particularly the Pretoria/Witwatersrand/Vaal (PWV) area that is now the Gauteng province and what became the province of KwaZulu-Natal" (Jilly Kelly, *To Swim With Crocodiles: Land, Violence, and Belonging in South Africa, 1800–1996* (Scottsville: University of KwaZulu-Natal Press, 2018, xxviii.)

17. Kelly, *To Swim With Crocodiles*, xxix.

18. Liz Gunner, "Jacob Zuma, the Social Body and the Unruly Power of Song," *African Affairs* 108, issue 430 (2009): 27–48.

19. "In May 2008 nearly 70 people were killed, many more were injured and over 100 000 were displaced in violent attacks on people perceived to be foreigners. . . . This kind of outbreak was repeated in April 2015, and both events were spectacularly captured in media images." Loren Landau, *Exorcizing the Demons Within: Xenophobia, Violence and Statecraft in Contemporary South Africa* (Johannesburg: Wits University Press, 2012); M. Neocosmos, "From 'Foreign Natives' to 'Native Foreigners': Explaining Xenophobia in Post-apartheid South Africa" (Dakar: Codesria, 2010); Danai Mupotswa and Dorothee Kreutzfeldt, "Xenophobia, Nationalism and Techniques of Difference," *Agenda: Empowering Women for Gender Equity* 30, no. 2 (2016): 13–20.

20. S. Hassim, T. Kupe, and E. Worby, *Go Home or Die Here: Violence, Xenophobia and the Reinvention of Difference in South Africa* (Johannesburg: Wits University Press, 2008).

21. Mbali Phala, "Jeppe Hostel Residents Say Their Public Image Is Affecting Service Delivery to the Hostels," June 9, 2016, https://www.thedailyvox.co.za/jeppe-hostel-residents-say-public-image-affecting-service-delivery-hostels/.

22. Nomsa Maseko, "Inside South Africa's 'Dangerous' Men's Hostels," May 13, 2015. http://www.bbc.com/news/world-africa-32692461.

23. Sakephi Mbatha, interview with the author, Mdukatshani, Msinga, 27 April 27, 2017.

24. Maseko, "Inside South Africa's 'Dangerous' Men's Hostels."

25. Greg Nicolson, "Gauteng Xenophobia: Gigaba and Mashaba Trade Accusations." February 28, 2017, https://www.dailymaverick.co.za/article/2017-02-28-gauteng-xenophobia-gigaba-and-mashaba-trade-accusations/#.WTj_sSN97s0.

26. Nicolson, "Gauteng Xenophobia."

27. Tankiso Makhetha, "Crime Surge in Eastern Suburbs," *Star Late Edition*, May 2, 2017.

28. Fezela Zwane, interview with the author, Jeppe Hostel, Johannesburg, June 4, 2017.

29. Sukelwa Mvelase, interview with the author, Jeppe Hostel, Johannesburg, June 4, 2017.

30. Sizakele Zwane, interview with the author, Jeppestown, Johannesburg June 4, 2017.

31. GG Alcock grew up at Msinga speaking isiZulu with the same fluency he speaks English (GG Alcock, *Third World Child: Born White, Zulu Bred* (Johannesburg: Tracey McDonald Publishers, 2015)). An *imisebenzi* is a return of the spirit ceremony that takes place one or more years after a person has died. An *umemulo* is a coming-of-age ceremony for young women, one purpose of which is to announce her readiness for marriage. The views in this paragraph were expressed in an interview with the author at Ehlathini, Johannesburg, on June 2, 2017.

32. Sakephi Mbatha, interview with the author, Mdukatshani, Msinga, April 27, 2017.

33. Manyathela Mvelase, interview with the author, Jeppe Hostel, Johannesburg. June 4, 2017.

34. Jonathan Clegg, "Dance and Society in Africa South of the Sahara" (BA Honors diss., University of the Witwatersrand, 1977), 74–75.

35. "In situations where there exists keen competition between groups or factions, the dance is an expression of group identity and membership" (Jonathan Clegg, "Toward an Understanding of African Dance: The Zulu Isishameni Style," paper read at 2nd Symposium on Ethnomusicology, September 6–24, 1981, Music Department, Rhodes University, Grahamstown (Grahamstown: International Library of African Music, Institute of Social and Economic Research, Rhodes University, 1982), 9.

36. Clegg, "Toward an Understanding of African Dance," 9.

37. Clegg, "Toward an Understanding of African Dance," 10.

38. Manyathela Mvelase, interview with the author, Jeppe Hostel, Johannesburg, June 4, 2017.

39. Sakephi Mbatha, interview with the author, Mdukatshani, Msinga, April 27, 2017.

40. Mbatha, interview with the author.

41. Louise Meintjes, *Dust of the Zulu: Ngoma Aesthetics after Apartheid* (Durham, NC: Duke University Press, 2017).

42. Terence Ranger, *Dance and Society in Eastern Africa, 1890–1970: The Beni Ngoma* (Berkeley: University of California Press, 1975).

43. Clegg, "Toward an Understanding of African Dance."

44. Penwell Dlamini and Alon Skuy, "Buthelezi Begs Angry Crowd to Calm Down As He Speaks against Xenophobia," accessed online on September 8, 2019, at https://www.timeslive.co.za/news/south-africa/2019-09-08-hostel-residents-march-against-foreigners-as-buthelezi-tries-to-appeal-for-peace/.

African Heritage Revealed through Musical Encounters and Political Ideologies

John Frederick Matheus and Clarence Cameron White's *Ouanga!* and Reuben Tholakele Caluza and Herbert Isaac Ernest Dhlomo's *Moshoeshoe*

INNOCENTIA JABULISILE MHLAMBI

INTRODUCTION

Shared traditions and communicative forms that extend to multiple cul-
turescapes in many African and diasporic communities have been a subject
of interest in turn-of-the-twentieth-century Black Nationalism debates and
expressive cultures. Revisiting these debates is important as significant off-
shoots such as gender, class, sexuality and ethnicity emerged from critiques
of this particular earlier version of Black Nationalist thought and praxis and
have been besieged by retrogressive race politics and the plurality of other
forms of nationalisms to emerge in the twentieth century. Of late, the world
has witnessed the resurgence of race-based or nationality-based nationalisms in American and European countries, xenophobia/Afrophobia in some
African states, and the betrayal of African national consciousness by African
postcolonial leaders. All these developments have led to a rise in racialised
fascism and bigotry throughout the world. Many of these movements have
reorganized themselves around old racial supremacist hierarchies in which
Black people, irrespective of their heterogeneity and diversity, continue to
be perceived as a homogenous group and always occupying the lowest rung

of racial categories. This includes bigotry in intra-Black hierarchies based on gradations of shades of Blackness or the status of individuals as foreigners, Others in a nation-state. These twentieth-century issues have scarcely changed as we moved into the twenty first.

Certain thematic trajectories in John Frederick Matheus and Clarence Cameron White's *Ouanga!* (1932), and Reuben Tholakele Caluza and Herbert Isaac Ernest Dhlomo's *Moshoeshoe* (1939), address broader Black historical consciousness awareness and are relevant to today's politics on race and nationalism. Recent examples of disturbing race politics and crises of nationalism cast doubt on anti–Black Nationalists' debates that urged for the abandonment of the twentieth-century version of Black Nationalism because of its homogeneous, essentialised discourses on the question of the Black race. A hundred years of racialised experiences by most if not all generations of Black people around the world suggest that twentieth-century Black Nationalism is a suspended revolution, abandoned and cut short before making significant advances regarding the question of the Black race. This observation is underscored by the fact that revivals of the question of the Black race in recent Black politics have not yielded significant inroads. Debates about the question of the Black race are being overtaken by politically correct ideologies and practices of minorities within the Black race itself. Further, mainstream Band-Aid packages in the form of Black economic empowerment, political participation in pseudo-democracy, affirmative action, gentrification of Black popular expressive forms all fail to address fundamentals of the right to be Black first and foremost, without fear and without the need to curry favour in any part of the world.

Revisiting this earlier version of Black Nationalism, particularly, its emphasis on cultural philosophies around African heritage is crucial for reviewing how contemporary Black politics are curtailed from appealing to Black people of the world in a manner Black Nationalism of the twentieth century failed to realise. Although the question of Black identity and the awareness of Black experience were common threads in earlier Black Nationalism, the dimension of its African heritage, with its emphasis on Afrocentrism as expressed by Asante remains a powerful thought modality for reading Matheus and White's *Ouanga!* and Caluza and Dhlomo's *Moshoeshoe*. Such an articulation of Afrocentrism could become a unifying factor for Black people and other oppressed peoples in the world. In current times, uncertainty exists in racial equality politics and there is also the re-emergence of racialised nationalism, where bigotry continues to be directed with impunity at people of colour, people of Africa, and people of African descent throughout the world. These disquieting instances of racial intolerance include those that happen among races that historically were occluded from racialised polarities that resulted from slavery and encounters with colonialism. It is within this larger framework of race and nationalism that I examine Matheus and White, and Caluza and Dhlomo's works, using earlier formulations of Black Nationalism and the context within which they were composed as organising tools for my analysis.

This chapter reinscribes into the Black Atlantic portrait a musical encounter, largely obscure, but central to the New African Movement around the turn of the twentieth century. Furthermore, this musical encounter is of import in the twenty-first century as the international stage has provided a vibrant arena for Black South African operatic activities. Even so, the presence of Black bodies, experiences, and consciousness remains an unwelcome reality in some economic and cultural landscapes of the dominant culture. The two music-accompanied works explored in this chapter present philosophies of being that depict a consciousness that illustrates how diverse Black nationalities show resilience, resistance, and reaffirmation of identities within the context of the older and more recent constructions of empire.

Matheus and White's opera *Ouanga!* narrates the rise and fall of Jean-Jacques Dessalines, a Haitian revolutionary leader of 1804. John Frederick Matheus, the librettist, and White drew from the political fallout of a historical figure, Dessalines, the fearsome leader of the Haitian war of liberation, to crystallise the subaltern's counterhegemony. The recreation of counterviolence in the operatic text underscores a Black (inter)nationalist political ideological standpoint as an inevitable consequence in the face of regimes of terror and dehumanisation. This standpoint is further shored up by the orality-based aesthetic of the opera, which serve as entertextualised forms that offer a different and alternative view to the dominant world, an alternative epistemology through which a Black consciousness discourse could reformulate its call for cultural kinship and consciousness among Black people and other oppressed groups. These oral forms link the aesthetic moulds of Matheus and White's opera to Caluza and Dhlomo's *Moshoeshoe*, which too has welded Western classical art forms with African popular oral verbal art and performance traditions. Caluza-Dhlomo's *Moshoeshoe* is one of the pageant musical dramas in a series composed in honour of past African kings in South Africa produced by the African Dramatic and Operatic Society. It centers on King Moshoeshoe (c. 1786–1870), of present-day Lesotho, and his rule of his Basotho kingdom during the wars of Mfecane/Lifeqane. The work further portrays Basotho tribal life, its daily rhythms, family life, court politics, inter-ethnic feuds, and significant ritual performances, including the Feast of the Harvest, believed to be the ritual of unification among Basotho.

This discussion investigates how Matheus and White's *Ouanga!* (1932) and Caluza and Dhlomo's *Moshoeshoe* (1939) engage issues of Black subjectivity, reclamation of identity, and (inter)national Black consciousness. I argue that these composers suggest that African heritage is the key to opening up broader philosophical discourses about resistance to slavery, colonialism, and the postcolonial state. In addition, the oral/African heritage is deployed in ways that indicate how ontological epistemes embodied in the past African oral world reveal intricate understandings through which subjected peoples reaffirmed their identities. By recasting subjugation periods in their compositions, Matheus and White, and Caluza and Dhlomo seem to signal that despite the dystopia that animated these periods (seen in *Moshoeshoe*), precolonial and pre-contact philosophical systems remain repositories and locations of indigenous knowledge systems that contribute in fundamental ways to the formation of contemporary counter-ideologies. These counter-ideologies are capable of rallying Black and other repressed peoples around common struggles. Entertextualised orality forms that these compositions use as a frame of reference illustrate how they are able to articulate and mediate presumptions to power whereby cultural dominance of the Western world is critiqued and how the critique can be a peg on which to stake an array of other contestations.

Tapping into Gilroy's Black Atlantic consciousness and turn-of-the-twentieth-century Black Nationalists tradition, I will demonstrate how the rise of Black art music in the Black Atlantic basin is predicated upon oral and performative traditions that were intended to produce a veritable transnational Black consciousness and renaissance. I base this argument on the similarities observed between Haitian and Basotho life in South Africa that Matheus and White, and Caluza and Dhlomo (respectively) appropriated for a Black cultural renaissance. For the purposes of illustrating this argument, this discussion will draw one theme from each composition: the African-derived Vodou religion in Matheus and White's *Ouanga!* and the Feast of the Harvest ritual celebrations in Caluza and Dhlomo's *Moshoeshoe*.

TRANSNATIONAL BLACK INTELLECTUALS AND THEIR CONTEXTS: COMPOSERS AND THEIR WORK

White's brilliant developments in Black art music, stellar performances at his concerts as a first violinist, and his violin pedagogy at the Washington Conservatory of Music and in several Black colleges (which included West Virginia State College (1924–1937) and Hampton Institute (1932–1935),[1] added fame and luster to his reputation as a leading figure in music. White is part of that first generation of Black composers who dedicated their talents to presenting and preserving traditional African American spirituals in the authentic style of their creators. Also in White's experimentations there are aspects that signaled that he was also a pioneer among Black music innovators. The opera *Ouanga!* attests to a preoccupation with newness in art music composition which relies on a general Black music consciousness but also draws upon European forms, particularly, opera, to develop a unique style. *Ouanga!* was a product of a "music and cultural ethnography" (Largey 1996, Bryan 2012) and offers dignity to Haitians in the face of cultural onslaught by European imposition. Through a depiction of postcolonial Haiti the opera gestures toward the centrality of Africa-based culture as a source of an alternative discourse and, ultimately, a vehicle for an alternative consciousness not only for Haitians but for all Black people in the Black Atlantic region who had also experienced the devastating aftermaths of European imperialism.

Largey (1996), following Gilroy's (1996) seminal views about the Black Atlantic, observes *Ouanga!* as "a product of the diasporic cultural process" that provides an instance for an exploration of the interconnectedness of the Black experience in different geographical regions within the Global North structures of political economy. For my chapter here, Gilroy's observations raise three important points as they relate to the African experience in South Africa: (1) the extension of this interconnectedness of diasporic consciousness with its other dimensions among elite Africans in South Africa (this will be brought in detail when Caluza and Dhlomo are discussed); (2) broader connections between the aesthetic discursive practices *Ouanga!* strike with precolonial and pre-slavery African epistemological understandings of social justice, an aspect White aimed to illustrate in representing Vodou in *Ouanga*; and (3) how Haiti at the turn of the twentieth century held significant esteem for African Americans with regard to the consciousness of the Black race in the northern hemispheric Atlantic regions. These points emerge after considering the broad sweep and effect of historical developments among Haitian elites, the New Negro Movement of the Harlem Renaissance, and the New African Movement in South Africa. Matheus's inspiration for the opera came from the Haitian revolution and he presented this history of the Haitian's struggle for liberation as a play *Tambour* (1928). The play was developed into a libretto to which White was to provide music. Matheus and White's interests with the Haitian revolution followed Harry Lawrence Freeman's *Voodoo* (1928) and the history was once again revisited by subsequent Black generations of art music composers such as Shirley Graham Du Bois in *Tom Tom* (1932) and William Grant Still in *Troubled Island* (1949). Altogether these operas began a wave of centralising this political epoch for Black transatlantic consciousness. The Haitian war of liberation highlighted and featured the beginning of an alternative world premised on the centrality of the African pre-contact culture in the formation of a Black consciousness.

Haiti, as the first and only Black republic at the opening of the 1800s, was founded on a successful slave revolt. For African Americans, it was a symbol of hope and reclamation of dignity of the Black race in faraway places that historically sought to berate and look down on what being African and Black entailed in the modern world. It was further considered a space where a fight against the commandeering of Black bodies for the benefit of European economies was waged successfully. To white supremacists, Haiti signaled sheer horror and anxiety about the backlash of the terror of slavery. For this sector, Haiti illustrated the aftermath of the regime of terror and that there is no monopoly in the ownership of the regime of violence and terror as these remain uncertain, fluid, and illusive.

Ouanga!'s African-based music, oral and performance arts distinguished White and Matheus for the directions that art music of this period was taking in the diaspora. White pursued this direction further through providing folk song materials for other composers. He intended to create a new American School of Composition, which was to focus on the deployment of Black folk idioms in music. As director of Hampton Institute, after Robert Nathaniel Dett left the post, he developed a course, "The History of Negro Music" (1935), which explored the relations of Black music and traced its development from Africa through slave songs in the United States and folk music in the West Indies. The year White took over the post of director of Hampton Institute was a watershed moment for South Africa's entry into that realm of art music. Caluza was at Hampton Institute to study for his first music degree. But even before Caluza set sail for America to study music, decades earlier, before the turn of the century, John Langalibalele Dube also went to

America and also studied at the Hampton Institute when it was under the directorship of Robert Nathaniel Dett. Dube came away from this institute with a renewed appreciation of Negro spirituals that he in turn taught to his students at Adams College in Durban, South Africa. Similarly, Caluza came away with a renewed sense of folk song in modern music in the tradition that White was visioning through studies in Black folk music.

The South African music theater scene to which Dhlomo and Caluza were to transfer this knowledge is an important starting point in the directions towards a merger of serious music and theater in Black performance cultures. When Dhlomo and Caluza collaborated in 1939 on *Moshoeshoe* (Coplan 1985) and perhaps also on *Ruby and Frank*, their experiment was seen as an advancement for taking musical dramas in a direction that would emphasise the unity of all the arts, which would also incorporate African traditional indigenous oral verbal and performance art forms.

Herbert Isaac Ernest Dhlomo (1903–1956) a founding figure of South African literature, worked as a governmental librarian and was a leading journalist for newspapers in Durban and Johannesburg (*Ilanga lase Natal, The Bantu World*). In his articles and editorials from the early 1920s he expressed great concern over cultural politics, the progress of Africans toward European modernity, the development of Black politics, the arts, and literature. His articles underscored his firm belief in African art forms; they were even necessary for the development of European classical ones and these directions could lead to a new relevance for Western classics. As a member of the New African Movement, he saw himself as part of a larger movement that included the greater African diaspora, even though he never had any experience internationally. Dhlomo, together with the rest of the New Africans, was inspired by the Harlem Renaissance of the 1920s and 1930s and accessed many writings of the progressive African American intellectuals such as W. E. B. Du Bois, Marcus Garvey, Alain Locke, and others.

Reuben Tholakele Caluza (1895–1969) was a leading Black South African composer who spent his early career (1915–1929) as a teacher at Ohlange Institute (Durban), and after traveling abroad he returned to Durban to became a professor of music at Adams College in 1936. Unlike Dhlomo, Caluza had extensive international experience. Beginning in 1930 Caluza's Double Quartet was invited to England, where they recorded more than a hundred songs for HMV Zonophone label; many of these songs were composed by Caluza and became bestsellers in South Africa. After England, Caluza studied in the United States from 1930 to 1935, first at Virginia's Hampton Institute and then at Columbia University.

While in the United States, Caluza was immersed in a rich, multi-textured musical world. Black Americans in increasing numbers were becoming involved in lyric theater, which gained momentum after Samuel Coleridge-Taylor's *Hiawatha* trilogy, op. 30, based on Henry Wadsworth Longfellow's poem ("Hiawatha's Wedding Feast," "The Death of Minnehaha," and "Hiawatha's Departure," 1898–1900). By the early 1930s, when Caluza first got to Hampton Institute, most pioneers in this space had carved out names for themselves. The formal classical nature of some of the African American music composition had a powerful impact on him and influenced his views on the constitution and the directions of modern Black music generally. For instance, he not only had an encounter with African American sacred music (e.g. spirituals), he also was in the company of stellar African American classical composers and singers whose compositions were inscribing a new understanding on notions of Black modernity. For instance, he came across the work of Robert Nathaniel Dett (1882–1943), who together with Harry Thacker Burleigh (1866–1949) revived and arranged African American slave songs. He also was immersed in the world of Paul Robeson, Marian Anderson, Roland Haynes, and Clarence Cameron White, whose work in bringing Black singing talent and compositions to mainstream America was being keenly felt.

From the turn of the century Black American art music, which foregrounded Black themes and its African heritage had gained momentum so that by the 1930s some compositions had a distinctive marker of Black composers' particular contributions to the classical music tradition. Short and long forms of art music such as symphonies and operas had been successfully staged and were making their mark in Black American classical spaces. These included Scott Joplin's *Treemonisha* (1911), Harry Lawrence Freeman's *Voodoo* (1928), Shirley Graham Du Bois's *Tom Tom* (1932), and John Frederick Matheus and Clarence Cameron White's *Ouanga!* (1932); a lot more were still to be produced, such as Dett's oratorio *The Ordering of Moses* (1937), William Grant Still's opera *Troubled Island* (1949), and many more symphonies that premiered in the late 1930s and afterward. Though ethnomusicologist Veit Erlmann (1991) laments that there is no traceable impact of Caluza's immersion from his studies at Hampton Institute and Columbia University, the titles of his music pieces, "Rondo for Orchestra," "Reminiscences of Africa," and "Go Down Moses," which he prepared for the string quartets he presented for his BS and MA degrees respectively, are telling of the new musical consciousness, direction, and discourses he had absorbed. Matheus and White, and Caluza-Dhlomo's work advance Black Nationalist discourses, the African intellectual's ideological crises, Du Bois's double consciousness concept, and, for Caluza and Dhlomo, a renewed search for a pan-Africanist consciousness that surfaced in national racial politics around the time of Caluza's return from the United States.

Caluza's return from the United States in 1936, on the political front, coincided with sedimentation of Africans' marginalisation by the South African National Party prime minister, James Barry Munnik Hertzog, and his Pact government. The four-year interregnum during which Caluza was absent from the country had seen rapid worsening of African lives across all classes. The African elite's traction as cultural proselytisers had begun to show signs of stagnation and reversal as they themselves realised that their aspirations for progress under white rule and acceptance by their white counterparts would never materialise. On the cultural front, as Erlmann points out, there were growing views from anthropological studies that had begun to contradict earlier perceptions regarding the centrality and function of African cultures. These "expert" views, responding to perceived cultural dislocations occasioned by liberal reform projects for Africans had a tremendous impact on the policy that shaped music education at Adams College where Caluza assumed a post at the School of Music. These policies had disastrous effects on apolitical and non-politics-aligned elites like Caluza; an exception was H. I. E. Dhlomo, who was fearless and outspoken about a range of sociopolitical and cultural issues. The views of these "experts" were in contradistinction to the context within which Caluza experienced the deployment of African heritage in the African American music theater.

Most scholarship on African aesthetics in African American art forms indicates that the presence of African heritage on Black American stages is intrinsic because musicals, opera, and dance-drama are forms that invoke romantic feelings. Such emotions subtly encouraged the audience to humanize the characters and consider the perspective of an emancipated Black race. Every instance of Black liberation in Black America generated interest in folk customs of African origin. Thus in Caluza's mind, the conviction of South African ethnomusicologists such as Percival Kirby and Hugh Tracey, who were influenced by the anthropological turn, represented a contradiction and a schism, where attempts at retraditionalisation for South African arts were far removed from the inscription of these African forms for racial pride.

At the Adams College School of Music in Durban, the music curriculum emphasised Bantu music and entailed an interest in African folk music; this was for the archival collection and recordings as well as for the teaching of this music to schoolchildren. This curriculum was strongly advocated for by Edgar Brookes of the American Mission Boards. On the cultural front, the cultural nationalist revivalism, signified by the founding of the Zulu Society in 1937, included a counter-stance. A number of African elites turned their interests to past ethnic nationalist symbols of a freer existence under ethnic kings and monarchs, and they brought these symbols to bear on the ravages and betrayal of European modernity by successive segregationist white governments. Dhlomo and Caluza's *Moshoeshoe* foregrounds precolonial existentialities that stem from this counterhegemonic stance. Nonetheless, beginning and continuing on from this period, Caluza's music turned to Zulu folk music, advocated for ethnic morality, essentialised notions of reinventing traditions, and drew copiously from African American spirituals (Erlmann 1991, 150). Erlmann laments that within a short space of time Caluza's educational efforts through this second phase of his musical career, together with those of Kirby and Tracey (key ethnomusicologists of Bantu music), laid the foundations of early apartheid educational policies, in which spirituals and ethnic nationalism were hijacked and used as vehicles to produce ideal African subjects for racial capitalism. This move towards the ethnicisation of the colonial subjects was coupled with the abolition of the Cape Franchise in 1935 and the passing of the Native Lands Amendment Act of 1936, which were political and administrative structures of the apartheid state's forms of the Bantustans, the homelands system.

Moshoeshoe's composition and staging in May 1939 happened after these significant shifts, which successfully destroyed African elite's conceptualisations of progressive modernity and which, according to their views, were supposed to be similar to those which produced the New Negro and the Harlem Renaissance. Caluza's turn to ethnic-inspired music coincided with Dhlomo's search for a nuanced relevancy of African drama and performance against the unyielding and bleak political future and cultural landscape. Caluza and Dhlomo's inclusion of traditional African epistemologies and cosmology evolved from their dismay with European modernity as well as the desire for complete autonomy of African arts and its artists from white control. The efforts of European anthropological "experts" to reshape future roles of African performance arts in education and its greater cultural and political impact in policy formulation contrasted dramatically with Caluza and Dhlomo's aesthetic goals of gravitating to autochthonous art forms in contemporary African arts. These artists saw the traditional arts as an opportunity for indigenous voices to expand what was considered prodigious in terms of arts and aesthetics within the larger global context.

TRANSATLANTIC 'TEXTSCAPES' AND THE ORAL WORLD

A reading that invites a focus on the aesthetics of oral arts if further extended by Robolin's (2012) recent work on literary (cross)migrations between African Americans and Africans in South Africa. Robolin's treatise is in itself an extension of Gilroy's analysis. Although Gilroy excluded a focus on South Africa's racial and cultural links (see Masilela 2001; Piot 2001), Robolin introduces newer interdisciplinary models that focus "on a wide array of past and ongoing social, economic, religious, ideological and cultural intersections, parallels, and divergences between the two countries or their various constituencies" (Robolin 2012, 82). These approaches are significant in bringing to light real and imagined cultural and textual symmetries of the underappreciated divergences between "(con)texts or authorial philosophies" and the "deep thematic resonance," more specifically, the "texts' performative intertextuality" that help illustrate a pattern of influence and cross-fertilization without flattening or collapsing together vastly different cultural arenas.

For studies on Black operatic transnational consciousness, the idea of exploring divergences while taking care not to flatten or collapse difference is crucial. With the compositions concerned, there are significant differences in how Black composers respond through oral forms to political and cultural experiences in their respective regions. Black identities represented in Matheus and White, and Caluza and Dhlomo's works share certain commonalities, yet they also entertain striking differences. The convergences and divergences available through transnational studies link up with the transmigratory and transmutable nature of oral forms and allow for transnational comparative analysis. Harnessing oral forms to histories of (pre) nationalist societal identities helps identify cultural interconnections, flows of people, cultural materials, and ideas across national borders (Hofmeyr and Gunner 2014, 3).

As a continent, Africa has enjoyed a longer history of being imbricated in a series of transnational world systems where there has always been constant mobility, migration, and circulation; these earlier crisscrossings of cultural forms translated to subsequent historical global flows and pathways. Nonnational constructions invoke pre-national forms of belonging, and enduring forms of ethnic allegiance. Colonially contrived forms of national identities may be seen as sovereignty-related identities. The national is a passing moment in the greater scheme of things, because nationalism, as a foreign, late twentieth-century political concept, was introduced to Africa as a continent that already had long established thick histories of the crisscrossing of materials, cultural movements, and peoples, who grappled with their histories without referring to nation or national identities.

When African anticolonial engagements assumed a nationalist stance from the middle of the twentieth century it gave impressions that anticolonialism had moved from nationalism to transnationalism. The transnational was then perceived as the undertone of a global Black consciousness. Nothing, however, could be further from the truth; it was African epistemological systems that defied nationalised identities and national boundaries. Indigenous forms generally favour a fluid-based continuum structure and affect a number of contexts in which they are found both on the continent and across the African diaspora. Therefore, symmetries and differences between the African and African American circulation of oral cultural forms, and how they are used in art music and music theatre generate a set of critical questions. First, what are the sociopolitical and cultural bases for North American and South African comparative analysis? Second, what are the sociocultural, material, and politico-ideological conditions of circulation, exchange, and interconnectivity that have yielded discernible patterns of influence, syncretism, and cross-pollination across the Black operatic transnational consciousness? Third, for a religion as demonised as Vodou, what aspects of it raise it above European Catholicism and links Vodou to African systems of justice and modalities of thought? Finally, how does intersubjective precolonial African life in *Moshoeshoe* interconnect with Haiti's postcolonial conditions of African descendants in *Ouanga!*? These questions will shape the discussion, as I now turn to the analysis of the music pieces.

VODOU AND THE NEW TRANSNATIONAL CONSCIOUSNESS

In *Ouanga!* there are constellations of transnationalist cultural ideas drawn upon to reflect on past pre-contact understandings of Black racial dignity and autonomy. Matheus and White drew upon these constructions for their Black Atlantic nationalist consciousness in this opera. Their focus on the spontaneity and sensuality of Haitian culture, however, interpreted as marked symbols of Black distinction, were ironically interpreted by mainstream discourses as a sign of Haitian barbarism and an antidote to the rationality of civilisation. Nevertheless, notions about Africa's "hidden knowledge," which link to wider beliefs of spirituality, invite different interpretations in the centralisation of Vodou in *Ouanga!*. According to Desmangles (1990, 477–78) there are two sects of Vodou strains that later characterised the Haitian Vodou religion prior to its banning by French officials:

> the Rada whose pantheons and religious traditions derived from the region of Arada, in Dahomey,[. . .] and the *Pétro* whose "creole" deities were *tertium quid*, New World creations born out of slaves' rage against the cruelty of their masters. In the days of the colony, as with Vodou today, the Pétro *loas* (deities) were known to be bitter, aggressive, and forceful, their characteristics deriving from the oppressive conditions of slavery and the spirit of revolution which they inspired. In contrast, the Rada *loas* have been identified traditionally with benevolent forces. The mythology which surrounded the Pétro *loas* was not African but Haitian for, as this mythology exists today in Haiti, they relate stories about slave's struggle for liberation.

Further, Desmangles outlines the trajectory of the religion over the period of history in its association with material conditions Haitian slaves were subjected to before the revolution. These findings relate to how the "generative materialism" internal to the dynamism of Vodou shape representations and interpretations of the regimes and repertoires of violence in Matheus and White's *Ouanga!*. Haitian history has described how the Haitian revolution was launched at the Bois-Caïmann ceremony, which was a sacred gathering celebrating the Pétro *loas*. The *loas* easily associate with the evolving polyglot flux, porous constitutions of Haitian society's structural makeup. The religion's encounter with the rigid institutionality of European regimes of control, which depended on regimes and repertoires of violence to extract obedience from colonial slave subjects, is matched with the ever-changing nature of the Vodou religion. The kinetic nature of Vodou presents it as disorganised and complex, with multilayered configurations and a rhizomorphic constitution that is best equipped to challenge and disrupt the seemingly organized logic of the old regime and the new-age empire. By disrupting these political economies, the assumed monopoly of the regimes and repertoires of violence are illustrated to be unpredictable and fluid. As such, they attach and detach themselves equally from one end of the continuum to the other. This is demonstrated in act 2 of the opera when Dessalines disrupts a ritual enacted to cast a curse on him. This occurs after he has ordered the killing of a Mamaloi. At his coronation ceremony, he is established as an invincible emperor through the legacy of his regime's violence. But this changes when the Papaloi challenges him (early in act 2, 21–22). The effect of this challenge saw his soldiers defying his orders to kill the Papaloi; they suddenly, without warning, turn against him. Equally, his intensions to kill the Papaloi with his sword are obstructed mystically:

> The Papaloi and mourners project themselves towards the advancing Des-salines, casting the "Voodoo Spell". Dess. stops short as if hypnotised, unable to lower his extended arm. The sword falls from Dess. Hand. The Papaloi lowers his arms, Dess. with a shudder comes to himself and slowly lowers his arm. He picks up his sword, turns and with slow uncertain steps goes out of the door quickly followed by Michel, Gerin and some of his soldiers.

Notably, some soldiers present during this confrontation later joined forces with the Vodou followers and conspired to end his life at the end of the opera (act 3, 24). Demonstrated in the above representation is the instability and migratory power of violence; Matheus and White capitalise upon fluidity of violence to portray how Vodou was central to unmasking the genocidal role of European Catholicism in its collusion with old and new-age empires' logic of capital in dehumanising and objectifying of Black people. The fact that violence moves freely between the powerful and powerless signals that violence can rehumanise Haitians subalterns and accord them human dignity as well.

Further, the complicity of the Catholic Church in the violence against Haitian slaves is also centralized in the opera. The Catholic Church hovers in the background and is always juxtaposed with symbolism that pertains to Vodou priests (the Vodouissants), Vodou places of worship, and the estranged lovers: Defileé and Dessalines (act 2). Within the context of the opera, the focus is no longer on the old colonial empire, but the new independent empire of Dessalines. The new king's contempt for Vodou and his campaign to drive it out of post-French rule in Haiti derive from political opportunism in which the indigenous beliefs systems are selectively chosen for the personal selfish gains by the ruling elite. Dessalines, having witnessed the power of Vodou during the revolution, is now part of the ruling elite and appropriates colonial French sensibilities of control in order to secure the regimes of violence and eradicate the power of Vodou in the popular imagination (act 3). Of course, it is expected that his sudden change, betrayal, and hatred of the religion will consume and destroy him; his very identity is carved into the religion and its internal dynamism of defiance that resists control. On the broader symbolic reading, which might have spoken to sentiments active during this period, some African American elites read the betrayal of their African capturers (who eventually sold them to slavery) as requiring a complete break with Africa. For this sector, Matheus and White illustrate that such moves to cut out Africa's connections from the new identities created by the African Americans in the New World would never diminish their link to African roots, as that would be tantamount to self-destruction.

The inability to delink the New World from Africa is further concretised by Dubois (2001, 100), who provides a historical framework for thinking about Vodou in the opera:

> Haitian Vodou situates the religion within a broader Afro-Atlantic historical context, one reshaped by the economic and political effects of the slave trade, the intense cultural encounters forged in the Caribbean, and the difficult development of human relationships within these contexts [. . .] the religion is far from being the antithesis of "modernity" that it has been often posed to be, in fact [it] provides a window into the profound aftereffects of the process of enslavement, production and cultural confrontation that have shaped today's Americas.

Considering the wedge driven between Dessalines (the tragic hero) and Defileé (the cultural heroine) by the former's conversion to French sensibilities and the latter's steadfastness to Vodou, it is clear that they embody two irreconcilable worlds. Several times the love bond shared between these lovers drew them together, but their love is also severed by complications (act 1, scene 2, 12–14; act 2, act 3, scene 1). Both believe in different visions of the future; in the case of Dessalines, Vodou has no part in it. For Defileé, the religion remains a relevant reality and salient force of resisting future encroachments to the freedoms attained by Haitians now that they are no longer slaves to anyone and have become true citizens of Haiti.

INTERSUBJECTIVE IDENTITIES AND THE UNIFICATION OF A (POST)APOCALYPTIC NATION

Focalizations on the Vodou religion and its symbols in *Ouanga!* are also orality elements and motifs that punctuate the narrative structure of *Moshoeshoe*. Vodou's ability to carve out Haiti's new nation in Matheus and White's *Ouanga!* is similar to King Moshoeshoe's forging of a new nation out of the ruins of Umfecane/Lifaqane in *Moshoeshoe*. Umfecane/Lifaqane generally refers to the nineteenth-century Zulu leader Shaka and his wars of expansion. These internecine wars were of apocalyptic proportions, just as slavery and settler invasion were on the continent of Africa, the Atlantic, and the Indian Oceanic basins. *Moshoeshoe* is a critique of the segregationist' state at retribalising South Africa's ethnic groups. Broadly, the musical drama explores the ideological and political maturation of African intellectuals. In similar ways, the work strikes chords with that of preoccupation of the Black American renaissance practitioners and artists around the same period, in the 1930s (Erlmann 1991; Peterson 2001). This period was characterised by heightened senses of connections to the African past and how the past can be positioned to illustrate its relevance for the new century. For the African and African American elites, the past was important in connecting newer struggles to economic access and the position of Africans and Black people in the new, post-contact social strata both in South Africa and in the United States of America. Moreover, the past was a vista for connecting both continents and offered these elites perspectives on how to think about the African American dream and transnational Black identity. Lastly, the past revealed how these elites on both sides of the Black Atlantic dealt with issues of double-consciousness as it affected notions of modernity (Du Bois 1901). All of these interconnectivities are convoked in the central questions raised by the ritual of the Feast of the Harvest in the music drama.

Loren Kruger (1999, 16–71) locates the musical play within the unfolding theatricality of the political occurrences of the time, arguing that Caluza and Dhlomo's musical drama belongs to that pantheon of counterhegemonic plays that are connected to "the visual publicity," works whose connections to contemporary politics were more oblique (ibid., 13). She further asserts that *Moshoeshoe* retained a "subjunctive force" in the sense that it is a representation of an unacknowledged history and possible future (ibid., 13), which are aspects that are also most pronounced in Matheus and White's final gestures in the opera. Kruger establishes her contentions in the dialogue of the only two white foreigners living the Basotho life recreated in the work and argues that "the performance of the play gives voice and body to the inheritance of *Moshoeshoe* while staging the gap between that legacy and the limits of contemporary agency" (ibid., 71):

> FRIEND: One would like to see things remain as they are. . . . But I see trouble ahead. Our own white adventurers and farmers push upwards.

Soon Moshoeshoe will be called upon to deal with problems of land-purchase, boundaries, trading, and other matters foreign to his mind . . .

MISSIONARY: . . . Moshoeshoe is a genius and builder; a man of triumphs and sorrows; a man consumed by the smouldering and devastating fire of thoughts wishing but fearing to be born, of smaller hopes against the greater Hope, of great expectations unfulfilled, of plans and ambitions whose very attainment would but give birth to plans and ambitions never attained" (Dhlomo, Visser & Couzens 1985, 260–61).

After focusing her contentions on these observations, Kruger comes to the conclusion that the Harvest Festival that concludes the play does not yield the expected solutions that locate this musical drama in the extra-textual political, cultural, and aesthetical exigencies that gave it birth. She says this despite the play's response to depicting the presence of ancient customs and the modern evaluation of the social fabric of contemporary South African society. It is in recognition of these debates that I argue that the dialogue above presents Caluza and Dhlomo's prophetic visions for the future which engages earlier visions African intellectuals had about the promises of Victorian liberalism and the progress made. Furthermore, the dialogue reveals discontent regarding unfolding racial fracas in the structural makeup of the country's political and cultural economies. The promises of European modernity were not working out as earlier envisioned, and the new political economy entailed more uncertainties, insecurities, and privations for all Africans.

Nonetheless, the dialogue above is not the crux of what the Feast of the Harvest is all about. While the reading Kruger arrived at offers one interpretation of this ceremony, there is also another that is also derived from focusing on the ritual performances central to this harvest and incorporates some of her conclusions. The point of departure in analyzing this ritual stems from the moment of enacting the performance as characterised by two symbolic harvest offerings: one embodied by the ontological epistemes associated with the physical performances of rituals (which involve tangible offerings brought by community members to the ancestors), and the other is symbolic, personal testimonies and offerings from the tortured souls of individuals within the community who bring in an empty harvest; this is represented by Moshoeshoe. These offerings simultaneously yield divergent outcomes. On the one hand, there is a regenerative vitality associated with the continuity of the cycle of life, and on the other, despondency and the sense of the end of times. Thus, the ritual in the context of the performance by and representation of South Africans embodies two interlacing aspects: (1) thanksgiving and chastisement and (2) appeasement. Caluza and Dhlomo, both having grown up in rural Natal, would not have been oblivious to these interpretations as these symbolic gestures formed part of the everyday rhythmic patterns of country life and the growing urbanizing Africans. As mission-educated Africans, though vacillating between this life and that of their forebears, they were well conversant with societal ontologically derived cultural knowledge regarding this ritual. These epistemes connected them to indigenous forms of knowledge about the intersubjective identities and relationships engendered in the performance of this ritual. Hence they fully grasped the implications it held for the broader interpretive process necessary in understanding this play.

To set the tone for these intersubjective identities and relationships, Caluza and Dhlomo recasts the Spirits (scene 6, 256–57), which are seen wondering and dancing about by innocent, young children. These Spirits will later be invoked to speak to Beauty and Truth (scene 6, 263–64), but at the moment, at the commencement of the ceremony, the Spirits avail themselves only to the chosen few whose virtue accords them with the ability "to see the hidden truths." These Spirits thereafter interface with the various characters and identities that populate the text, setting up a harmonious relationship between them. The environment that is the last strand connecting the intersubjective triad between the spirits of the ancestors and the humans has been productive, as there is merriment and the shouts of deference, "*Pula*" (rain) to the Spirits and the king, who is also saluted as "*Sefabatho! Ntate oa se Chaba*" ("Feeder of the people, Father of the Nation," scene 6, 257). After their invocation, these Spirits rise from the ground and their recitation speaks of rebirth and the promises of life bountiful and unending in the presence of its maker:

SPIRIT OF BEAUTY: When Beauty rises in the Human East
    Goodness will swell like yeast
    Reborn, the sons of man will blossom fair . . .

SPIRIT OF TRUTH: Then shall the rains of Truth, Love, Mind all fall . . .
    And wave-like, man will boil with new-born thought,
    And, like sea-vapour, rise noiselessly still,
    And purified, and charmed with Light and Love,
    Return to heaven from whence at first he fell.

The cyclic regeneration of life is at the core of the Feast of the Harvest. This promise derives from the thanksgiving and conciliatory nature of this supplicatory process, which is repeated every season.

The other strand, which touches on rebuke, derives from unfortunate humans who, because of misdemeanours, failed to ensure this intersubjective relationship. Ideally, the wise Mohlomi (the wanderer), whose encounter we witnessed earlier on (scene 1, 235–40), returns again after the Spirits have left. Outside the context of this play, Mohlomi, just like Moshoeshoe, was a historical figure who was chiefly by birth and once ruled over his chiefdom. Mohlomi's representation as a wanderer in the play is symbolic of the pariah status of chiefs like him, and their subjects, who are in that state because historically Moshoeshoe dispossessed them of their lands. Mainstream historiography presents Moshoeshoe as a great peacemaker whose diplomacy not only ensured the safety of his subjects but also united scattered nations (scene 1, 234), gave dignity to dehumanised people (scene 1, 238–39), and rehumanised others, such as the cannibals (scene 3, 243). But there is also the little-known history of his participation in land grabs that went into the making of his mountain kingdom. Historically, Mohlomi was his blood relative, but Moshoeshoe sold Mohlomi out to the English colonialists and the Afrikaner Boers in order to appropriate his lands and that of other chiefs. Scholars including the Comaroffs (1997) and Cobbing (1988) describe how during the white settlers' clamouring for more land from the colonial administrators, later turned into labourers and pariahs African rulers who appropriated fertile lands and dispossessed their subjects; and forced others to form the large proletariat class that populated urban centers. The complicity of African rulers and earlier Christian converts in these activities gained them prosperity, which went on to establish their progeny as the first, second, and third generations of African intellectuals; their privileged position contrasted sharply with that of the rest of the African masses. The actions of these African rulers and earlier converts set the tone for segregationists' policies of land ownership in which Africans gradually lost lands until none could own any land under South African laws.

This historical detail read against the articulation of Moshoeshoe in the play, as well as the missionary dialogue Kruger brought into her analysis, are suggestive of the kinds of harvest different constituencies of the Basotho kingdom bring to their ancestors. In the broader social context outside the play, right up to the point of the commemoration of Moshoeshoe's Day, on the 11th March annually, it is mainly the general populace that brought sacrifices befitting their ancestors and in return are promised regeneration and future abundance. However, for rulers like Moshoeshoe and African intellectuals who harbour dark secrets of betrayal, an empty harvest filled with uncertainty and no future prospects is what they bring to the ritual of the Feast of the Harvest.

> MOSHOESHOE: The seasons come and go: the world moves on.
> All pain, all joy, birth, death—all is but motion!
> 'Twas not for pain or joy Man came upon
> This star. Souls come and grow up—evolution!
> Like as a river . . . so my pain flows endless!
> Like unto stars, my thoughts shine far beyond me!
> Like wind, I'm here, there, gone—but am! O sadness!
> Fain would my soul soar high to God and be!

Moshoeshoe's invocations read against the simultaneous chastisement and appeasement dialectics, as well as against his perennial pensive mood and the tension-filled, travel-honed wisdom (this is equally baffling) of Mohlomi, are telling of Caluza and Dhlomo's excavation of the African ontological epistemologies deployed in driving Black Nationalist sensibilities. Despite the celebratory mood at this ritual by the general populace, the constituency that brings an empty harvest could not join in the festivities (scene 6, 266). Moshoeshoe's pan-ethnic form of nationalism is punctuated by colonial designs, even though this pan-nationalism is still regarded as capable of transgressing limits of the old and new empires in reclaiming African dignity and humanity. For Caluza and Dhlomo, the much-needed cultural renaissance ought to begin with a reassessment of history and the role that the African elite, both royal and educated, played in undermining their own yearnings for social and human justice.

In conclusion, turn-of-the-twentieth-century Black subjects across northern and southern regions of the Atlantic embodied philosophies of being that induced reflexivity. For Caluza and Dhlomo, the pan-ethnic consciousness with its introspective reprisals is the necessary beginning before a broader pan-Africanist or international Black consciousness can be sought. Theirs is an ideology worked from their connections with African American cultural renaissance discourses. Their deployment of orality speaks to the African heritage and past world orders, which are systematic channels to foreground common philosophies about existential questions. These reactions reveal their contemplative reflexivity about complexities that move beyond binaries introduced by the colonial encounter. In the case of Matheus and White in *Ouanga!*, while specifically Black cultural and transnational consciousnesses are critical to the formation of new Black identities, the expanse and depth of philosophical meaning embodied by the indigenous cultural art and performance forms—especially in creating these new cosmopolitan transnational identities—have highlighted multifaceted, abstruse ways through which Black epistemologies in other regions are made to engage one another and speak to humanity projects such as justice and the restoration of human dignity.

The ability of turn-of-the-century Black folks, even at this early stage, to negotiate the intermediate spaces of the contact zones between Africa, the United States, and Haiti displayed ways that move beyond the narrow confines of the Black condition. The Afrocentrism that prevails in these two works, though mystic in tone at times (as if under the cloak of mysticism glancing to the past), could be called a new symbol of how to challenge racism and the toxic nationalism that have defined the position and identity of the Black race in the modern world. Tokenism in racial upliftment programs through gender, class, sexuality, and ethnicity discourses has been a reaction to the advances of turn-of-the-twentieth-century Black Nationalism and has not yielded notable successes for the Black race in its entirety, save for a few token Black people epitomised as success stories in Black upliftment politics. Such a fallacy is shattered when racism and toxic nationalism intermittently rear their ugly faces.

NOTE

1. There is much disagreement in his scholarship regarding his tenure at Hampton Institute. Carl G. Harris (1974) in "Three Schools of Black Choral Composers and Arrangers," set at 1935–1941. I am persuaded, however, by recent scholarship, mainly Edwards and Mark (1981) and Michael Largey (1996).

WORKS CITED

Bryan, K. M. 2012. "Clarence Cameron White's *Ouanga!* in the World of the Harlem Renaissance." In *Blackness in Opera*, edited by N. André, K. M. Bryan, and E. Saylor, 116–40. Urbana: University of Illinois Press.

Caluza, R. T., and H. I. E. Dhlomo, 1939. *Moshoeshoe*. In *HIE Dhlomo (1903–1956): Collected Works*, edited by Tim Couzens and Nick Visser. Johannesburg: Ravan Press.

Cobbing, J. 1988. "Mfecane as Alibi: Thoughts on Dithakong and Mbolompo." *Journal of African History* 29 : 487–519.

Comaroff John, and Comaroff Jean 1997. *Of Revelation and Revolution, Volume 2 The Dialectics of Modernity on a South African Frontier*. Chicago: University of Chicago Press.

Coplan, D. 1985. *In Township Tonight! South Africa's Black City Music and Theatre*. London: Longman.

Desmangles, L. G. 1990. "The Maroon Publics and Religious Diversity in Colonial Haiti." *Anthropos* 85, no. 4/6: 475–82.

Dhlomo, H.I.E, Visser, N and Couzens, T. 1985. *H.I.E. Dhlomo Collected Works*. Johannesburg: Ravan Press.

Du Bois, W. E. B. 1901. *Souls of Black Folk*. Chicago: A. C. McClurg.

Dubois, L. 2001. "Vodou and History." *Comparative Studies in Society and History* 93, no. 1 (Jan.): 92–100.

Edwards, V. H., and Michael L. Mark. 1981. "In Retrospect: Clarence Cameron White." *The Black Perspective in Music* 9, no. 1: 51.

Erlmann, V. 1991. *African Stars: Studies in Black South African Performance*. Chicago: Chicago University Press.

Gilroy, P. 1996. *The Black Atlantic: Modernity and Double Consciousness*. Cambridge, MA: Harvard University Press.

Hofmeyr, I., and L. Gunner. 2014. "Introduction." *Scrutiny* 10, no. 2: 3–14.

Kruger, L. 1999. *The Drama of South Africa: Plays, Pageants and Publics Since 1910*. London: Routledge.

Largey, M. 1996. "'Ouanga!': An African-American Opera about Haiti." *A Journal of Interarts Inquiry* 2: 35–54.

Masilela, N. 2001. "The Black Atlantic and African Modernity in South Africa." *Research in African Literatures* 27, no. 4: 88–96.

Peterson, B. 2001. *Monarchs, Missionaries and African Intellectuals: African Theatre and the Unmaking of Colonial Marginality*. Johannesburg: University of the Witwatersrand Press.

Piot, C. 2001. "Atlantic Aporias: Africa and Gilroy's Black Atlantic." *Southern Quarterly* 100, no. 1: 155–70.

Robolin, S. 2012. "Black Transnationalism: 20th Century South African and African American Literatures." *Literature Compass* 9, no. 1: 80–94.

White C. C. 1932. *Ouanga! Opera in a Prologue and Three Acts Based on the Haitian Drama by John F. Matheus*. Piano/vocal score. Paris. Néocopie Musicale. Held in Clarence Cameron White Collection, Schormburg Center for Research in Black Culture, New York Public Library.

Discussing the Play Angalia Ni Mimi! and a Performance by the Playwright Marthe Djilo Kamga

FRIEDA EKOTTO

"The impossible return,
not here, not there,
wandering in the depths of myself . . ."
  Djilo Kamga

In this era of migration, artists perform the important work of reminding us that displacement occurs not only in the physical sense, but also at the very core of our beings. In her one-woman theatrical performance *Angalia Ni Mimi!*, Marthe Djilo Kamga, a Cameroonian artist and activist who emigrated to Belgium as a young woman, explains how she has come to define herself in a world that has, again and again, placed her at the margins. Moving between past, present, and future, Djilo Kamga demonstrates how, as an African woman, an immigrant, and a woman who loves other women, she has often found herself without the language or models from which to form her own identity. *Angalia Ni Mimi!*, which Djilo Kamga translates as "Look, it's me!," is her creation story, her contribution to a new archive, one of African women and their place in modernity.

To look at Djilo Kamga, to see her and to hear her, readers and viewers must resist approaching *Angalia Ni Mimi!* via established Western discourses. Although performed orally by an African woman, the piece cannot simply be assigned to traditions of African oral poetry; although Djilo Kamga addresses same-sex love, one cannot classify the piece as a lesbian (surely an antiquated term) coming-of-age story, or even within the broader LGBTQ catchall, for those terms, and the identities they denote, were developed within cultural circumstances that do not entirely pertain to Djilo Kamga and the work she presents here. In this critical reading of her performance, I offer a theoretical framework that allows readers to understand the piece beyond this kind of categorization, and instead to see it as an invitation to be transformed by Djilo Kamga's presence and work.

Angalia Ni Mimi! redefines and problematizes prejudices about African women's place in modernity, thus engaging the concept of *reprendre*, or "retaking," à la V.Y. Mudimbe in his reading of "The Colonial Library." In his seminal text *The Invention of Africa*, Mudimbe shows how the West has accumulated knowledge in the "Colonial Library" and in so doing has *invented* and *constructed* the imaginary landscape known as Africa. This "Colonial Library" is the archive of knowledge on Africa that is inevitably drawn from when any person speaks, writes, or thinks about Africa today, and it is the central resource, Mudimbe argues, that African artists must return to and excavate ideologically in order to rearticulate epistemologies of Africa on their own terms.

Djilo Kamga's beautiful and insightful performance is an example of the new epistemologies currently being formed by African women artists and activists, who live between countries and continents. In this chapter, I begin by theorizing how Djilo Kamga presents displacement to suggest that there is not only movement in space, but also in time. Her narrative travels between past, present, and future, allowing her to write her own narrative as a female postcolonial subject. Rather than remain an object of the past, she rewrites it as she experienced it, thus changing the way we see it, as well as the present and future. Next I address in Glissantian terms how the audience encounters her performance, demonstrating how Djilo Kamga makes clear the political nature of her performance even as she creates space for an important intervention through play with language and expectations.

With her stories Djilo Kamga creates snapshots that move in both time and space. In Deleuzian terms, we can understand these snapshots to be showing movement *as* time. In *Cinema 2: The Time-Image* (1985) Deleuze develops the concept of the "crystal-image," a shot that combines (often in an indiscernible manner) the past-ness of a recollection with the present-ness of its experience. The crystal-image is the keystone of Deleuze's "time-image," or cinema as a direct image of time. *Angalia Ni Mimi!* contains a variety of magnificent "crystal-images" that encourage us to recognize the importance of time as a continuum in her experiences of life on the margins.

By mixing snapshots from her childhood with reflections about her parents and her children, Djilo Kamga creates "crystal images" that suggest her self-actualization is always deferred, always moving toward the future. For example, a few moments into the performance, an artful sound bridge creates an effect of continuity between her two iterations of the powerful line: "I want TO BE who I am." Not only does she articulate this iteration in the past, but she repeats it again toward the end of her performance. In this and other "crystal-images," Djilo Kamga effectively elaborates a cinematic effect in which, as Deleuze puts it, "time is no longer the measure of movement, but movement is the perspective of time" (1985, 21). Djilo Kamga's complex and multifaceted engagement with movement asks the audience to consider how long a journey toward self-actualization is, not in terms of miles, but in terms of time. She asks us to consider when the time arrives to be the self, or as Aimé Césaire would say, when "l'heure de nous-même a sonné." ["Our time is now."]

Djilo Kamga makes clear that the audience, too, is part of this movement, for the process of performing actively includes the audience. Although originally from Cameroon, the audience with which Djilo Kamga participates is not an African one, as is implied by comparing it with traditional African poetry. Rather, her audience is the cosmopolitan mixture of individuals found in contemporary European cities. As Lisa McNee reminds us in her book *Selfish-Gifts: Autobiographical Discourses*, this aspect of audience is important for its role in constituting the performance of the autobiographical self. "This process actively involves others, for in constructing a textual self or selves, the autobiographer must also imagine an audience or the responses of the audience before her" (2000, 150). In the intersubjective activity that is autobiographical performance, the individual's place is always part of an exchange. As such, it is imperative not to consider this work within a tradition African oral poetry, but rather as involved in an exchange with contemporary Western and diasporic audiences. For example, when Djilo Kamga speaks of her family, this is not only because it is characteristic of African oral poetry (indeed this feature is found in most autobiographical work from many cultural contexts), she is asking the audience to understand the heft of her origins so as to understand the weight of her exile.

To take up a Glissantian image, this intersubjective aspect of exchange is part of the fabric in which her stories are woven. For example, in her opening lines, Djilo Kamga speaks her names, those she was given, and those she has chosen to call herself. She then addresses the audience directly, challenging it to hear these names and encounter her in a space that moves beyond the theater itself.

> *My name is Marthe Alphonsine Djilo Kamga,*
> *I could have been called Marthe or Dijlo, or even Kamga,*
> *I could have been called something else,*
> *But my name is Marthe Alphonsine Djilo Kamga.*
> *I am speaking to you,*
> *The scene exceeds the theater and so I speak to you, you!*
> *I love women, well one or two, maybe three, sometimes, well I mean . . ."*
> *You can see what I mean!*

In *La poétique de la relation* (*The Poetics of Relation*, 1990), Glissant sketches a literary history of cultural identity, noting the tension between a vision of human culture that tends to extol unity, essentialism, universal truths, and one that mixes, relativizes, and particularizes. He traces the developments that have been formed out of or against these elements, such as tropes like the nomad and the exiled, processes such as diaspora, creolization, and migration, and theories including identity and culture. Overall, Glissant aims to propose an open-ended model of being, and he envisions a process of self-definition that is predicated on Relation as opposed to Unity: an identity that is forged through encounters with others.

A Glissantian poetics of relation is complex and can be read in contradictory ways. Rather than perform an extensive reading of Glissant's poetics of relation, there are a few specific elements that are salient to *Angalia Ni Mimi!*, which I will briefly outline here. In particular, I will discuss in some detail how the notion of *encounter* works in *La poétique de la relation* and what *opacity* contributes to this poetics.

First, in Glissant's poetics, the self is created out of interactions with people, places, and cultures, one's own and, more importantly, with "others." What Glissant takes care to complicate is that even when the encounter contains an element of chance or surprise, the conditions that make the interactions possible may be historically contingent. In other words, not all encounters are created in equal conditions. So while in his poetics, relation (encounter, interaction, transformation) is positively charged, the circumstances and the moment of encounter itself may produce or be the product of violence and deep injustice.

But a Glissantian poetics of relation also honors "opacities." By this Glissant acknowledges and makes room for that which cannot be assimilated, or that which cannot be limpidly translated in the moment when one "I" encounter another "I." In an elegant phrase, Glissant declares, "Des opacités peuvent coexister, confluer, tramant des tissus dont la véritable compréhension porterait sur la *texture* de cette trame et non pas sur la nature des composants" (204) ["Opacities can coexist and converge, weaving fabrics. To understand these truly, one must focus on the texture of the weave and not its individual components" (Wing 190)]. Glissant envisions opacities as coexisting threads that can weave a fabric or a story, as "une trame" in French means both the weave of a textile and the plot of story.

Angalia Ni Mimi! challenges its audience to be aware of the politics of its encounter and to make space for her stories to exist along with those more commonly told. Her stories, which include those of her ancestors and descendants, demonstrate how the modern subject is composed of heterogeneous parts. They underline, with the utmost clarity, concrete ways in which interiority is shaped by marginality, as well as how trajectories are marked by the absence of paths to follow. Djilo Kamga must create the self and invent her own paths. Indeed, she shows us how the identity of the performer *comes from* her paths, which are then *transformed* when the audience watches the performance, encounters it, and engages with it, within the conditions that it offers.

Part of the transformation occurs on the level of language, which Djilo Kamga redefines for herself and the audience. Take for example this statement, which comes directly after she has addressed the audience:

> I love women, well one or two, maybe three, sometimes, well I mean . . .
> You can see what I mean!

Her language here is willfully vague. She does this to create dramatic tension (how many women does she love?), but also to play with, expectations of language and time. Indeed, her vagueness is a means to control French on *her own terms* à la Mudimbe. She chooses not to be specific, either in terms of temporality or in terms of number. She wills language to open up to possibility.

This deceptively simple moment sends a powerful message. In his work, Frantz Fanon showed clearly that there was no hope of actually escaping the world of the European because the European was constitutive of its colonized

Negro; not even speech could be uttered by this Negro outside of a European worldview, as in order to be taken seriously the Negro is forced to speak in a European tongue, which turns him further into a colonized object by making him assume a colonized subjectivity: "To speak means to be in a position to use a certain syntax, to grasp the morphology of this or that language, but it means above all to assume a culture, to support the weight of a civilization" (pp. 17–18). In the film *Vibrancy of Silence: A Discussion with My Sisters* (2017), Djilo Kamga addresses this challenge and her work to change language from something that controls her to something that she controls:

> The truth is that French was forced upon me, and now I want to gain control of it. Gaining control means that I want to . . . use it differently. Sometimes I say things, I say words, and people say "Why did you it that way? It's incorrect." And I say: "No, I want to say it that way to express this." See? The question of language . . .

> I don't think language is static. They change, so I think we need to know how to speak the master's language, we need to know the master's tool, in order to be able to deconstruct it, or control it in a different way, instead of the way in which it was supposedly passed on to us as an inheritance.

For Djilo Kamga, the "gift" of language she has been given does not meet her needs, as both a colonial subject and as a woman who loves other women. She must therefore take it and transform it.

In a telling scene from her childhood, she recounts how she would not allow language to control her. When it became clear to her that she wasn't interested in boys, Djilo Kamga had to learn to defend herself from their words by learning new ones.

> *I have to say, there was a snot-nosed kid, who one day called me "frigid,"*
> *This word, which I didn't know, became the engine of my future vocabulary!!!*
> *I took the habit of learning words in the Larousse dictionary by heart so that I could WIN our daily verbal jousts!!!*
> *It was necessary that I distinguish myself at something, that I was the best at something!!!*

Djilo Kamga knew she was not frigid, so to prove it, and to take control of a word that was intended to control her, she set out to learn the entire French dictionary. Now, as a powerful storyteller, she has found that more than the right word, she needs to convey her meaning by changing language. Even more, she must challenge the audience to accept her changes and the space it opens for her stories. As writer and scholar bell hooks has written so powerfully about her relationship with English, "I know it is not the English language that hurts me, but what the oppressors do with it, how they shape it to become a territory that limits and defines, how they make it a weapon that can shame, humiliate, colonize" (1995, 296). It then becomes the subaltern's role to reshape language in a way that takes back agency and subverts power. hooks continues, "In the mouths of Black African in the so-called 'new-world,' English was altered, transformed, and became a different speech. Enslaved Black people took broken bits of English, fragments, and made of them a counter language. They put together their words in such a way that the colonizer had to rethink the meaning of English language" (297). Djilo Kamga performs this control through play, play with words and with our expectations. Through play she gains control. In this sense, she inscribes herself in this new archive that African women are creating for new generations. She opens up and exposes idiosyncrasies and errors, showing what doesn't make sense in the master's language. The rules of the game have been established, and they are not fair, but just as when she was a child, with her skillful play, Djilo Kamga will win the game.

She will play with our idea of African women's sexuality (how many lovers does she have?). But rather than bow to racial and sexual fetishizing, she will own her joy, her beauty, and her power, the power she has created for herself on the margins. As she puts it she is:

> *Marginal, free to live otherwise extravagantly, whimsically, sensually,*
> *erotically . . .*
> *A Black woman who loves other women,*
> *who dreams of a harem . . .*

Here, by playing with—and controlling—language, Djilo Kamga articulates her identity on her own terms. As for the performance's place in Western-centric notions of queer culture, we must resist the ease of describing same-sex identities and relationships in Western terms, whether as lesbian, queer, homosexual, or otherwise. As Naminata Diabate writes in her discussion of my novel *Chuchotte pas trop* [*Don't Whisper Too Much*]:

the term "homosexual," travelling through the centuries with a host of meanings, is a highly unstable term and using it amounts to perpetuating epistemic violence. As for lesbianism—understood as a mode of resistance against patriarchal and compulsory heterosexual economies—it is partly applicable to the characters as they seek to decolonize their bodies by refusing to comply with male expectations. However, unlike Cherly Clarke's lesbians or Wittig's materialist lesbians, [Ekotto's] female characters operate within the patriarchal paradigm. They give birth, get married, and fulfill some of their naturalized functions. Put differently, they negotiate the complexities of their lived experiences with multiple and interrelated identities as African, neocolonialized, women, rural, and uneducated. (2016, 56)

Although Djilo Kamga doesn't figure in among the rural and uneducated, her experience is not confined to Western contexts, and therefore attempts must be made to listen to her work, to see her and understand her in her own terms, and even in places where English or French terms don't exist.

In this way, through her powerful stories, which transform our notions of time, movement, and even language, Djilo Kamga creates a new archive, an important archive for other African women around the world. As Michel Foucault wrote, the archive is the first law of the sayable; its absence is precisely that which renders it invisible. By displacing patterns enacted by colonial discourse, and questioning language, symbols, gaps, and silences, Djilo Kamga allows us to see, theatrically, a new representation of Africa *and* the West. We experience the colonial world through an African woman's lens, and we hear its language with an African woman's ears. Djilo Kamga allows us to see and hear the significations of colonial and postcolonial discourses, how it has defined Africa, and particularly African women, and how it can be used *by African women* to *redefine* Africa and *rewrite* the texts that have described it. With Djilo Kamga, the audience sees her goals, achievements, hopes, dreams, and struggles. It appreciates her need for a new language. The need we all have for a language that will allow these stories to be told.

Angalia Ni Mimi! has been performed in Brussels, Belgium, in 2016 at the Massimadi Film Festival (the only Black LGBTQ+ festival in Europe). In 2017 *Angalia Ni Mimi!* was performed at the University of Michigan, Ann Arbor in a graduate seminar on women and gender and at the Mellon Workshop in Maropeng, South Africa. In 2018, at the XXI International Conference on "Revisiting Cosmopolitanism" in Puri, India, organized by Forum on Contemporary Theory, Baroda, *Angalia Ni Mimi!* was performed again. This is the first joint publication of Djilo Kamga's text and my theoretical comments. Enjoy!

WORKS CITED

Deleuze, Gilles. 1985. *Cinéma II: L'image-temps*. Translated as *Cinema 2: The Time-Image*. London: Bloomsbury Revelations, 2013.

Diabate, Naminata. 2016. "Geneologies of Desire, Extravagance and Radical Queerness in Frieda Ekotto's *Chuchote Pas Trop*." *Research in African Literatures* 47, no. 2:46–65.

Djilo Kamga, Marthe. 2016. *Angalia Ni Mimi!*. Play Performed.

Fanon, Franz. 2008. *Black Skin, White Masks*. Translated by Richard Philcox. New York: Grove Press.

Glissant, Edouard. 1997. *Poetics of Relation*. Translated by Betsy Wing. Ann Arbor: University of Michigan Press.

hooks, bell. 1995. "'this is the oppressor's language / yet I need it to talk to you': Language, a place of struggle." In *Between Languages and Cultures: Translation and Cross-Cultural Texts*, edited by Carol Maier and Anuradha Dingwaney Needham. Pittsburgh: University of Pittsburgh Press.

McNee, Lisa. 2000. *Selfish-Gifts: Autobiographical Discourses*. Albany: State University of New York Press.

Angalia Ni Mimi!

Therapy of a Thwarted Artist

MARTHE DJILO KAMGA

I am Marthe daughter of Kamga
Also named Djilo and Alphonsine,
My name is Marthe Alphonsine Djilo Kamga,
I am the maman of Priscilla Kristy, Bryan Austin
And of Malaïka Aziliz

I learned to grow with Priscilla,
She is my constant companion
Bryan allowed me to put life in perspective,
To get to the essential
I rediscovered myself through him,
He allowed me to accept myself completely.
He is my strength,
He is also my greatest weakness,
My distress, my anguish,
But how he pushes me, I love that.
The figure of autism for me is him, Bryan My son

Malaïka, she, she's . . . how to put it,
She is the serenity,
I am me with her,
I continue to be me,
I want TO BE who I am,

Marginal, free to live otherwise extravagantly, whimsically, sensually,
erotically . . .

A Black woman who loves other women,
who dreams of a harem . . .☺☺
I am 50 and plus,
I think I have accumulated some knowledge, experience, an organic mind.
That I want to convey today,

My leitmotif,
The permanent quest for identities,
The linchpins: social, cultural, intellectual, geographic, historic.
In short, questions of transmission, of silence, of muteness, of memory
blow me away!
How to be oneself, against all winds and tides. . . .
How to conjugate, articulate, cultivate one's marginality,
One's singularity without living for it on a deserted island?
My name is Marthe Alphonsine Djilo Kamga,
I could have been called Marthe or Dijlo, or even Kamga,
I could have been called something else,
But my name is Marthe Alphonsine Djilo Kamga.
I am speaking to you,
The scene exceeds the theater so, I speak to you!
I love women, well one or two, maybe three, sometimes, well I mean . . .
you can see what I mean!

(Silence,)
I am hungry for exoticism, eroticism, sensuality!
Tonight there will be secrets, raptures, Ndole, and Makossa,

I was frightened 1983

(Silence)
I don't remember all that well.
Everything is blurry, mixed up in my mind!
Intertwined with a million things, difficulties, dreams unfulfilled, strategies to
    be in the middle of a whole in which all the world exists and yet no one is.
I remember all that.
On the other hand I don't remember much.
I remember I was 17!!!
But how long ago it was my 17th year,
I also have a hard time remembering it.
Is it a selective, voluntary amnesia?
Or simply that there weren't any notable events?
I am going to try and think,
To reflect,
To introduce myself to myself, tenderly,
Into my past, to remember . . .

The reflex I have when I recall my memories is to say to myself,
So which class was I in that year?
For me studies were beneficial, but especially a release.
I took refuge in my studies.
I was 17 in 1983.
Just the year before one of my brothers had immigrated to France to pursue his
    studies in pharmacy.
Two years before my mother, she, had immigrated to Gabon.
Five years before my father he had migrated definitively to the great beyond.
Three years that I lived with my second host family after my father's death.
Already my second migration,
Intra-familial, to be sure, but a migration nonetheless.
My parents, my mother,
I'm not really sure what to say,
The story goes that when she was pregnant with me,
She was always on the road,
Her husband in prison, she was looking for a way to get him out
Me, I came into the world in motion!!
Already wandering, in my own country.

On exile before I even came into the world.
I have the same name as my mother's aunt, DJILO, which means in Band-
*   jounais, etymologically, "feel like crying"*
How am I supposed to know. . . .
My great-aunt, I think I saw her once in my life?
I don't really remember more.

And then what else to say about maman?
That she left home when I was about three-and-a-half, I think.
I saw her again at my father's death.
I was twelve.
She was in my memory, a myth, an ideal!!
Later I admired her for having left my father during that time period,
If she preferred to leave, without us, her children,
It was because she had her reasons, good reasons,
In any case, she couldn't have done otherwise!
Not with the patriarch, not with my father.

I don't really know her,
She doesn't really know me either.
She finds me rebellious, insolent, standoffish.
She says that I am the one who makes the event in the family.
We never know when, or what kind of upheaval I'm going to cause next!
We respect each other, nonetheless.
We have in common: risk taking, swimming against the current.
She worked hard so that I, each of us, could have a good education.
She gave me a taste for effort and perseverance . . .
She's a complex woman, strong,
Whom I found, and I still find, very beautiful!
I hope she finds peace, that her own demons will be gone before her.
Thank you, maman, for giving me life.
Thank you for having travelled with me as you could, with your tools, and
*   your baggage!*

If we speak of maman,
We must also speak of papa, aye. My father,
I am the daughter of Kamga, my father.
Kamga, it's a noble name in the chiefdom of Bandjoun.

His own parents had been exiled, banished from the village.
I don't know why.
I have the exile anchored in me like a gene. . . .

Michel Gaspard Kamga, that's him, he called me Alphonsine,
as a first name.
The first name of his first daughter,
That he had in Congo, in Brazzaville.
I saw her one time, my sister.
Michel had been in the infantry of the French army, during the war, the sec-
ond.
He came back from the war alive, his gun on his shoulder.
I remember the gun well because it was never far from papa's chin
when he wasn't well, which was often. . . .
War memories to be sure!!

Having come back alive from the war, the motherland's reward
Was a training at the school of French colonial administration.
The motherland, our ancestors, the Gauls, the Great France!!
A civil servant upon graduation, he started his life in the colonies, French.
I would make a pilgrimage, soon, following his traces, from before . . .
To Congo Brazza where I still have a brother and My sister.
I've been angry with him for a long time.
I remember when I was 17 I wanted to kill him.
But I lacked a body, he was already gone!
I reconciled myself with him dead. After having seen my homonym, my sister
with the same name.
Later, I gradually dropped Alphonsine,
To reappropriate myself as Marthe my only real name in my opinion.
My father, he gave me the pleasure of learning,
Of all kinds of knowledge, the aesthetics of awareness,
But especially the love and the practice of the French language, its elegance.

I remember that in 1983 I was 17, I was in the Seconde C class at the Lycée de
New-Bell in Duala, Cameroun, my native country.
With my baggage, my emotions, my tools . . .
It wasn't really my choice.
It was that of my brother, who had given himself the role of father.

I remember that I wanted to study literature.
Even if I was good at math and science.
I remember that I was pretty good in school.
But also passionate about sports.
I loved sports, I tried everything: basketball, volleyball, track, soccer, and many
  more. I was even a part of the lycée and other outside sports teams, with
  which I practiced and felt pretty good.
When competitions came, despite my selections,
I didn't participate, because my brother and mother banded together to argue
  that it didn't matter.
And that nothing other than studies had a rightful place.
I gave in despite myself and after a while my place was relegated to the side-
  lines, and then to that of a supporter.
I considered the appearance of my injury
As an opportunity to notify to my different teams that I had become unfit for
  intense athletic activity.
On the sidelines then, already the margins . . . Since always!

I remember, too, that it was a period when I wasn't well in my soul,
I wasn't well at all in my body, in my head.
I did not look like nothing beside my peers they said.
Since I was 13,
I never stopped hearing that all the time, that I wasn't as beautiful as the other
  girls in the family.
That I was a tomboy—a botched boy,
That I would never find a husband,
Always relegated on the margins, Marthe!
This margin started to become my safe haven, my place of comfort.
From there I could see everything.
Over what could happen within the pages, therefore. You know.
It was, in its own way, very secure.
I would find myself alone, in dialogue with myself.
I did not mean anything to anyone.
Well, yes, I did mean a little to my cousin, one of my cousins in the group of
  cousins, the cousins of my age, my peers.
Her name was Eurézie.

We were between 14 and 19 and we all hung out, often together, all the time.
I remember,
That it was the time of first loves.
They all had one or two boys who hung around them, except me.
The boys too had often heard that I was not a "real" girl.
What could they do with a botched boy?
A girl unlike the others, a boy unlike the others.
So what then? An alien? Or simply a freak of nature?
What to make of if not a whizz kid?!
We would make the alien into a whizz kid
Maybe more boy than girl, because you know.
I hung out more with guys, whom I dominated in every way.
Physically, I had strength that would make even Goliath go pale!!
I fought like no one else.
It could go on for a whole day.
With pauses, of course, but a fight to the finish,
Until somebody throws in the towel.
I never did.
I stopped fighting around the age of 17, actually.
I sent one of my cousins to the floor with a blow to the head.
He ended up at the hospital unconscious, with a concussion thrown in for good
*   measure.*

And so, I had to find something else . . .
I have to say, there was a snot-nosed boy, who one day called me "frigid,"
This word, which I didn't know, became the engine of my future vocabulary!!
I took the habit of learning words in the Larousse dictionary by heart so that I
*   could WIN our daily verbal jousts!!*
It was necessary that I distinguish myself at something, that I was the best at
*   something!!*
That I escape into something!!!!
I hung out with the boys, because I didn't really understand the girls.
I continue to struggle to understand, today, that my most ardent desires are
*   only for them.*
But, I dream of a harem of discovery, exploration, similarity, mutual compre-
*   hension and, of course, ecstasy.*

Yes, the first loves, we had to experiment, to know how this all happened before facing the boys!

The tries, it was between us, between girls in the family, understood in its largest sense!

My cousins, I mean my cousins and the cousins the cousins.

Sometimes there were boys, younger ones.

But that didn't count at all.

The fact is that it was especially between the girls that it happened.

This mess in which we have to meander around to find our place.

For experimentation, and where some g-i-r-l-s came out without too much trouble.

They knew the codes, not me.

Yet we had all been bathed in it since we were small.

Me, I never came back, I stayed in this eternity that doesn't say its name, this ideal!

So I fell madly in love with Eurézie. . . .

She was the designated prettiest one, the leader.

And she chose me, me, for the private parties,

Without our band of peers.

I was happy.

I believed it.

For the first time in my life,

I saw myself as part of a group, the norm.

It was the insouciance of adolescence.

I dreamed the moment.

Maybe I was becoming like everyone else!

But no!

For her it was a game, an experience, like all the other girls.

All the sudden everything stopped: the group, the games.

Each girl got it on with a guy for real . . .

I didn't know that it was like that.

I didn't know.

And with my favorite cousin it was also over.

It wasn't the rule anymore.

And me, and me, and me . . .

I stayed by the side of the road.

The train let me off.

It left without me on board.

I hadn't understood the rules. . . .
Until I figured out that I couldn't.
That I couldn't be anymore.
I had to appear to be. Simply fade away.
I found myself again on that margin to which I'd always been assigned.
Not a girl, not a boy . . .
This margin where I had fled for a time, to realign myself.
Where I did my reckoning, in the end.
No, I hadn't understood a thing.
I would never be like the others.
Like anyone.
It was a fact that I had to live with!
Convinced by myself that I was me.
A girl, convinced I was one.
A girl who desired other girls to be sure! And then what?
I couldn't live like this!!!
Impossible, unthinkable, incorrect.

I relegated myself to fantasy and the sublimation of my being.
I entered into silence, oblivion, mutism.
I found refuge in learning, in all the kinds of knowledge, possible and imagin-
*   able, to which I was inclined.*
I remember that I wanted to become a nun.
It was easier . . .
And then I wanted to die,
So that it would all stop!
I also thought for a while that I was crazy.
I became an amnesiac of my ME.
Until I understood how to deal with all this.
It took me time.
Lots of time.
I remember that despite the fact that my studies focused on the sciences.
Thanks to my sister's books,
I discovered literature.
Molière with Les femmes savant, Andromaque, Emile Zola with Germinal,
*   Richard Wright Black Boy, Kafka with the trial, Albert Camus, Jean Paul*
*   Sartre with dirty hands, Césaire with his return to a native land, Rous-*
*   seau, Senghor, and many others.*

A few texts, just enough to enlighten me.
To tell me that I wasn't swimming in complete delirium.
A little while later, I discovered philosophy.
The "net plus ultra" for me.
The right to counter argue a thought.
It was a total blast for me!!!
I had a good teacher.
He made me love the matter
It was my way out!!!
I devoured it!!
Under the pretext of philosophy I could speak once again.
And I used it to keep my place on the margin
while being connected to others.
And then, and then, and then . . .
I was lost!!!
(Silence)

Between 1983 and 1988, I was lost.

I remember after having understood nothing,
I was lost, lost in the depths of myself.
I understood less than nothing,
My history—personal, familiar, holes, pieces, here and there.
I didn't know how to shape myself, which future, which career, which ME.
I had to finish the three years that separated me from University, the promised
  land, sweet freedom!
These high school years taught us to analyze, question, the inner-workings of
  thought.
They prepared us to become the adults of tomorrow.

It was pretty cool,
But how can you do it if you're not holding all the cards?
I remember that we learned about the triangular trade, the explorers, the wars,
  the two wars, colonization, and then the independences, the wars of inde-
  pendence, the underground, and many other things, far, very far from us.
In the end, they taught us what the textbooks made for us in France wanted
  to tell us, you know. The motherland, our ancestors the Gauls, la grande
  France!!!
It made me think about Michel, the infantryman.
I told myself that if he hadn't survived, if he hadn't met my mother, I wouldn't
  be here, now, to ask myself all these questions, without even a glimmer of
  an answer! And if, and if, and if,

And then I remember too that at home we would talk from time to time about
  my grandfather Joseph, my mother's father.
He had been killed at his own home, on his veranda, in June 1960, a little after
  independence, not long after the return of his daughter my aunt.
She had been kidnapped during the struggle for independence,
She had spent months in the underground,
I don't know much about it,
No one is clear about these things in the family,
No doubt it's hard,
We don't really talk about it,
It's taboo.
What happened to her in the bush?

I know nothing about it.
She lost an arm, from her trek, my aunt.
Joseph, the indépendantiste, was punished,
He let go of nothing, he paid with his life . . .
I didn't know him, this brave man!!

I remember struggling with all these stories, familial, national,
African, and even beyond.
It was the period of great PanAfrican leaders.
The great, celebrated Thomas Sankara, to name only him.
We were enthusiastic.
We wanted to change the world.
We had to vote for the first time.
We hoped, we really believed in it.

It was hard to understand.
We were hearing new words: "civil society," "multi-party system," "democracy,"
    "election," "NGO," "opposition" . . .
But most of all, "Cap Liberté."
One of the first NGO's for populist political education in Cameroon then.
You can imagine that incidentally
My engagement wasn't far off.
But then once again, my mother!
This time, she was nice about it.
She gave me a choice:
Keep hanging out with Cap Liberté,
Or keep out of it, pass the BACC and go study abroad.
Me, I said: Senegal, Ivory Coast, Burkina Faso,
She decided:
I would go study medicine in Belgium!

And then I went cold, in my head, in my body, in my soul, I went cold.

(Silence)

In 1988, and thereafter, I was cold!!

I remember being separated from my town, Douala, in the most heat of eve-
ning aboard a Sabena flight, the first flight of my life!

My mother, being who she was, had bought me one of those beautiful outfits
for a party, a suit with a skirt, pffff . . . come on, what I wanted was my old
jeans!

I felt like I was wearing a disguise.

I don't remember very well anymore who went with me,

But I remember that there were many people there for the event, lots of people
at the airport.

And also that excitement was bubbling up around me

That maman wanted to stay to the side, even though she had made the trip
from Libreville to come and help me prepare for my trip.

I remember having taken off on this Sabena flight,

The morning of August 28, 1988.

On this, my first step towards the outside,

I almost turned back,

That was how cold I was,

In my suit

Of silk,

I was cold!

I wanted to go back, return toward, my land, my roots.

I discovered, instantly, that I had within me, roots.

Yes, strong roots, which I had just pulled out without really understanding,
and which would henceforth be, distant.

This wind, so cold, so strong, tried to take me back to my native land.

O Cameroon, my dear, beautiful country! Cradle of our ancestors!

I felt too, at that moment, my soul swerve far away from me

as if it stayed on that plane.

I understood then that hereafter, I would run after my soul,

Which remained in the air

Wandering.

I remember that

At that exact moment,

The possibility of no return occurred to me,
I remember too that I quickly chased that idea from my mind.
I had a mission to accomplish, and things could not come full circle
if I did not return to my native land.
Unimaginable to consider the possibility of no return, impossible!!

I was cold in 1988 and the years that followed . . .
I discovered the seasons and their set of contradictions,
The autumn, with its shining sun that does not warm.
And me trembling in a shirt, like in the burg
The cold that greets me outside is like no other!!!
I miss my country, I miss people, I want to leave,
But I am stuck, here, I am stuck in my body.
I do not know when I will be able to see my family,
I am sad, I am cold, I am cold in my soul,
Solitude, melancholy, nostalgia, all of these made me cold!!!

Then I learned to cover myself, to dress myself, seasonally . . .
I had landed at 14, rue du Laboratoire 6000 Charleroi, in a home
A home for young girls, run by nuns, Catholic sisters.
The home emptied out every Friday night.
I survived the weekends with the sisters and Rita, the only white woman of the
*   group.*
I stayed cloistered in my room.
I only came out for basic, primary needs . . .

I was surrounded by the gilded youth of the great Congo of the time.
Every Friday evening, the girls would go home to their families in Brussels,
Or to the family home in Waterloo, La Hulpe, etc.
Without their parents who were still in Congo.
I was invited a few times to spend the weekend with them!

I had some wonderful times at Charleroi.
Bus trips, with the elderly.
They allowed me to discover Belgium, differently, with the elders, their stories,
*   their experiences!*
They would tell me stories, tell each other stories, during the excursions.

I remember, on the return trip, the bus would stop at a club
To give the elderly a chance to have a party, a dance in the middle of the
*   afternoon!!*
These were my only moments of real escape, the buoy that kept me from sink-
*   ing into the solitude.*
I did not know that in leaving my burg I was going to be so alone!
Yet I had been accustomed to being alone, alone among the others!

I remember that in the years that followed,
My leitmotif—and that of the great majority of my contemporaries—was to
*   finish our studies and to return to our countries,*
To serve it, to build it . . .
Then the years passed,
The echoes that came told us not to think about returning,
In any case, not immediately, to postpone it, because things were going badly,
*   in the country*
And that the outlook was, so to speak, hopeless.

I remember having discovered after arriving in Brussels some new words,
Until then, I was familiar with the category of foreign student, of which I was
*   a part.*
Then I discovered: "immigrants," "refugees," "asylum seekers," "undocumented
*   immigrants," and so on.*

New phrases . . .
"Management reserves the right of entry."
"Private club," "For members only,"
And the spaces are more and more restricted, confined, relegated!!!
And you find yourself unable to move, hereabouts,
With the uncertain hope of returning one day to the burg.
After 28 years, the myth of the return little by little cedes its place to its corol-
*   lary the impossible return!*
The impossible return, not from here, not from there, wandering in the depths
*   of myself . . .*
Vulnerability, resilience, acculturation, re-acculturation, henceforth are the
*   words/sorrows that accompany me.*
I am neither from here nor from there, even if I feel myself to be a true Bruxel-
*   loise, a real zinneke! Truer than true, even with offence to some of them!!*
Brussels is my town, in any case today and now I'm a Bruxelloise!!

I am going to be 50 next July 29th!!!! Wow, already 50!!!

I remember when I was 20 I wanted to be 40!!!

Today I am 50 and I would like to be ten years older, although I feel like I still have so many things to do, to live!!!

For a long time I lived without, what I would now call, eruditely, the memory of my body.

My memory has again become present, I have again become ME, and then, being smitten, swept of my feet, bowled over, and all that's happened since but that is not at all the same . . .

I love life, I love who I am, who I am becoming,

All that I am living now, even if it's painful, at times.

It still seems in the singularity of the margin that characterize me . . .

I am gonna be 52 years old you know!!!

Things are changing in my gut, easy come, easy go.

I'm not too sure what's happening, I don't understand a lot.

From time to time, I seek

And then things evade me, and I let them go.

I am scared

I am cold

I am lost

I am torn apart

I am hungry for love,

I love!

It's charnel,

It's transcendental,

It's historic,

It's political,

It's also nostalgic

I want to be,

I don't know how,

I no longer know how,

I don't know where,

Everything tumbles around in my head,

In my body,

In my being,

I no longer know how things stand,

Even, if, I always know who I am.

And maybe a little bit what I want.

No doubt it is simply TO BE
I am a Black woman,
A woman who spends
A woman who loves,
A woman who suffers,
She who hungers,
A lost woman,
A strong woman,
I am THE Black woman
The one with the big ass and nice thick lips,
I am a seductress, sexy,
Me, I puff up for the girls.
I am a female Panther,
I am a Black Panther for some,
Black desire for others
Phara from *Pharaoh*

. . . .

Space, the question of spaces
Which, how??
Vulnerable, I am,
I have become, by the force of circumstance, situations!
I am fragile from being uprooted,
From wandering, permanently!
Even if I appear to be sedentary
Nomadic in the soul since always, I am.
What makes me vulnerable,
It's this question of the impossible return,
Which in my case, in addition to the rupture of acculturation,
Of re-acculturation,
Is increased by the fact that I am a woman who loves women,
Finally, one, two, three, you know the song . . .
And it's not . . .
How should I say . . .

I don't want to die a martyr,
But I also don't want to go back into the closet!!!!

Being from here, or from there, why do I have to choose
I don't want to choose,
I want to be from nowhere, but here, now, at the moment when I speak to you.
Situations make me vulnerable,
Not my identities, which forge me, found me.

I am tired
Of hearing, seeing, sensing you,
Every day, these voices, these looks
Which interrogate you, again and again,
Where are you from?
"From Brussels, fieu!!!
No, I mean . . . Before, you know?
Ben non, I don't know, I don't have the slightest idea.
What do you want to know?
We aren't friends, you could guess that probably,
We've just met, for the first time,
Immediately my pedigree?
Why? What's yours?

I am tired of hearing,
But you're clearly very African!!!
And yet you're so calm, you're so Zen!!
That must come from your culture, huh?
Ben oui, all of us in Jette, we act with a super natural. . . . Uh. . . .
It's exhausting!!
You can be resilient, for a while, not forever, after a while you can't handle it
*   anymore!!!*
You want to break everything!
You want to throw it all away!
You even want to become a volcano.
You see what I mean?
And then you have too much love in yourself,
Love for others,
Love for humanity,
So, so, then one more time, you make the effort.
The effort to not be eaten by the hate!

So you make love, again and again,
Untillllllllllll the infinity that doesn't even exist!!

I am part of that generation of Africans who were dispossessed
Of their history, their cultures, their customs, their languages.
Me, I grew up in French, at home, at school, in the neighborhood, with my
*   peers. . . .*
My heart could have been like my parents', my ancestors', beating in another
*   language, I could have been able to breathe in another language, love in*
*   another language, find pleasure in another language . . . MY LANGUAGE*
I am the pure product of decolonalization, of the post-colony, we say?
Neither from here, nor there.
I am a mixture of something which only I, have a deep sense of. . . . some-
*   times . . .*
I don't know my history, the history of my country, the one in which I was
*   born,*
I am trying to construct it, to construct myself today, now.
One has to pass something on, no?

Ladies and gentlemen
The crisis,
The 50th and plus,
It's mine,
I hope to survive it peacefully.

Angalia Ni Mimi!
(Look, it's me!)
Thank you

Gendered Messages of Social Change

Surviving Gender Violence

Activating Community Stories for Social Change

ANITA GONZALEZ

South Africa's prolific history of theatre performance for social justice ascertains that community-based theatre can effectively influence cultural transitions. Theatre performances for social change, however, must partner with community organizations for greatest effect. While ongoing and sustained engagement with activists can change social attitudes about gender-based violence, only community input can ensure participants remain committed to ideals of change introduced through performance. Historical patterns of intervention, from colonial rule to apartheid protests, demonstrate how performance has supported an evolving sense of race and gender consciousness in South Africa. Some critical volumes, like Kruger's *The Drama of South Africa: Plays, Pageants and Publics Since 1910* (published in 1999), articulate how songs, dances, and stories animate public plazas and spaces where communities gather in response to repressive, often racially based injustices. Less apparent are South African theatrical productions in intimate spaces where actors engage audience members in dialogues about difficult personal issues.

This chapter examines the efficacy of theatre for social change through the lens of two Johannesburg-based social activist performance projects: *Songs for Khwezi* by Refilwe Nkomo and *We Are Here* by Antonio Lyons. Both productions are solo performances that tackle issues of sexual violence through differently gendered lenses. While *We Are Here* was developed as a male response to the feminist project "16 Days of Activism," Refilwe Nkomo's *Songs for Khwezi* is a personal exploration of the political implications of a publicly prominent rape. Collectively, the two productions advocate for social changes around rape and gender violence. Yet the playback of stories surrounding gender-based violence may not be enough to create real change in practice. Real intervention in gender-based violence requires ongoing education imbedded in family and community organizational structures. Both artists currently seek to expand the impact of their work by activating existing community networks. By connecting the performance work with a wider matrix of arts and social service agencies, they continue to influence activists promoting social change.

PUBLIC SPACE AND THEATRICAL STORYTELLING

Antonio Lyons paces the space of the community hall, entering through the audience while confronting audience members with his gaze. He is a tall man who could easily tower over most individuals, yet he is warm and welcoming. Using an easy tone of voice coupled with welcoming arm gestures, he beckons audience members while inviting them to listen to stories told by men about their response to violence against women. The viewers quiet themselves as he softly begins.

> I won't be silent anymore as a firestorm swirls around me
> An inferno seeking to consume my soul and my identity
> My manhood, the fuel feeding the flames, as they rage out of control.[1]

His hands waft around his head, loose wrists creating an imagery of flames. In his next speech, Lyons describes himself as a "beacon on a hill" calling upon men to testify about their experiences, to break silences surrounding what they know about gender-based violent acts. This one-man evocation of the power of stories to reveal deep-seated secrets or lost histories is emblematic of a new forum for a continuing form of social activism within the context of South Africa.

Public spaces have long served as a forum for South African performance. Traditional practices of the many ethnic communities that make up the nation privilege open community spaces as a site of storytelling. Activating spaces with public storytelling is a way of foregrounding indigenous systems of knowledge that have played a crucial role in African society. Nomusa Happiness Mdlalose notes that there is a continuity between precolonial forms and modern-day art forms.[2] Her work considers the evolution of the art form of narration within Ndebele communities, focusing on NGOs as a site of employment as artists use the spoken word to grapple with twenty-first-century social issues. Historically, protest theatre was an ideal way to incorporate precolonial forms of chanting, music, poetry, and storytelling into dialogues pertinent to contemporary society.[3] Today the power of storytelling persists as a means of connecting and educating regional populations—in schools, community centers, prisons, and traditional theatre spaces—about pertinent issues.

During the 1970s and 1980s theatres of resistance that used Brechtian techniques of testimonial to draw attention to oppressive conditions appeared in many townships. Plays developed with local populations would incorporate colloquial languages, worker's voices, and women's perspectives. These traditional practices became institutionalized when European theatre artists, sympathetic to resistance struggles, established organizations like *The Market Theatre* in Johannesburg[4] to promote a theatre of protest emerging from primarily British aesthetics. *The Market Theatre*, founded by Manni Manim and Bernie Simon when apartheid was rampant, played a major role in providing a voice to the voiceless. Today, it continues to offer programming designed to advance social justice through storytelling. *The Market Theatre* used a combination of European and African forms to move theatre repertory from the street to the stage. Fuchs describes the founders as "culture brokers" who, with input from leaders of the Black consciousness movement, revolutionized the content and form of commercial South African theatre.[5]

During the early 1990s, community theatre became an alternative way of addressing health and social issues in the country. The AIDS crisis prompted national and international NGO agencies, as part of their AIDS prevention programs, to promote performance companies that used techniques of Paulo Freire and Augusto Boal to educate communities.[6] An example of this work is the project of Lynn Dalrymple, a professor and activist who worked at the University of Zululand to develop programming for secondary schools. Performances delivered by university students educated rural communities about AIDS and HIV. Dalrymple developed pedagogies for enhancing life and health skills through activist performance.[7] The twenty-first-century artists whose work I discuss, Refilwe Nkomo (from South Africa) and Antonio Lyons (based in South Africa and Los Angeles), follow in the footsteps of earlier community theatre artists who chose to work in local meeting halls and theatres, spaces conducive to dialogue about the intimate topic of gender violence. Central to their work is the notion that stories can capture hidden histories and respond to charged social situations that may not reveal themselves in more formalized interactions.

Live storytelling is a well-recognized mechanism for remembering histories, engaging with trauma, personifying an event, or offering an emotional response. Even though community and personal histories may be communicated through literature, film, or musical expressions, the powerful presence of the living performer charges the air, activating possibilities for dialogue and discussion generally unavailable in other expressive forms. At the same time, personal stories retold in public spaces invite political action or intervention because live audiences can respond to the performers, even shift the performance outcome. Kuppers writes about how community performance helps to re-evaluate the everyday as a site of political action and community development.[8] When an artist encourages community members to relate a story, the artist becomes a catalyst for new interpretations of memories evoked by the story. "Storytelling is the mother of all the other creative art forms. Whether you want to write songs or drama, storytelling is the mother of them all."[9]

At the same time, storytelling intervenes when audiences cannot access written materials because of educational or access restrictions. In some ways, this accounts for the popularity of this artistic mode in disenfranchised communities. Theatre communicates through the human body rather than through technology, making it accessible as a mode of messaging in an outlying, nonurban setting or as a way of connecting to an unschooled populace at community sites. Because it vocalizes internal emotions, it inherently contradicts silences attached to sexual violence. And activists regularly adopt theatre as a preferred mechanism for educating and activating populist response. For example, Mmatshilo Motsei, the author of the book *The Kanga and the Kangaroo Court: Reflections on the Rape Trial of Jacob Zuma*, is a healer and speaker who advocates for justice for rape victims. In her writings, she polemically urges activists to fight against the conspiracy of silence attached to rape through comprehensive community educational campaigns:

> Educating the public about their legal rights cannot be limited to the written word in a language that not everyone understands. Given that about three million adults in South Africa are completely illiterate, between five and eight million are functionally literate, and ten million are alliterate, such an educational campaign should occur within a context that is culturally relevant to the target population[10]

Theatre and the spoken words of storytelling directly address her concerns about bringing educational messages to target populations through oral performance forms.

Motsei's anger inspired her to write about the specific endangerment of Black women within the landscape of South Africa. By using the trial of Jacob Zuma as a mirror, her account reveals the hidden yet public forms of violence against women in their homes, marriages, and churches. In a similar way, Refilwe Nkomo, responding to the same set of circumstances, used the stage as a mechanism to protest ongoing violence against South African women. While Motsei analyzes the social and political environment that allowed Zuma to prevail, Nkomo extrapolates the experience of the rape by the public figure of Zuma to all young women who might—at some time—become a victim of sexual violence. Her performance text capitalizes on the personal as a way of accessing the political. In her play, she writes:

> *One day this girl will wonder*
> *Why she wore a kanga that day*
> *Would jeans have been a less easy access point*
> *She'll replay that night*
> *8:05*
> *10:30*
> *02:08*
> *05:10*[11]

Nkomo's writing implies that any of us, perhaps all of us, could at some time be that vulnerable girl.

Theatrical storytelling educates using gesture and imagery. Not only does storytelling adapt to specific languages of local populations, it can also use symbol and metaphor to incite response. In the excerpt above, the writer deliberately uses a recitation of time to signify how slowly the hours might pass while the violence continues. At the same time, the writing foregrounds the event through the lens of the protagonist, the woman who is being raped. The potency of using stories as a way of educating and intervening in silenced narratives is one reason social activists prioritize theatrical techniques. Image and gesture communicate the unspeakable, opening up possibilities for direct engagement with submerged traumas and fears. This is particularly useful when addressing issues of sexual violence.

RAPE: A SOUTH AFRICAN NIGHTMARE

Rape is one of South Africa's enduring nightmares, and sex abuse has become normalized in the country.[12] In 2017–18 the police recorded 40,035 rapes, or an average of 110 rapes each day.[13] The violent abuse of women and men remains ingrained as an acceptable social practice in Johannesburg communities. Social and political contexts that differ from those in the United States undergird the differing ways in which "violence against women" is perceived. Historically, violence has been used to subdue and subjugate Black men. Women, separated from male communities through displacement, tend to raise their children away from male communities. At the same time, youth unemployment in South Africa has risen to 58 percent, leaving many young men without financial security.[14] While rape in the United States is often viewed as a private sexual act perpetrated by one individual against another, in the South African context, rape is more closely associated with masculine rites of passage and group solidarity. The proliferation of disenfranchised groups of young men may lead to increasing incidents of rape in the country. On the other hand, Puma Dineo Gqola's book *Rape: A South African Nightmare* situates rape as an act of gender-based violence perpetrated in both public and private spaces.[15] Her writings argue that rape is normalized through historical stereotyping of Black women as sexually available and therefore unrapeable. "The same White supremacy that constructed the stereotype of the Black man as rapist, created the stereotype of Black woman a hypersexual, and therefore impossible to rape."[16] She advocates for public conversations about rape that hold society accountable for communal acceptance of rape culture. Related to the rape crisis is the prevalence of AIDS as a human health risk in the country. Seven million people, or about 19 percent of the population, live with HIV.[17] Not only is rape violent, it can also be deadly if the perpetrator carries the HIV virus.

Antonio Lyons and Refilwe Nkomo insert their theatrical work into this sociopolitical landscape. Both artists use storytelling monologues to educate, creating empathy by actively voicing stories that might otherwise go unheard. While Lyons bases his stories on interviews and conversations with men, Nkomo creates movement and monologue scores which reinterpret the anguish of rape victims. Lyons trained at the Master of Applied Theatre program at the City University of New York.[18] Students in this program learn how to use theatre to address social issues in a wide range of settings. Theory and practice are linked, as participants apply their theories about arts practice to experiential settings, where they develop work with and for community settings. Notably, having lived and worked in South Africa, both artists also chose to focus on issues of rape.

There are certain aspects of rape culture that resonate in the types of stories that emerge within each artist's performance works. They craft their text and dialogue to counteract common misconceptions about rape such as:

- Women should only talk to other women about rape
- Rape is between men and women
- Perpetrators are monsters
- Rape is inappropriate sex
- A rape survivor is not a credible authority to discuss rape
- A woman cannot be raped by her husband
- Women ask for rape by wearing seductive clothing or walking alone or being drunk

For example, in one of his monologues, Lyons demonstrates how sexual violence is about more than the relationship between a man and a woman. It also involves the complicity of others. There are consequences inherent in witnessing a violent act without taking an action. Lyons, in one scene of his solo work, describes himself as a man on the street waiting at a bus stop for the bus to arrive. It's a hot day, too hot. The character/actor sees a man and a woman in an altercation. He says:

A violent wind is blowing.

She pushes him and jumps in his face. He sidesteps and moves forward. She spins around unwilling to be dodged. He feints left and brushes her away determined to continue his forward motion. Her insistent demands. Him unwilling to stop, listen and address her needs. She so concerned with driving her point she misses the mark . . . misses the signs that on a too hot day anything can happen.[19]

As the character watches the pending violence unfold, he is tense, sweaty. He doesn't know if, or how, to intervene. As the couple realizes others are watching, they calm down and disengage. The mere act of witnessing has, in effect, defused the confrontation. Now Lyons (as the character) reflects:

(tone more to self. like doing an inquiry) whose fault? I wonder if my temper would have held. I wonder what is it that kept him from jumping down her throat. What made her so mad that she had to go in on him on this bustling sidewalk. Why did I listen and avert my eyes? What dangers live in his mind?[20]

Lyons, by calling attention to his role as a witness, implies that everyone who observes the pending abuse of women has the potential to intervene. Witnessing becomes an act of complicity where the responsibility is shared by all. His writings humanize victims and perpetrators alike.

Nkomo, in contrast, focuses on why women might not come forth to report their abuse. While impersonating a woman who has been raped, the performer speaks about the internal feelings of her character in the third person:

> One day this girl will sit in a courtroom
> In oversized clothes
> Instructed to hide her heritage
> She'll listen as men dissect her life
> Her choices
> As her pain becomes the knife that severs her
> She'll listen as she's accused of abnormal behavior
> Because
> One day this girl will have a normal reaction
> To an abnormal act
> As they call her a liar
> As they call her a slut
> As they lose her last name
> And forget her first
> She'll wonder about her first
> Can she love and be loved
> Again
> Can she touch and be touched
> Again.[21]

As informed activists, Nkomo and Lyons deliberately animate stories and experiences that provoke dialogue and discussion about misconceptions surrounding rape. Lyons also does this by casting men, not women, as actors in performances. In these types of performances, the men collectively discuss their experiences with sexual violence and reflect upon male attitudes toward these experiences. This approach enables Lyons to engage with male perpetrators as well as female victims of sexual violence and humanize men who might be misogynist. Nkomo contrasts this approach by personifying voices of many women who tell a similar story of unjust humiliation. While her imagistic song and dance phrases directly respond to the rape of Fezekile Ntsukela Kuzwayo (Khwezi),[22] they also represent the thoughts and emotions of a multiplicity of women. Below I place the work of these two artists in context.

ANTONIO LYONS AND THE *WE ARE HERE* PROJECT

Antonio Lyons is an actor whose work bridges the worlds of social justice and commercial film. He was born in Florida and lives in Los Angeles, yet he considers South Africa to be his second home. He has appeared in the commercial films *Hotel Rwanda* (2004), *The Sum of All Fears* (2002), and *The Book of Negroes* (2015). Commercial film work exposes Lyons' work to broad international audiences and enables him to enter the sphere of social justice performance with "star" status. In addition to his theatrical performance work, he also produces poetic house music albums that blend text with dance music. Albums like "We Dance, We Pray"[23] emphasize spiritual aspects of bodies in motion, while the 2007 album "Human Jewels"[24] provides a more techno rendition of poetic song. The music production work supports Lyons' theatrical projects. In workshops and rehearsal settings, Lyons uses music to relax actors and bring them into a common space where they can freely express their feelings.[25]

Lyons' activist theatrical project is titled *We Are Here*. He describes it as a one-man show and a social campaign whose sole purpose is to explore identity, masculinity, and gender-based violence. One aspect of the project is a performed series of monologues developed through interviews with men about their experiences with rape and gender based-violence. Sixteen sketches performed by Lyons express the diversity of male voices. The monologues present multiple perspectives by aggregating a range of responses to gendered interactions. For example, Lyons delivers one monologue from the perspective of a man who responds to the beauty and vivacity of a woman at a party, while another captures the feelings of a man whose daughter has been raped. The crafted writing encourages audience members to consider their own complicity or perhaps lack of response to situations where gender violence may emerge. Performances of the monologue are always followed by talk-back sessions where viewers identify trigger moments within the work. They are able to engage in dialogue with one another about the nuances of social interactions. Lyons writes:

> Often men and boys of color feel invisible, unheard, under-represented and un-acknowledged. Spaces in which we exist are led by feminist pedagogy. I found that the only way to bridge the disconnect between the two was to find a way to speak to men about the issues that impact women and girls and themselves and therefore the entire community.[26]

As I mentioned earlier, the project began as a response to the feminist project "16 Days of Activism" in Johannesburg.[27] In South Africa, the campaign is associated with former President Jacob Zuma, who in 2014 announced his desire to have it as a year-long initiative, one not limited to sixteen days. As I will discuss later, many women saw this as a hypocritical stance because two years after actively promoting the antiviolence campaign, Zuma was accused of raping Fezekile Ntsukela Kuzwayo (Khwezi), an accusation he publicly denied. For Lyons, it was marketing surrounding the sixteen-days campaign that inspired him to develop *We Are Here*.

> I had been in South Africa for 7 years at the time. Every year there is a campaign called 16 days of activism. Every year I would notice this campaign and feel a little uncomfortable and I couldn't articulate why. All of the images I would see were all of women and children and men were absent or were only present in the role of perpetrator. I was disturbed because I didn't see me or anyone I knew in this campaign. What do we do with that and how to we raise awareness around that. If the majority of men were really like this it would be a slaughterhouse. I complained and people prompted me to do something. So, I wrote a poem a day during the campaign.[28]

These poems became early drafts of monologues he would later use to elicit dialogue with male community members. Lyons staged the monologues ritualistically using minimal props and costumes so viewers would understand the performance as a cleansing space, an open portal where the actors and audience members could heal through the power of language. He deliberately included folk elements such as praise songs to connect the event to familiar local art forms. Director Lindiwe Matchikiza worked with Lyons to shape the story poems into a narrative. Matchikiza, a theatre practitioner, actor, director, deviser, and producer, is the granddaughter of the legendary journalist Todd Matshikiza, who composed the South African musical *King Kong*. Lyons met her while working on a production of Leroi Jones' *Dutchman*. When he decided to stage the *We Are Here* monologues, he chose to work with Lindiwe because he wanted a female director to represent a contrasting gender experience. He was also looking for someone who could work collaboratively and was skilled in devising physical theatre.

Matchikiza theatricalized the written text by placing the narrated experiences within spatial arrangements that evoked intimate relationships. Each story was set in a particular area of the ritual circle to create variety and emotional impact for the viewers. In one section, for example, Lyons speaks to a doll-like figure while seated on the floor, in another he dances throughout the space as if re-enacting a party. The entire work becomes an immersive experiment in text and movement that offers perspectives on relationships between men and women. The solo performance work toured extensively both within South Africa and internationally, yet this first rendition, the performed monologues, were only one part of a much larger vision Lyons had of what *We Are Here* might accomplish.

The second part of the *We Are Here* project is a social campaign that has recently become a part of a two-year activism program called iStarshipp. The 2017 summer plan was to tour the project in two provinces (Gauteng and KwaZulu Natal) and four districts. Accompanying the performances was a five-day curriculum with in-depth workshops about HIV/AIDs preventive care and testing. The United States Information Agency partnered with the NGO SisterLove to sponsor and promote *We Are Here* as community engagement that aimed to facilitate community dialogue and foster nurturing environments where men and boys can engage constructively with complex identities and roles in society. Project leaders train community ambassadors to lead conversations about sexuality and to elicit monologues and stories from participants about their experiences with and attitudes toward various gender identities. Within the parameters of the engagement project discussions of alternative gender identities and sexuality practices complement workshops about sexual violence, sexuality, and what it means to live in a gendered world.

The 2017 iteration of the *We Are Here* project built from a previous engagement with actors from Tembisa township, who participated in devising workshops and used them to develop a response to the original Lyons solo show. Their rendition of the project features ensemble work coupled with drumming and highly emotional content. This time local actors contributed stories drawn from their own experiences. Lyons' 2009 text describes this version of the work as a three-part journey. It begins with a choral incantation titled "HOW WE CAME TO BE":

> *We gathered together to find the pieces we didn't know were missing.*
> *To bind our wounds*
> *Heal our souls*
> *To find the source of the grief*
> *We journeyed into ourselves*
> *Crossed ancient bridges*
> *Got lost*
> *Got angry*
> *Got hurt again*
> *Got help*[29]

The personal stories that follow illustrate male responses that differ significantly from Lyons' approach to the topic. The South African (primarily isiXhosa) actors talk about the Bible; they talk about fear. One actor named Mongezi talks about his son and the way they used to play soccer together, a ritual of father-son unity where they share a physical world. As Mongezi describes the intimacy of his relationship with his son, the hopes he has for their collective future bleeds through in the text.

> *Here we have outside toilets, dirt paths, broken schools, no jobs, houses of mud*
> *and tin and cardboard and missing windows.*
> *While just over there is a new highway and on televisions I see a life far away*
> *from my own.*
> *The rainbow nation has promised me much but the start hasn't been so great.*[30]

I am struck by the contrast between Lyons' hopeful intonements of the beauty of manhood and the local actor's self-assessment of the challenges they face in escaping the limitations of their lives. When these men describe the women in their lives they lament those who have been murdered by violent partners or describe their beauty that is too often defiled by groping hands of desire. Descriptions such as "She ran from a culture of undervalue and taxi drivers rubbing legs too close or accidentally rubbing against her breasts" portray a less poetical and more tactile world than the artistic responses created by Lyons and Nkomo. From my perspective this speaks to the less-advantaged circumstances of the actors in Tembisa township as they approach the subject matter.[31] Actors who participated in the ensemble version of *We Are Here* eventually formed their own township-based theatrical group called TX Theatre Productions, which, as of 2019, has become a much-lauded company in South Africa. Company director Mxolisi Masilela has expanded his work on include ongoing performances with female artists who can bring their perspective to social justice issues.

In some ways, *We Are Here* follows the genre of playback theatre, a theatrical technique where audience or group members tell stories from their lives and watch them enacted on the stage. The first official "playback theatre" company was founded in the Hudson Valley of New York in 1975 by Jonathan Fox and Jo Salas, who drew from their experiences in improvisation and psychodrama. It is similar to Augusto Boal's forum theatre in style and approach. Audience members recount a story from their lives, and then actors re-enact the event, allowing audience members to change or shift the story as they see it replayed. Endings can change and new characters can enter the performance as participants develop solutions for imaginary conflicts depicted in performed scenes. Each improvised ending allows actors and audience members to analyze the nature of conflict within the story and to consider what might be done to resolve a complex situation. Of course, the notion of open-ended storytelling is not a new idea. Indeed, most traditional storytellers reframe or adapt their material for their audiences, allowing for feedback to influence content. Lyons trained in playback theatre and other community-engagement techniques at the Masters of the Arts Applied Theatre program at the City University of New York. Yet his experiences working with community organizations in Johannesburg and its surrounding villages led him to believe that playback or forum theatre would best engage South African audiences in discussions of gender violence.

REFILWE NKOMO: KHWEZI TALKS BACK

The second artist I discuss in this chapter is Refilwe Nkomo, a female curator and producer who has worked closely with Antonio Lyons. Refilwe graduated from New York University with a Master of the Arts degree in arts and politics. Her performance of the choreopeom *Songs for Khwezi* originated while she was traveling in the United States. Nkomo says:

> I first performed *Songs for Khwezi* at NYU as part of my master's project. It was this idea of thinking about myself as dislocated and in another country and having to deal with traumas happening in South Africa and in a sense, I got out. I was able to look back into the country and city that I love and that holds so much pain. It was an interesting thing to interrogate. I had no real words to articulate despondence and dissonance and it was coming out in movement, so it became a movement practice. I started thinking about songs and songs of women and poetry.[32]

She developed the work first in New York City and later at the University of Michigan, where she did an in-process showing sponsored by the Department of Afroamerican and African Studies. The short presentation included songs, audience interaction, and dance movement depicting the suffering and isolation Nkomo imagined Khwezi undergoing. As I mentioned earlier, the recently deceased Khwezi (Fezekile Ntsukela Kuzwayo) was most known for accusing Jacob Zuma of rape in 2006. Her allegations were publicly denied and considered a threat to the Black liberation movement, as Zuma was then the deputy president of the African National Congress. He remained in that position until December 2017. Zuma's trial and Khwezi's accusations highlighted the discrepancy between male patriarchy and the rights of women.

> Zuma pleaded not guilty. During the trial, the president infamously said he had taken a shower after having sex with Kuzwayo so as to avoid contracting HIV. The president also testified that Kuzwayo was wearing a *kanga* (a traditional cloth) at the time and that he interpreted the dress as an invitation to have sex with her. Throughout the trial Kuzwayo faced harassment, slut-shaming, victim-blaming and threats from many Zuma supporters.[33]

Steven Robins asserts that the trial "highlighted the deeply entrenched character of patriarchy in South African society."[34] Private matters became a public concern. The ANC rallied around Zuma, painting Khwezi as a disruptive conspirator against the nation. The image below illustrates forces at work to criminalize Khwezi for pursuing her accusations. With ingrained institutional forces working against her, she became a martyr for feminist activism. Nkomo was drawn to the story of Khwezi because it connected her to a dis-

Political cartoonist Zapiro (Jonathan Shapiro) comments on corruption in the rape trial with this cartoon. Rape of Justice©2008 Zapiro. Originally published in *Sunday Times*. Republished with permission.

turbing part of her culture, which was largely unacknowledged internationally and was especially not known in metropolitan New York.

At the same time, performing and developing *Songs for Khwezi* rekindled Nkomo's interest in women's issues and social activism, paving the way for Nkomo to re-enter the arts landscape of Johannesburg and present the work at the 2016 Cape Town Fringe festival. She states, "At the Fringe, it was about the idea of bringing it back home, and I could add nuances and things that people would recognize back here. Working with a South African director allowed us to interrogate abuse and assault at different ages."[35] Public response to the performance focused on the politicized nature of the content rather than on the storyteller or the form of the work. While the artist suggests the work developed its aesthetic from Ntozake Shange's choreopoem *for colored girls who have considered suicide when the rainbow is enuf*, I found the work to be more of an imagistic dance/movement presentation with calls and recorded songs incorporated at strategic points. Its effect was more symbolic than narrative, offering moments of reflection rather than telling a story.

The language of the text moves fluidly between the Setswana, Zulu, and

English languages, and the general narrative is one of empowerment as the central character comes to accept herself as a survivor with agency. As I mentioned earlier, Nkomo speaks about herself in the third person throughout. Chapter 5 of the work, titled "How to Survive," has the central character reciting "the good news is that it will get better." By the end of this monologue, the violated woman is breathing, feeling tingling sensations in her hands and her feet. Ultimately, she is able to release her nightmares, able to "Wake up. Sit up. Get up. Wash teeth." The performer says directly, "she won't die." The final section of the work evokes images of water; a warrior woman arrives like a phoenix from the fire.

> *I am coming for you*
> *With glistening rains on my back*
> *Riding serpent winds*
> *Dressed in kanga*
> *I am coming for you*
> *In your kangaroo courts*
>
> *and freedom for a few*
> *I am coming for you*
> *On your golden seats*
> *With all you stole from us*
> *I am coming for you*
> *On mountain tops*
> *Through vaginal volcanoes erupting*
> *Spewing generations of rage*
> *I am coming for you*
> *And I will set fire to this house*
> *And it will burn*
> *Cause when we burn*
> *There is ash*
> *And I will rise from it*
> *I am coming for you*
> *We are coming*
> *For you.*[36]

This closing monologue implies that the spirit of Khwesi lives in every woman who survives sexual violence and is able to live a meaningful life afterwards.

There is something mythical about the way Nkomo describes the woman dressed in a kanga who is able to descend from a mountaintop with a vengeance. *Songs for Khwezi* captures the pain and the anger of a woman violated, then transforms those sentiments into a strong statement of empowerment.

Nkomo's performances were well-received, although critic David Fick from *Broadway World* suggests the artist could grow into the piece and consider how modalities of live music, spoken words, or sung songs could enhance the experience of the performance.[37] What is clear about *Songs for Khwezi* is that it intends to foreground women's resistance to established patriarchal systems by rehashing an uncomfortable moment in the history of South Africa. While many supported Khwezi in her pursuit of rape charges, others considered her to be a traitor to the cause. Motsie, in her book *The Kanga and the Kanagaroo Court: Reflections on the Rape Trial of Jacob Zuma*, quotes women like Sthembile Ndwandwe, who maintained, "This mama is speaking lies because she was in Zuma's room with that (kanga) on and he could see everything."[38] The drama of the kanga permeated the press, rehashing a familiar trope that women ask for rape by wearing seductive clothing. Nkomo's choreopoem, performed ten years after Zuma's acquittal, opened up an old national wound.

In an unusual coincidence, the Cape Town Fringe production of *Songs for Khwezi* closed on the day that Khwezi, living as an exile in Amsterdam, finally died from HIV complications. The artist found this to be unsettling. "She passed away the day that I was performing her, so that was very sad and I felt a kinship without having met her, although I know people who know her and are friends with her. She passed on and it was very bizarre because to this day she is remembered as Zuma's woman who accused him of rape." Khwezi lived and died in the shadow of the rape trial, with her legacy determined by the politicizing of a personal intimacy with a powerful man. Zuma has survived multiple legal challenges, a rape trial, and other attempts to oust him. In May 2017 party leaders called for his resignation because of his 783 business corruption charges.[39] Khwezi's silence, in exile, replicates the silence surrounding discussions of sexual violence in a country where this same violence is prolific. Is it possible for theatre storytelling to intervene in narratives of normalized gender violence?

The complicity of the community is an essential component of the work of Nkomo and Lyons. Merely re-enacting stories may stir memories, but it cannot incite the kind of community-based activism that changes attitudes. The performances must be paired with ongoing dialogues, connections with community services, and sustained opportunities for community members to challenge prevailing notions about gender norms. Lyons' *We Are Here* project is beginning to address these concerns through the sponsored community workshops he envisions as a part of the funded expansion of the work into community centers and rural provinces. Nkomo speaks of reaching out to youth, young women who are still developing their perspectives about empowerment and self-esteem. Each of these approaches, while admirable, merely scratches the surface of what is needed as resources, cultural expectations, health concerns, and community support systems merge to support sustained education. While both projects began as artistic ventures, they must ultimately engage with social solutions to the issues they raise.

On the other hand, the two projects do raise awareness about important educational issues surrounding rape. Earlier I mentioned a series of myths surrounding sexual violence. Each of the artists addresses these myths in some way through their storytelling. One of the most obvious is the presumption that women should only talk to other women about rape, or that rape only concerns survivors and perpetrators. Both artists break this assumption about silence by bringing the topic into the public sphere. Because Lyons focuses his project on male voices, he dispels the notion that perpetrators are monsters. Instead, he works to expose the humanity and vulnerability of all men, so participants in performances and workshops can see how male attitudes and presumptions might lead to inhumane behaviors. Using the specific circumstances of Khwezi, Nkomo challenges the social amnesia about the details of the Zuma case where the "seductive" kanga and the existing domestic relationship between Zuma and Khwezi influenced public sympathy for Zuma. She presents the vantage point where the community wants to negotiate the terms of rape; the play demonstrates that rape is never something that can be renegotiated in retrospect.

Advocacy against gender violence remains a relevant concern in Johannesburg and elsewhere. Nkomo told me one of the lessons she learned through her international travels is that North Americans perceive gender violence to be an intimate, domestic crime, while in South Africa a person may be raped on the street or in public spaces. "So where is a woman safe?" she asks. "She is not safe in her home, and she is not safe in public spaces, so what can we understand as a safe space when your own body is not safe." Lyons extends this paradigm to men and to all forms of gendered encounters, seeking to improve human relationships by encouraging healthy social interactions.

We Are Here and *Songs for Khwezi* intervene in dialogues about rape and gender violence through the vehicle of theatre. As Guarav Desai has eloquently argued, "African popular theatre has continually articulated itself as an educational medium, and thus as a primary arena for social struggle."[40] Lyons and Refilwe reimagine the arena of popular theatre as an opportunity to redirect social justice discourse from its historical context of racial struggle to a contemporary engagement with issues of sexual justice; they educate South African audiences about gender based violence through reiteration and replay of humanized stories within a community context.

NOTES

1. Antonio David Lyons, *We Are Here (IMPAACT Theatre Chicago)* (n.d., script provided by the author), 2.

2. Nomusa Happiness Mdlalose, "Transformation in the South African Storytelling Tradition: Stylisation and New Genres in Storytelling NGOs" (PhD diss., Witwatersrand University, 2018), 15.

3. Mdlalose, "Transformation in the South African Storytelling Tradition," 15.

4. http://markettheatre.co.za/.

5. Ann Fuchs, *Playing the Market: The Market Theatre, Johannesburg*, rev. and updated ed. (New York: Rodopi, 2002), 33.

6. Loren Kruger, *The Drama of South Africa: Plays, Pageants and Publics Since 1910* (London: Routledge, 1999), 191–209.

7. Emma Durden and Keyan Tomaselli, "Theory Meets Theatre Practice: Making a Difference to Public Health Programmes in Southern Africa. Professor Lynn Dalrymple: South African Scholar, Activist, Educator," *Curriculum Inquiry* 42, no. 1 (2012): 80–102, DOI: 10.1111/ j.1467–873X.2011.00575.x.

8. Petra Kuppers, "Remembering Histories," in *Community Performance: An Introduction*, ed. Petra Kuppers (New York: Routledge, 2007), 30.

9. This is a quote from the actress and storyteller Gcina Mhlophe in the introduction to her play "Have You Seen Zandile," in *Black South African Women: An Anthology of Plays*, ed. Kathy Perkins (New York: Routledge, 1998).

10. Mmatshilo Motsei, *The Kanga and the Kangaroo Court: Reflections on the Rape Trial of Jacob Zuma* (Johannesburg: Jacana Media, 2008). The figures she cites are from 2004 as quoted by Elinor Sisulu during a keynote address at the symposium on the cost of a culture for reading, Centre for the Book, Capetown, September 16–17.

11. Refilwe Nkomo, *Songs for Khwezi* (2015), 5.

12. Rebecca Davis, "How Rape Became South Africa's Enduring Nightmare," *The Guardian* (South Africa), September 29, 2015. https://www.theguardian.com/world/2015/sep/29/south-africa-rape-nightmare-crime-stats.

13. https://africacheck.org/factsheets/factsheet-south-africas-crime-statistics-for-2017–18/.

14. https://tradingeconomics.com/south-africa/youth-unemployment-rate.

15. Puma Dineo Gqola, *Rape: A South African Nightmare* (Johannesburg: MFBooks, 2015).

16. Ggola, *Rape*, 3.

17. https://www.avert.org/professionals/hiv-around-world/sub-saharan-africa/south-africa.

18. https://sps.cuny.edu/academics/graduate/master-arts-applied-theatre-ma.

19. Lyons, *We Are Here*, 7.

20. Lyons, *We Are Here*.

21. Nkomo, *Songs for Khwezi*, 5.

22. Khwezi was a public figure allegedly raped and ultimately delegitimized by Jacob Zuma, past president of South Africa.

23. https://www.youtube.com/watch?v=gT35fjo01KM.

24. https://open.spotify.com/album/33IgEQ0yy1bKuPKFFelmAK.

25. https://www.imdb.com/name/nm0529014/bio.

26. Antonio Lyons, Skype interview with the artist, April 2, 2017.

27. For an example of the kind of promotion that surrounded Lyons' work in the campaign, see https://www.youtube.com/watch?v=tF3t32YWl10.

28. Lyons, interview.

29. *We Are Here (Tembisa)*, reimagined by Antonio David Lyons and TX Productions, script provided courtesy of the author (2009), 2.

30. Lyons, *We Are Here*, 5–6.

31. To view video documentation of the Tembisa performances, see https://www.youtube.com/watch?v=OmhGcWbLnxg.

32. Refilwe Nkomo, Skype interview with the artist, April 20, 2017.

33. Alyssa Klein, "Khwezi, Fierce Advocate of Women's Rights and the Fight against Rape in South Africa, Has Died," *okayafrica.International Edition*, October 9, 2016, http://www.okayafrica.com/in-brief/remember-khwezi-fezekile-ntsukela-kuzwayo-dead/.

34. Steven Robins, "Zuma's Rape Trial," in *The South Africa Reader: History, Culture, Politics*, ed. Clifton Crais and Thomas McClendon (Durham, NC: Duke University Press, 2014), 530.

35. Nkomo, *Songs for Khwezi*. The South African director was Refiloe Lepere.

36. Nkomo, *Songs for Khwezi*, 12.

37. David Fick, "BWW Review: Powerful Choreopoem 'Songs For Khwezi' Is Theatre That Can Disrupt and Heal," *Broadway World*, October 7, 2016, http://www.broadwayworld.com/south-africa/article/BWW-Review-Powerful-Choreopoem-SONGS-FOR-KHWEZI-is-Theatre-That-Can-Disrupt-and-Heal-20161007.

38. Motsei, *The Kanga and the Kangaroo Court*, 145.

39. Robyn Dixon, "South African President Has Survived a Rape Trial, Corruption Charges and Many Bids to Oust Him," *Los Angeles Times*, May 29, 2017, http://www.latimes.com/world/la-fg-south-africa-zuma-noconfidence-20170529-htmlstory.html.

40. Guarav Desai, "Theater as Praxis: Discursive Strategies in African Popular Theater," *African Studies Review* 33, no. 1 (April 1990), 70.

Gangsters, Masculinity, and Ethics

Underground Rapping in Dar es Salaam

DAVID KERR

INTRODUCTION

Since becoming a popular music phenomenon in the 1970s, hip hop has engendered strong critical engagement from scholars and cultural commentators. Hip hop has been variously celebrated as the authentic voice of marginalised subjects, decried as a moral danger to young people and characterised as the apotheosis of music's commercialisation (Osumare 2007; Haupt 2008; Rose 1994; Forman 2002; Spence 2011; Jefferies 2011). Halifu Osumare suggests that hip hop has the potential not only to articulate ideas of resistance but to bond practitioners across the globe who experience forms of marginalisation because of race, class, and age in what she terms "connective marginalities" (Osumare 2007, 72; Osumare 2012, 83). Early scholarship on hip hop in Africa focused on its role in articulating the social and political concerns of youth and its ability to express "the shout of city dwellers that are condemned to silence" (Benga 2002, 81; Fenn and Perullo 2000; Remes 1999; Ntarangwi 2009). Another branch of scholarship has viewed African hip hop as extolling of "individual stardom, consumption, and success over ethnic, familial, and national affiliations and older political hopes of a socialist or Pan-Africanist state" (Shipley 2009, 646).

Tanzanian hip hop can provide a provocative counterpoint to these arguments. The role of artists as the *kioo cha jamii* (the mirror to society) or social commentator, has a long history in Tanzania, bolstered by postindependence state-sponsored cultural policies. Artists who use their voice to express sociopolitical commentary might, in fact, be read as a conservative adherence to societal norms, and songs that foreground consumption and wealth as a more radical departure. Using the work of both Michel De Certeau and Saba Mahmood, this chapter explores how rappers negotiate the competing discourses they are subject to. Rapping is not only a linguistically creative act but one that is deeply social and corporeal. In this chapter I examine how this practice of embodiment acts as a medium through which transnational and local moral and ethical conceptions are inhabited. Rappers in Tanzania, I argue, appropriated forms of style, practice, and signifiers from the transnational image of hip hop to cast themselves as "thugs" or "gangsters."

Drawing on De Certeau's insights into cultural users pursuit of "relational tactics (a struggle for life), artistic creations (an aesthetic), and autonomous initiatives (an ethic)," I seek to complicate notions of rappers as simply either resisting domination or embodying modes of individuated consumption (De Certeau 1985, ix). I argue that rapping is a means through which young men in Dar es Salaam engage with the masculine, ethical and political discourses they are subject to. The everyday practices which rappers engage in are a tool through which discourses are embodied, resisted and transformed. Saba Mahmood suggests that we should be attuned to the "practical ways in which individuals work on themselves to become the willing subjects of a particular discourse" (Mahmood 2001, 210). Drawing on Saba Mahmood complex conception of the relationship between subject and discourse, I explore the multiple modalities of hip hop practice in Tanzania. Rapping, I argue, is a at once a tool of subjection to and subversion of hegemonic national discourse.

Hip hop is a medium through which rappers in Dar es Salaam negotiate both the legacy of Tanzania's socialist past and its neoliberal present. While the Tanzanian state has largely abandoned Ujamaa following neoliberal reforms in the late 1980s and 1990s, many of the concepts and ethics associated with Ujamaa continue to circulate in the Tanzanian imaginary. As Anne Pitcher and Kelly Askew have argued, socialism in Africa "left institutional, aesthetic, psychological and discursive legacies" (Pitcher and Askew 2006, 11). Rappers in Tanzania engage with these legacies in complicated and, at times, ambiguous ways.

Through a set of social and bodily practices, Tanzanian rappers embody the masculine figure of the gangster, seeking to inhabit this transnational symbolic image while imbuing it with ethical conceptions associated with Ujamaa. Embodying the "gangster" intertwines transnational images of masculinity with the "repetition, transformation, and reactivation" of ethical and ideational values associated with Ujamaa (Foucault 2002, 31).[1] I view the ethical work of rappers as engaging not with abstract categories, norms, and values but in the ordinary ethics of the everyday (Mahmood 2001; Lambek 2010; Bray 2013). That is an ethics "founded upon particular forms of discursive practice, instantiated through specific sets of procedures, techniques, and exercises" (Mahmood 2005, 120). This chapter examines not only the verbal texts produced by rappers but also the discourses, praxis, and techniques that circulate as part of the practice. An enquiry that for Veena Das calls for a "descent into the ordinary" in which "work is done not by orienting oneself to transcendental, objectively agreed-upon values but rather through the cultivation of sensibilities within the everyday" (Das 2012, 134).

HIP HOP IN DAR ES SALAAM

In the early 1990s a significant local hip hop scene developed in Dar es Salaam. The year 1991 saw the first major rap competition "Yo Rap Bonanza," and the release of the first Tanzanian rap recording in Swahili, "Ice Ice Baby—King of Swahili Rap" (Charry 2012, 15; Lemelle 2006, 235). Liberalisation of the media in 1993, the development of FM stations not directed by state cultural policies, and the use of Swahili as the language of performance led to what has been called a "Bongo Explosion" (Reuster-Jahn and Hacke 2011, 8).[2] Much of the early rapped music in Tanzania was characterised by the sociopolitical or "conscious" nature of its lyrics. Rapper Sugu described this early generation of rappers as "like *hali halisi*, we were rapping for the people, we were rapping real life you know"[3] (interview, Dar es Salaam, 2006). As rapped music has moved from the margins to the mainstream in Tanzania, a heterogeneous range of genres and subgenres have incorporated rapping into their forms (Omari 2009, 4). The ideological and gendered meanings ascribed to these genres and subgenres are contested by artists, popular culture commentators, and fans of Tanzanian popular music. A frequent source of deeply ideological discussion was which of the genres, Bongo Flava or hip hop, is autochthonous. Rapper King Crazy GK describes hip hop as indigenous: "Hip hop is a culture, Bongo Flava it's in hip hop. Hip hop is the mother of Bongo Flava" (interview, Dar es Salaam, 2006). Another common trope among hip hop fans in Dar es Salaam is contrasting the "realness" of hip hop with the "fakeness" of Bongo Flava. For some performers, cultural intermediaries, and scholars, Bongo Flava has become a "hybrid culture that is based on "extravagant consumption" and consumer capitalism, ripe with imitations of American pop culture" (Kibona Clark 2013, 8). The rapper D-Knob describes commonly held opinions among rappers on the gendered and technical distinction between the genres. He suggests that in hip hop you rap "about lots of things, about street things" while Bongo Flava artists sings "about 'oh I love you baby'" (interview, Dar es Salaam, 2011). D-Knob represents hip hop as tough, masculine, and more meaningful than Bongo Flava and suggests that "to be a man you are supposed to rap" (interview, ibid).

UJAMAA, CULTURE, AND THE STATE

Before turning to the practice of rapping, I will explore how the discursive legacies of Ujamaa continue to animate everyday political and ethical discourse in Tanzania (Becker 2013; Askew 2006). Since independence in 1961 the Tanganyika African National Union (TANU), renamed Chama Cha Mapinduzi (CCM) in 1977, has been the sole political party to govern the country. After adopting the Arusha Declaration in 1967 Tanzania began to follow the distinct political philosophy of Ujamaa, or African Familyhood. Central to Ujamaa was a belief in a return to "traditional" African values such as "democracy, human rights, egalitarianism, education for self-reliance and women's liberation" (Stöger-Eising 2000, 129). Ujamaa continues to be, at least nominally, a founding principle of the state, and the Tanzanian constitution's call for "the pursuit of the policy of Socialism and Self Reliance which emphasizes the application of socialist principles" (United Republic of Tanzania 1977, 13). In the late 1970s Tanzania experienced a series of economic shocks, and from the early 1980s adopted several structural adjustment programmes aimed at liberalising the economy. In 1985 Julius K. Nyerere resigned as Tanzanian president in part over his unwillingness to accept further economic restructuring.

While economic policies in Tanzania have altered following the neoliberal reforms of the late 1980s and 1990s, the state has continued to invoke Nyerere as a legitimising figure and Baba wa Taifa (Father of the Nation) (Becker 2013, 253). The symbol of Nyerere and the values of Ujamaa associated with him continued to play a significant role in contemporary everyday social, ethical, and political discourse (Fouere 2014). As Priya Lal and Pat Caplan have shown, memories and understandings of Ujamaa are constantly being re-evaluated, reinterpreted, and reinvented by Tanzania's citizens in their everyday lives (Caplan 2007; Lal 2012). Concepts such as *kujitegemea* (self-reliance), *haki* (justice), and *kazi ya jasho* (hard work) continue to be important markers of moral value in Tanzania's contemporary social-political discourse (Sanders 2008, 117; Dancer 2015, 103). Julius Nyerere is frequently invoked in contemporary musical production: rapper Sugu referred to himself as the *Nyerere wa rap* (Nyerere of rap) and film of Nyerere is used in videos such as the 2011 song "Tanzania" by Roma. In 2011 Bonta released a song called Nyerere which ends its chorus with the words "kila kitu Nyerere" (everything is Nyerere). Ideas associated with Ujamaa and its architect Nyerere continue to be invoked by contemporary artists to legitimate their voice and to haunt politicians of the present.

During Ujamaa the state played an active role in national culture. Nyerere emphasised the important role of culture in building the newly independent nation in his inaugural presidential address: "I believe that its culture is the essence and spirit of any nation. A country which lacks its own culture is no more than a collection of people without the spirit that makes them a nation" (Nyerere 1966, 186). The notion of a "national culture" had a profound influence on Tanzanian cultural policies over the next forty years. State and parastate organisations were the largest patrons for musicians. The state, to a large extent, dictated what was recorded in state-owned recording studios and played on state-controlled radio. Musicians were tasked with praising political leaders, celebrating the nation's achievements, and helping to mobilise the population (Nyoni 2007, 247). Popular culture occupied a space in which the new nation of Tanzania was imagined and a site of contestations over the national political, ethical, and social order. While control over cultural production is now exerted by private studios and FM radio stations, contemporary hip hop artists continue to seek to imagine the nation (Mwangi 2004). As suggested earlier, the idea of artist as social commentator or *kioo cha jamii* (the mirror to society), reflecting the spirit of society, continues to have salience in contemporary Tanzania.

PERFORMANCE, PUBLIC SPACE, AND UNDERGROUND RAP

In 2009 I was introduced by an old friend and rapper Hashim Rubanza to Mwinjaka ally Mwinjakaw, known by his artist name Mbaya Wao, or "Bad Man." Following this meeting I was quickly initiated into a community of rappers who met each Monday, the only day that Mbaya Wao was free from work. We gathered at his family compound in Kijitonyama. These encounters started in the morning and would last until evening as members of the community congregated to recite lyrics, receive feedback, and discuss the latest developments in their lives. Meetings were held on a street corner outside of the family compound, which was marked with the graffiti clearly situating this space as a site of "hip hop" performance. Discussion and performance would ebb and flow and were sustained by coffee and cigarettes purchased from passing *wamachinga*, (street traders). Members of the group arrived in dribs and drabs, and on occasion passing members of other rap communities would stop to greet Mbaya Wao. This community became a central node in a wide network of *mandagraundi*, or underground rappers I came to know. *Mandagraundi* are defined through absence either of the ability to "release an album" or to "experienced success on a larger scale" (Reuster-Jahn 2008, 56; Englert 2008, 75). These are largely young men without the financial or social capital necessary to participate in the commercial world of music making.[4] All the rappers I encountered at Mbaya Wao's compound considered themselves to be *mandagraundi*.

The physical occupation and resignification of space is essential to underground rap performance. Excluded from the formal, commercial spaces of performance, underground rappers congregate at sites of male socialising called *maskani* (base, dwelling, or abode). It is principally at *maskani* that underground rappers practice and perform and it is within these social networks that their identity as a rapper is recognised. Through their practicing of hip hop at *maskani*, underground rappers in Dar es Salaam forge new masculine identities. When performing for large groups, rappers regularly adopt a masculine pose of bending their knees and using their hand to grab the crotch of the trousers. This pose, as well as the emphasis placed on the masculine body of the performer, has become something of a trope in Tanzanian rap performance. Rappers' masculine identities are performed through rap lyrics, the adoption of pseudonyms, and sartorial style, as well as a set of corporeal practices. The act of rapping produces not only verbal texts but a set of bodily practices. Rappers physically exert themselves projecting their voice in time to the rhythm and with sufficient volume to be heard. The act of rapping is often accompanied by a set of bodily movements including hand gestures, head nodding, and stepping back and forth, emphasising the rhythm of performance that allows rappers to dominate the space surrounding them. Heads rock back and forth in time with the rhythm, in something

of a "classic" hip hop pose. This set of physical practices, of gesture and posture, borrow from the circulating images of the global hip hop genre. Sartorial style associated with hip hop, including baseball caps, large T-shirts, and
Timberland boots, are equally appropriated by rappers. Through their bodily
movements, posture, and gestures when performing, as well as their clothing
strategies, rappers embody the transnational mediatised persona of a rapper.

Rappers adopt or are given nicknames, such as Mbaya Wao, which they
come to embody. Mbaya Wao related being a "Bad Man" to his independence
from familial control, his familiarity with urban life, and his willingness to
traverse the city, including its informal settlements, any time of day or night.
It was his self-sufficiency, knowledge of city life, and fluency with different
social classes that made him a "Bad Man." Familiarity with the city is not just
a process of acquiring knowledge but is displayed in an easy physical comportment when inhabiting city space. Through greeting members of other
maskani, strolling through the narrow streets and alleyways of *uswahilini*,
this familiarity and habitation of space is displayed.[5] Being a rapper became
part of Mbaya Wao's subjectivity, his very being in the world. As he expressed
it, "you're born a man so you have to show the world I am a man" (interview,
Dar es Salaam, 2009).

The masculinity of the rapper, of being a Bad Man, is expressed not only
through bodily gestures but also through the use of voice. Underground
rappers meet in groups, sit closely together, and listen intently as freestyle
raps are performed. It is through the body that the lyrics of the rapper are
produced. Whether raps are delivered slowly or quickly, loudly or quietly,
forcefully or listlessly, is determined by the rapper's body. For underground
rappers, the timbre of the voice was understood as projecting either a masculine toughness or feminine softness. Those such as Mbaya Wao who adopt a
distinctly masculine persona perform this through their use of voice to sonically dominate space. The body projects the voice, which in turn enables the
body to occupy space beyond the confines of the skin. Masculinity is not only
embodied in the voice but also in the lyrics, which are used "to speak different
problems, the life that we face which is basically based on a society especially
on economics and politics and what and what. The problem facing society."
(interview, ibid).

Amka chakalika faidika kwa maisha yako
Wake up hustle and profit from your life

Usiache shunghuli zako ukafuatilia maisha ya wenzako
Mind your business don't focus on other people's life

. . . . .

Nasimama kwenya hoja sitaki kungoja nipate jasho langu
I put my foot down I no longer want to have to wait to reap the benefits of my
    sweat (work/labour)

Sitaki kesho nakaza msuli nakua jasiri mwanao
I don't want to wait for tomorrow, I strengthen up and be brave.

These lyrics, delivered at his *maskani*, encourage a form of ethical masculine agency located in individual agency, strength and struggle. Mahmood in *Politics of Piety* posits a form of moral habitus "acquired through human industry, assiduous practice, and discipline, such that it becomes a permanent feature of a person's character" (Mahmood 2005, 136). Her focus on bodily disposition and practice are instructive for understanding underground rapping. Rappers engage in forms of routinized self-making. Embodying being a rapper or gangster is achieved not only through the frequent acts of rapping but by adopting forms of deportment in the everyday. Rappers as part of their daily routinely adopt masculine modes of gesture and posture, which are part of the practice of being a rapper. This disciplining of the body is a form of work through which rappers construct a masculine ethic. Being an underground rapper in Dar es Salaam, I suggest, is a technology of the self that seeks to generate a mode of being in the world. This mode of being is not fixed but rather emerges from the discourses that rappers are subject to from both transnational imaginaries and local sociopolitical discourses. Poststructural adjustment discourses that appeal to individual self actualistaion, Ujamaa ideas of self-sufficiency and hard work, and transnational conceptions of masculinity are combined to create a masculine everyday ethic.

This social construction of masculinity is reinforced through rappers referring to themselves as *msela* and *mchizi*, terms equated in Tanzania with the masculine persona of the "gangster" or "thug" (Reuster-Jahn and Hacke 2011, 5). Derived from the English word sailor, *msela* is frequently used by young men in Dar es Salaam to refer to each other as a friend (Suriano 2007, 218). Drawing on ideas of the camaraderie, independence, and toughness of sailors who set off from Tanzania's shores during the colonial period, being *msela* signifies a masculine mode of being in the world. A *msela* is, as Mbaya Wao said:

> you know someone call you *msela* it's someone who is ready for anything. [. . .] If you call yourself *msela* it means you can live in any way and you don't follow anyone. You live as you can, you depend on yourself even though sometimes you live with your family. (interview, Dar es Salaam, 2009)

The terms *msela* and *mchizi* are not unique to rappers and circulate widely through popular culture and hip hop.[6] As rappers make clear, however, and as this chapter will demonstrate, the notion of the gangster is distinct from long-standing characterisations of artists as destructive *wahuni* or hooligans (Graebner 1997, 110; Perullo 2005, 76; Suriano 2007, 208). While *wahuni* are destructive, feckless, and unproductive, the gangster is for rappers in Tanzania a figure who can survive on his own wits in the tough city, who is skilled and productive as a rapper, and who shares with the other members of the community.

Underground rappers appropriated a stylistic and discursive framework from the genre of hip hop and referred to themselves, their practice, and musical output as "thugs" and "gangsters." The term "gangster" circulated in various forms. For instance, Ally Mohammedi, an underground rapper from Msasani, adopted the artistic title of "Gang Star." Rappers frequently used the term "gangster" not only in reference to themselves but to their forms of musical practice. For O-Key "the gangster is hip hop." Salim Muba, a rapper from Kiwalani, during a freestyle[7] performance, described the language in which he had just performed as "the gangster language, Kiswahili" (performance, Dar es Salaam, 2011). The term gangster was written upon walls adjacent to the sites of several of the *maskani* I attended. O-Key, an underground rapper from Keko, describes the genre of music that he made as "gangster music." Lyrics from one of O-Key's freestyles, which I quote below, demonstrate this linguistic and discursive borrowing from the global genre of hip hop.

Na switch off punchline na switch on swag,
I switch off punchline and switch on swag,
. . . .

Kila siku nahustle nia kupata salari,
I hustle everyday to get a salary (some money),

Make more dow baadae iwe better day,
Make more money so that you can live a better day,

Lose control machizi wakukufanye.
Lose control and guys will do you.

The use of terms such as punchline and swag as well as references to the hip hop trope of husting situate O-Key's lyrics as part of a wider transnational rap practice. In both freestyles, it is the lone masculine figure who through hard work, struggle, and daily hustle can fend off the dangers of losing control. The lyrics speak to a daily social and economic environment that is unstable and can be briefly tamed by men through the adoption of daily rigorous struggle. As with Mbaya Wao's lyrics quoted earlier, the masculine traits of hustle, strength, and control are referenced as essential ingredients that make it possible to "live a better day."

O-Key continued his description of the gangster as "a person who comes from the real hood, the poorest street," a "man of the people who used to share ideas, to chill with 'hommies' and share ideas with friends" (interview, Dar es Salaam, 2011). The music of the gangster is that which "tells about reality, real reality of life in our country" and performs not only "for his life but . . . sung for the people" (ibid). A member of O-Key's *maskani* and fellow rapper Kizito expands upon O-Key's definition, suggesting the "gangster" is a "person who shares with people" (interview, Dar es Salaam, 2011). From the description outlined by Kizito and O-Key, their conception of the "gangster" is one principally moored in ethical values. This concept of the "gangster" embodies a form of ethical value that is used by rappers to navigate the complexities of both the discursive legacies of African socialism and the realities of the neoliberal present.

On occasion members of *maskani* organised larger musical and dance performances, called *kampu* or *vigodoro*/small mattress. These events are held in *uswahilini* and, with the hiring of speakers and building of stages, dominate informal neighbourhoods spatially and sonically. As I have argued elsewhere, *kampu* act as a means for young people to gain recognition and to contest their marginality from participation in the local music economy (Kerr 2018, 74). *Kampu* contravene the conventional order through their domination of physical, social, and sonic space by younger people. These performances might well be read as a form of tactical trickery, from which "there is a certain art of placing one's blows, a pleasure in getting around the rules of a constraining space" (De Certeau 1985, 18). Underground rappers' temporary control over space (physical, sonic, and social) represents a subversion of the conventional order. Networks of *kampu* are held throughout the city, with members of *maskani* inviting each other to perform. Performing at *kampu* grants rappers a form of value through recognition by their peers. Rapping at *kampu* creates opportunities for local forms of celebrity in which rappers' names and reputation travel through both space and time. *Kampu* and *maskani* also act as a space for collective action, a means through which money is raised and events organised. They may occasionally have a wider role in the members' lives contributing to celebrations and funerals. A collective of rappers from the KGM *maskani* in the Mburahati and Kigogo area of Dar es Salaam described their aim as a form of *kujitegemea* (self-sufficiency). They wished to be able to record their own music and sought collectively to contribute money, expertise, space, and equipment for the establishment of a functioning recording studio. For this collective, the concept of *kujitegemea* was embedded in political discourse and the idea of self-sufficiency as a guiding principle of Ujamaa. In Ujamaa ideology *kujitegemea* addressed both the notion of national self-sufficiency as well as that of the individual citizen. Self-sufficiency began at the level of the people's struggle to provide for themselves and their families, moved to the level of the community, and finally to the nation.

As the Arusha declaration of 1967 stated:

> If every individual is self-reliant then ten-house cell will be self-reliant; if all the cells are self-reliant the whole ward will be self-reliant; and if the wards are self-reliant the District will be self-reliant. If the Districts are self-reliant, then the Region is self-reliant, and if the Regions are self-reliant, then the whole nation is self-reliant and this our aim. (Nyerere 1968, 248)

Thought written during the decade of independence in the 1960s, these goals of collective collaboration are still active in gangster rap. Following the states abandonment of Ujamaa the concept of *kujitegemea* has continued to circulate discursively in the neoliberal era. This use of ideas associated with Ujamaa and the figure of the "gangster" do not only circulate as concepts but as forms of practice. Through these forms of collective activity, rappers put into action some of the collectivist values associated with Ujamaa. Uthman Issa, a rapper from Kijitonyama, suggested that these discursive values associated with Ujamaa were emblematic of the "original people involved in hip hop" (in Dar es Salaam) (interview, Dar es Salaam, 2009). For Uthman the real hip hop community had "implemented Ujamaa among themselves" (ibid). This was evidenced in their *umoja* unity, lack of class differentiation, collective support for each other, and lack of selfishness. Being a gangster, real and not fake, sharing and not selfish, is not only a matter of rhetoric but of social practices. For rappers in Tanzania, their creative potential is not only exhibited in their ability to create texts but in the power to form and shape social relationships. References to the values of Ujamaa were made by rappers through direct citation of concepts associated with Ujamaa, such as *kazi ya jasho* (hard work), *haki* (justice), *kujitegemea* (self-sufficiency), and equality. Mbaya Wao invoked the notions of *kazi ya jasho* and *kujitegemea* as part of being both a rapper and a man. Members of the KGM *maskani* used these terms as a lens through which to critique contemporary Tanzanian society. The justice of the Ujamaa period, and the humility and simplicity of Julius Nyerere's life, were used as a counterpoint to the current national situation.

For O-Key, studying the history of Tanzania, revolutionary books from the 1960s and 1970s, as well as the speeches of Nyerere were part of the inspiration for his lyrics. This knowledge was for him an essential part of being both a gangster and a rapper. For others, while the values of Ujamaa were explicitly linked to the practice of hip hop, these values were described in broader communal terms of fairness, humility, and equality. For rappers, the notion of being a gangster and of practicing values associated with Ujamaa were linked. For O-Key, being a "gangster" entails being real, understood in part as a form of authenticity gained by being from the "real hood" and representing the "real life" of the streets of Dar es Salaam. Being real, however, requires more than the authentic representation of life in Dar es Salaam. Among rappers who identified as "thugs" and "gangsters," "fakeness" was equated with being both "a snitch" and "selfishness." Emphasising what he considered behaviour with its origins in the ideas of Ujamaa, Uthamn said "hip hop is real, someone like Mbaya Wao would buy a soda and offer everyone, a fake person would buy a soda and drink it by himself" (ibid). The real is associated with ethical forms of behaviour, which include sharing and supporting one another.

SYMBOLIC PRESENCE: TUPAC AND NYERERE

American hip hop stars, such as 50 Cent and Tupac Shakur, have become ubiquitous figures in Tanzanian popular culture, appearing in popular newspapers and on TV, radio, and barber shop walls (Sanga 2010, 152; Reuster-Jahn and Hacke 2011, 2; Perullo 2011, 108 Weiss 2009, 126). For a number of rappers, including O-Key, Tupac represented an ideal and inspiration, as O-Key said:

> The only one who inspired me to do music in this world is Tupac, because I get the tape of Tupac, so when I went to school I used to listen him. So he inspired me too much to do this game. I do want to do like him so it make me to like hip hop and go in hip hop. (interview, Dar es Salaam, 2011)

For many of the underground rappers that I interviewed Tupac signifies an important masculine role model. Tupac's representation of thug life based upon "hyper-masculine values (gang values of toughness, fighting ability)," as well as his role as "political advocate, educator and motivator," is recast in Tanzania (Iwamoto 2003, 46; Stanford 2011, 20). Many of the rappers I interviewed were only able to understand fragments of Tupac's lyrics and had picked up stories about his life and untimely death from his songs, interviews, magazines, or other rappers.[8] It was the persona of Tupac that rappers referenced as their inspiration rather than individual songs. Many of those inspired by Tupac were largely unable to understand his lyrics, and it was a sense of what he represented that captured their imagination. Free from being read solely through his lyrics, Tupac becomes a symbol for a particular masculine mode of being. For O-Key, Tupac is both a role model and teacher, someone from whom he "used to learn so many things . . . how to be a real man, how to be strong in decisions, how to write rhymes" (interview, Dar es Salaam, 2016).

During a discussion with Uthman he described the parallels he saw between Tupac and the former president and father of the nation Julius Nyerere. Among the most important common attributes was the ability of both men, despite their elevated positions, to "spend time with anyone." Tupac achieved huge commercial and financial success during his musical career yet was renowned for having a close connection to the neighbourhood he had grown up in and his friends. This was reflected in the lyrics of his songs, which for O-Key "talk about the real life that you live." Nyerere is revered in Tanzania as a man of the people who lived the austere and simple life, returning to his family home in Butiama to farm during holidays. For O-Key, there are similarities in their use of voice and the power of their utterances. As he describes, "they listen to the people, people can understand what they say.

Tupac used his career to sing for the people, to convince people when he tried to say things and Nyerere used his power to organise people together, build the nation, to work as a team, as a family, Ujamaa, he introduced Ujamaa in Tanzania" (interview, Dar es Salaam, 2016). Nyerere and Tupac, for Uthman, used their voices as mediums of communication, forms of power, and vehicles of human artistry. These are voices that call new worlds into being, voices that convince, shape, build, and organise the world around them. To return to O-Key's definition of the "gangster," Tupac is, like the gangster, "a man of the people" who "sing his music for the people who have problems" (interview, Dar es Salaam, 2011).

Uthman suggested that Tupac and Nyerere shared a desire to represent the poor, marginalised, and deprived. Both men, according to Uthman, used their voices to articulate an ethical position about justice and equality. On songs such as "Part-Time Mutha" and "Brenda's Got a Baby," Tupac reflects elements of working-class African American lived experience. He uses his voice to raise sociopolitical issues and question the oppression and marginalisation of African Americans in wider American society. Nyerere frequently took up positions both in relation to international affairs and domestic policy in support of colonised people, those facing racial oppression and the poor. Tupac represents a form of masculine struggle against poverty and the fight for equality and justice for underground rappers. The well-documented struggles of Tupac's life were read as a model of masculine *kujitegemea* to which rappers aspired.

As a symbol, Tupac comes to represent a form of masculine ethics that embrace many of the principles of Ujamaa, self-sufficiency, hard work, and the fight for equality and justice.

The themes of self-sufficiency and the struggle against injustice can be seen in Uthman's freestyle,

> *Masela mnakaa hamna kazi maisha magumu,*
> *Thugs saying without a job life is hard*

> *Raisi anasema lakini maisha ni malaini lakini*
> *But the president says life is easy*

> *Washkaji msiwe na hofu na jitihada tu ndio kila kitu*
> *Guys don't you worry effort is everything.*

In his lyrics, as with those of Mbaya Wao and O-Key, Uthman refers to the importance of hard work and effort to self-improvement. The hard life, opportunities, and experiences of *masela* (thugs) are contrasted with those of then Tanzanian president Jakaya Kikwete (born 1950) and the political elite. Uthman uses his voice to represent the experiences of marginalised young men in Dar es Salaam while animating the desire for hard work and effort.

De Certeau asserts that speech and discourses are "systems of representations or processes of fabrication" that "no longer appear only as normative frameworks but also as tools manipulated by users" (De Certeau 1985, 21). This notion of the manipulation of speech and discourse by users in their struggle, aesthetically and ethically, proves instructive for our analysis of how symbols are appropriated and modes of being are generated by rappers in Dar es Salaam. De Certeau conceives of everyday activities by marginalised subjects as a form of resistance to the dominant order through which the weak "use, manipulate, and divert" (ibid, 30), a resistance whose primary technique is that of *la perruque* (poaching), the trick of taking time or resources from the dominant order. Ideas and values associated with Ujamaa, I maintain, represent a means for young people to strategically inscribe themselves into, while at the same time refashioning, social and political discourse. Uthman Issa, by suggesting a connection between the figures of Nyerere and Tupac, stressed that this did not necessitate a belief in Ujamaa. Indeed, when discussing the achievement of Baba wa Taifa (Father of the Nation), Nyerere and then Tanzanian president Jakaya Kikwete, he suggested that both could be evaluated as *nusu kwa nusu*, or fifty-fifty. While for Uthman, Nyerere was clearly the more venerated politician, he distanced himself from *mambo ya siasa* political affairs. For Uthman, Nyerere had been someone who spoke the truth but had not always been able to accomplish this in his actions. Their invocation of these concepts is, however, multifaceted. Through invoking ideas from the legacy of Ujamaa, they frequently explicitly disavowed the Ujamaa project itself. Underground rappers' engagement with the legacies of Ujamaa is complicated and critical; overall, they are not nostalgic for Ujamaa.

CONCLUSION

In this chapter, I have engaged with the role neoliberal economic changes have played in enabling new possibilities to produce popular culture and in the circulation of practices and symbols from the global mediasphere. These have been appropriated and reanimated by rappers in Dar es Salaam. The figure of the "gangster" has, I maintain, become a space for the transformation and reactivation of concepts associated with Ujamaa. My primary locus for this analysis has been the practices of underground rappers, whose performances represent a politics of presence, an assertion of identity and a strategic inscription of young men into public space. Young people adapt to their surroundings using the tools available to them, including their voice, space, and the circulating concepts and symbols to constitute themselves. One lens through which this might be read is as the "clever tricks of the 'weak' within the order established by the 'strong'" (De Certeau 1985, 40). This reading might lead us to view rappers' borrowing of mimetic language, gestures, and style from the global genre of hip hop as users subverting the concepts and symbols of national political and transnational musical order. I propose, however, that the situation is more complex. To read the young men who rap as simply marginalised figures capable of tactical action does not account for the full intricacy of their practice.

Through their mobilisation of concepts associated with Ujamaa, underground rappers make themselves legible to wider society. This is not a practice simply of poaching, taking "advantages of 'opportunities' . . . 'seized on the wing'" (De Certeau 1985, 37). Rappers situate themselves strategically in relation to mainstream social and political discourse. While Ujamaa policies in Tanzania may largely have been abandoned by the state, the chief architect of Ujamaa, Julius Nyerere, remains an important legitimising force for the state and for CCM, the governing party. Here I think we should be attuned to the nuances and contradictory nature of popular cultural production. As I have suggested earlier, embodying a sociopolitical role as commentator can be read as the normative position for an artist to adopt in Dar es Salaam. Displays of consumption and wealth may therefore be read as a more revolutionary challenge to the norms of everyday social and moral discourse. I think it productive to here return to Mahmood's insights into the role of human industry, practice and technique in discipling the self. Rather than exclusively functioning as an act of resistance, we can also understand rapping as a willing subjugation to a different discourse. The act of rapping can be considered a practice of embodying new transnational and neoliberal forms of masculinity. I wish to suggest that the picture is more complex, rapping acts as a space for embodying the transnational figure of the rappers while simultaneously enabling the reanimation, reinterpretation, and reconfiguration of the conceptual legacy of Ujamaa. Rapping, I argue, acts in multiple modes. It is at once a tactic of subversion, a tool for resisting new dominant neoliberal order of meaning, and a strategy that enables the inscription of young people into legitimating discourses.

INTERVIEWS

D-Knob, Dar es Salaam, 2011
King Crazy GK, Dar es Salaam, 2006
Kizito, Dar es Salaam, 2011
Mbaya Wao, Dar es Salaam, 2009
O-Key, Dar es Salaam, 2011
O-Key, Dar es Salaam, 2016
Salim Muba, Dar es Salaam, 2011
Sugu, Dar es Salaam, 2006

NOTES

1. This article is based on ten months of ethnographic fieldwork on popular music in Dar es Salaam conducted during four trips to Dar es Salaam in 2006, 2009, 2011, and 2016, with follow-up research conducted through electronic communication. During my two lengthier periods of fieldwork in Dar es Salaam I spent time with a number of groups of underground rappers in the neighbourhoods of Kijitonyama, Msasani, Kiwalani, Kinondoni, Mwananyamala, Keko, Buza, and Mikocheni. These neighbourhoods were in many ways heterogeneous. Msasani and Mikocheni were largely planned settlements with pockets of *uswahilini*, informal settlements, within them. Keko, a short three-kilometre journey from the city centre, is one of the oldest *uswahilini* areas of Dar es Salaam. Buza is a periurban area on the outskirts of the city, close to the larger planned area of Mbagala in which livestock and small farming plots are interspersed between houses. All interviews quoted here were conducted in person in Dar es Salaam.

2. This form of rap, delivered in Swahili, came to be referred to as Bongo Flava. Bongo is derived from the Swahili word *ubongo* or brain, and *ubongo* has become shorthand in Tanzania to describe the city of Dar es Salaam, a city that requires the use of the brain, and cunning, to survive. Once outside of Tanzania the whole of Tanzania becomes "Bongo." Bongo Flava is the musical flavour of Dar es Salaam, or Tanzania, and was used as a term to describe rapped music or hip hop delivered in Swahili and emanating from Tanzania.

3. The term "*hali halis*," or the real situation, has become a reference point for conscious hip hop in Tanzania, used in albums, videos, and song titles.

4. While there have been a number of notable female rappers in Tanzania, such as Witnesz, Zay B, Sista P, and Stosh, this chapter explores how rapping acts as a space for performing a particular form of masculine identity.

5. The term *uswahilini* (the area of the Swahili people) has its origins in the racial colonial division of the city, though more recently the distinction between *uswahilini* and *uzunguni* draws on the provision of services "such as schools, roads, clinics, electricity and pipe water" and class "segmentarity" (Lewinson 2007, 206; Sanga 2013, 389–90).

6. These terms are not the preserve of underground rappers and have been used by commercial rappers, for example TMK Wanaume and Mangwair's song "Msela Msela."

7. A form of oral performance without recourse to written lyrics, these draw on memory and invention.

8. The popular press in Tanzania, for example newspapers such as *Kiu*, *Sani*, and *Ijumaa*, frequently carried stories about famous rappers and transcribed lyrics on a weekly basis from popular songs.

WORKS CITED

Askew, Kelly. 2006. "Sung and Unsung: Musical Reflections on Tanzanian Postsocialisms." *Africa* 76, no. 1: 15–43.

Becker, Felicitas. 2013. "Remembering Nyerere: Political Rhetoric and Dissent in Contemporary Tanzania." *African Affairs* 112, no. 447: 238–61.

Benga, N. A. 2002. "'The Air of the City Makes Free': Urban Music from the 1950s to the 1990s in Senegal—Variete, Jazz, Mbalax, Rap." In *Playing with Identities in Contemporary Music in Africa*, edited by M. Palmberg and A. Kirkegaard. Uppsala: Nordiska Afrikainstitutet.

Bray, Francesca. 2013. "Tools for Virtuous Action: Technology, Skills and Ordinary Ethics." in *Ordinary Ethics in China*, edited by C. Stafford. London: Bloomsbury.

Caplan, Pat. 2007. "Between Socialism and Neo-Liberalism: Mafia Island, Tanzania, 1965–2004." *Review of African Political Economy* 34, no. 114: 679–94.

Charry, Eric. 2012. "A Capsule History of African Rap." In *Hip Hop Africa: New African Music in a Globalizing World*, edited by Eric Charry. Bloomington: Indiana University Press.

Dancer, Helen. 2015. *Women, Land and Justice in Tanzania*. Woodbridge: James Currey.

Das, Veena. 2012. "Ordinary Ethics." In *Companion to Moral Anthropology*, edited by Didier Fassin, 133–49. Chichester, West Sussex: John Wiley & Sons, Blackwell Publishing.

De Certeau, Michel. 1985. *The Practice of Everyday Life*. Berkeley: University of California Press.

Englert, Birgit. 2008. "Ambiguous Relationships: Youth, Popular Music and Politics in Contemporary Tanzania." *Wiener Zeitschrift für kritische Afrikastudien* 14: 71–96.

Fenn, John, and Alex Perullo. 2000. "Language Choice and Hip Hop in Tanzania and Malawi." *Popular Music and Society* 24, no. 3: 73–93.

Forman, Murray. 2002. "The 'Hood Comes First: Race, Space, and Place." In *Rap and Hip-Hop*. Middletown, CT: Wesleyan University Press.

Fouere, Marie-Aude. 2014. "Julius Nyerere, Ujamaa, and Political Morality in Contemporary Tanzania," *African Studies Review* 57, no. 1: 1–24.

Foucault, Michel. 2002. *Archaeology of Knowledge*. Abingdon: Routledge.

Graebner, Werner. 1997. "Whose Music?: The Songs of Remmy Ongala and the Orchestra Super Matimila." In *Reading in African Popular Culture*, edited by Karin Barber. Oxford: International African Institute/James Currey.

Haupt, Adam. 2008. *Stealing Empire: P2P, Intellectual Property and Hip-Hop Subversion*. Cape Town: HSRC Press.

Iwamoto, Derek. 2003. "Tupac Shakur: Understanding the Identity Formation of Hyper-Masculinity of a Popular Hip-Hop Artist." *The Black Scholar* 33, no. 2: 44–49.

Jefferies, Michael. P. 2011. *Thug Life: Race, Gender, and the Meaning of Hip-Hop*. Chicago: University of Chicago Press.

Kerr, David. 2018. "From the Margins to the Mainstream: Making and Remaking an Alternative Music Economy in Dar es Salaam." *Journal of African Cultural Studies* 30, no. 1: 65-80.

Kibona Clark, M. 2013. "The Struggle for Hip Hop Authenticity and against Commercialization in Tanzania." *Journal of Pan African Studies* 6, no. 3: 5–21.

Lal, Priya. 2012. "Self-Reliance and the State: The Multiple Meanings of Development in Early Post-Colonial Tanzania." *Africa* 82, no. 2: 212–34.

Lambek, Michael. 2010. "Introduction." In *Ordinary Ethics: Anthropology, Language, and Action*, edited by Michael Lambek. New York: Fordham University Press.

Lemelle, Sidney J. 2006. "'Ni Wapi Tunakwenda': Hip Hop Culture and the Children of Arusha." In *The Vinyl Ain't Final: Hip Hop and the Globalization of Black Popular Culture*, edited by Dipannita Basu and Sidney J. Lemelle. London: Pluto Press.

Lewinson, Anne S. 2007. "Viewing Postcolonial Dar es Salaam, Tanzania through Civic Spaces: A Question of Class." *African Identities* 5, no. 2: 199–215.

Mahmood, Saba. 2001. "Feminist Theory, Embodiment, and the Docile Agent: Some Reflections on the Egyptian Islamic Revival." *Cultural Anthropology* 16, no. 2: 202–36.

Mahmood, Saba. 2005. *Politics of Piety: The Islamic Revival and the Feminist Subject*. Princeton, NJ: Princeton University Press.

Mwangi, Evan. 2004. "Nationalism and Masculinity in East African Hip Hop Music." *Tydskrif vir letterkunde* 41, no. 2: 5–20.

Ntarangwi, Mwenda. 2009. *East African Hip Hop: Youth Culture and Globalization*. Urbana: University of Illinois Press.

Nyerere, Julius K. 1966. *Freedom and Unity: Uhuru na Umoja*. Dar es Salaam: Oxford University Press.

Nyerere, Julius K. 1968. *Freedom and Socialism: A Selection from Writing and Speeches 1965–67*. Dar es Salaam: Oxford University Press.

Nyoni, Frowin Paul. 2007. "Music and Politics in Tanzania: A Case Study of Nyota-wa-Cigogo." In *Songs and Politics in Eastern Africa*, edited by Kimani Njogu and Herve Maupeu. Dar es Salaam: Mkuki na Nyota.

Omari, Shani. 2009. "Tanzanian Hip Hop Poetry as Popular Literature." PhD thesis, University of Dar es Salaam.

Osumare, Halifu. 2007. *The Africanist Aesthetic in Global Hip-Hop: Power Moves*. Basingstoke: Palgrave.

Osumare, Halifu. 2012. *The Hiplife in Ghana: West African Indigenization of Hip-Hop*. Basingstoke: Palgrave.

Perullo, Alex. 2005. "Hooligans and Heroes: Youth Identity and Hip-Hop in Dar es Salaam, Tanzania." *Africa Today* 51, no. 4: 75–101.

Perullo, Alex. 2011. *Live from Dar es Salaam: Popular Music and Tanzania's Music Economy*. Bloomington: Indiana University Press.

Pitcher, M. Anne, and Kelly M. Askew. 2006. "African Socialisms and Postsocialisms." *Africa* 76, no. 1: 1–14.

Remes, P. 1999. "Global Popular Musics and Changing Awareness of Urban Tanzanian Youth." *Yearbook for Traditional Music* 31: 1–26.

Reuster-Jahn, Uta. 2008. "Bongo Flava and the Electoral Campaign 2005 in Tanzania." *Wiener Zeitschrift für kritische Afrikastudien* 14: 41–69.

Reuster-Jahn, Uta, and Gabriel Hacke. 2011. "The Bongo Flava Industry in Tanzania and Artists' Strategies for Success." Working Paper 127. Mainz: Institut für Ethnologie und Afrikastudien.

Rose, Tricia. 1994. *Black Noise: Rap Music and Black Culture in Contemporary America*. Hanover, NH: University Press of New England.

Sanders, Todd. 2008. "Buses in Bongoland: Seductive Analytics and the Occult." *Anthropological Theory* 8, no. 2: 107–32.

Sanga, Imani. 2010. "The Practice and Politics of Hybrid Soundscapes in Muziki wa Injili in Dar es Salaam, Tanzania." *Journal of African Cultural Studies* 22, no. 2: 145–56.

Sanga, Imani. 2013. "Musical Figuring of Postcolonial Urban Segmentarity and Marginality in Selected 'Bongo Fleva' Songs in Dar es Salaam, Tanzania." *International Review of the Aesthetics and Sociology of Music* 44, no. 2: 385–405.

Shipley, Jessie-Weaver. 2009. "Aesthetic of the Entrepreneur: Afro-Cosmopolitan Rap and Moral Circulation in Accra, Ghana." *Anthropological Quarterly* 82, no. 3: 631–68.

Spence, Lester. K. 2011. *Stare in the Darkness: The Limits of Hip-Hop and Black Politics*. Minneapolis: University of Minnesota Press.

Stöger-Eising, Viktoria. 2000. "'Ujamaa' Revisited: Indigenous and European Influences in Nyerere's Social and Political Thought." *Africa* 70, no. 1: 118–43.

Stanford, Karin. 2011. "Keepin' It Real in Hip Hop Politics: A Political Perspective of Tupac Shakur," *Journal of Black Studies* 42, no. 1: 3–22.

Suriano, Maria. 2007. "'Mimi Ni Msani, Kioo Cha Jamii': Urban Youth Culture in Tanzania as Seen Through Bongo Fleva and Hip Hop." *Swahili Forum* 14: 207–23.

United Republic of Tanzania. 1977. The Constitution of the United Republic of Tanzania. Available at http://www.judiciary.go.tz/wp-content/uploads/2015/09/constitution.pdf.

Weiss, Brad. 2009. *Street Dreams and Hip Hop Barbershops: Global Fantasy in Urban Tanzania*. Bloomington: Indiana University Press.

Songs of Protest and Activist Opera

Seditious Songs

Spirituality as Performance and Political Action in Colonial-Era Belgian Congo

YOLANDA COVINGTON-WARD

INTRODUCTION

Can songs destroy colonialism? Groups of people can achieve social transformation and political action through a variety of means, from civil disobe-
dience to widespread protest and violent rebellion. This chapter considers
Baptist hymns as forms of social and political action within the context of
Simon Kimbangu's prophetic religious movement in colonial-era Belgian
Congo in 1921. Often (but not always) paired with vigorous trembling caused
by the Holy Spirit (*zakama* in KiKongo), I see these songs and the public
actions of the crowds who sang them as types of *performative encounters* that
challenged the hegemony and authority of Belgian colonial administrators
and Catholic, Baptist, Swedish, and other missionaries stationed in the Lower
Congo.[1] The lyrics, actual performance, and composition of the hymns that
were popular during Kimbangu's movement were sites of both coded and
explicit resistance and subversion on the part of Kongo people facing colonial
oppression and Christian organizational hierarchies. At the same time, however, Kimbangu's movement reified many of the beliefs, forms of conduct,
and hymns that were created by Baptist missionaries. It was after his arrest
that his followers gave more attention to the creation of hymns by Congolese
people themselves within this particular movement. This chapter will examine the concept of performative encounters, the background of Kimbangu's
movement, the meaning of the hymns for Kimbangu and his followers, the

interpretation of those same hymns by administrators and missionaries of different denominations based on analysis of four separate encounters,[2] and the persecution and arrest of those who sang the hymns. In 1921, these songs were a form of collective protest, public acts of refusal, a means for a population seeking many different ends to try to affect change in the world around them. Yet they are still relevant today as contemporary churches that emerged from Kimbangu's *kingunza* movement embrace hymns received through visions and dreams rather than Western-authored hymnbooks that populate the pews of the local mission-established Protestant churches.

PERFORMATIVE ENCOUNTERS

The analysis in this chapter will be developed around the concept of "performative encounters." I define performative encounters as moments when the body is used strategically in interpersonal interactions to disrupt the status quo in ways that transform existing social relationships in meaningful ways (Covington-Ward 2016). I bring together J. L. Austin's concept of performative utterances where phrases accomplish an action (*to say something is to do something* [1962, 12]) and Judith Butler's concepts of performatives (where gender is constituted through everyday performative acts), with Erving Goffman's idea of the social encounter (the natural unit of human interaction) to explore when *doing something is doing something more.* Moreover, my work is inspired by the ideas of Kelly Askew, whose book *Performing the Nation* outlines how nationalism, national identity, and interpersonal relationships are constituted through musical performances. Building upon these theories, my own work asks: What are the situations where what we do in social interactions has larger social consequences? This chapter builds upon my previous examination of performative encounters in my book *Gesture and Power: Religion, Nationalism, and Everyday Performance in Congo* (2016). In this chapter, however, I turn my attention to the songs themselves as collective forms of performative encounters, a topic that received very little attention in the book.

The most important characteristics of performative encounters are that they are incidents where restored behavior, behavior that is not for the first time and is in fact "twice-behaved behavior" (Schechner 1985, 35–41), is used in a public context to challenge the existing status quo. This behavior is a performance because of the use of restored behavior with the awareness of an audience observing the performance, but it is also socially transformative. In this case, four examples of incidences of performative encounters will be examined to demonstrate the utilization of Baptist hymns to deconstruct the colonial relationship between Congolese subjects and Belgian and other Western administrators and missionaries in the Belgian Congo in 1921.

CHRISTIANITY AND THE PROPHETIC MOVEMENT OF SIMON KIMBANGU

Christianity has a centuries-long history in West Central Africa, specifically through precolonial kingdoms such as the Kingdom of Kongo. Believed to have been formed in the mid-fourteenth century (Thornton 2001, 119), the Kingdom of Kongo converted to Catholicism in 1491 after years of contact with the Portuguese. By the 1920s, several centuries later and after the spread of European colonialism, the massive African colony (which included much of the former Kongo Kingdom) was first known as the Congo Free State, later as the Belgian Congo, and was Christian in many areas.[3] Most of the rest of the colony eventually became Catholic as this was the religion of the colonial state and Belgian Catholic missionaries were given preferential treatment compared to other missionaries (Covington-Ward 2016, 77). The Lower Congo province, where Nkamba was located, however, proved to be more complex because this area had a large number of Protestant missionaries who had established mission stations along the Congo River during the colonial period (Covington-Ward 2016, 76). By the time of Kimbangu's movement in 1921, the major Protestant missionary societies in the Lower Congo were the American Baptist Foreign Mission Society (ABFMS), the Svenska Missions Förbundet (Swedish Mission Covenant Church, SMF), the Christian and Missionary Alliance (CMA), and the Baptist Missionary Society of England (BMS) (Covington-Ward 2016, 76). Simon Kimbangu was a member of a BMS-founded mission church before starting his prophetic movement.

Born in 1889 in the village of Nkamba to his mother Lwezi and his father Kuyela, Simon Kimbangu's parents both died when he was a child (Mahaniah 1993). He was raised by his maternal aunt Kinzembo and was baptized in and became a member of the Baptist church at Wathen (Ngombe Lutete) in 1915 (Frame 1921). After having visions for a number of years, Kimbangu left to work in larger cities, but was not successful. After returning home, he asked to become the evangelist for Nkamba, but the elders there denied his request. Not long after, in mid-March 1921, he laid his hands on a sick woman while praying in the name of Jesus (Pemberton 1993, 205). This successful healing sparked a religious movement rooted in Protestant Christianity and Kongo forms of embodiment. Kimbangu's body would tremble vigorously when filled with the Holy Spirit, a form of embodied practice that was similar to how *banganga* (traditional ritual-specialists) moved when possessed by territorial spirits. Yet he also read from the Bible, used Baptist hymnbooks, prohibited secular dancing and drumming among his followers, and admonished people to get rid of their powerful objects, which missionaries called fetishes. People came from all throughout the Lower Congo, across the border in French Congo and Portuguese Angola, to be healed by Kimbangu. Thousands of people traveled to Nkamba with their sick or dying loved ones, and other prophets began to emerge almost immediately. As railroad and other workers left their jobs and clinics and hospitals emptied, colonial administrators and missionaries began to worry about the implications of this emerging movement. After some investigation, including a visit to Nkamba, the colonial government decided to try to suppress the movement by arresting first its leaders and then its followers. As the *kingunza* movement spread, it began to take on an antiwhite character, with people refusing to pay taxes, awaiting the arrival of the dead, and waiting for God to kill white men in the Congo so that the Congolese could rule themselves. Eventually, the mere act of singing Protestant hymns was seen as cause for arrest. What were these hymns exactly? What did these songs, which were largely Protestant hymns taken from hymnbooks of the Baptist missionaries in the area, mean for the Kongo people themselves who were a part of this movement in 1921?

HYMNS FOR THE SPIRIT

For Simon Kimbangu and other prophets who emerged, the singing of Baptist hymns played an integral role in working with the Holy Spirit.

> Kimbangu had already said that the hymns must be sung loudly and enthusiastically, for then he would be given the power of healing. The louder the song, the stronger became the spirit. The prophets therefore tried to get men with good voices to be their assistants most of whom also experienced ecstasy . . . loud instrumental music was used in addition to the singing and dancing in order to produce the desired condition. (Andersson 1958, 58)

Thus the loud singing was crucial for Kimbangu to be able to harness the Holy Spirit and heal sick patients. When Kimbangu began his work as a prophet, he built a *lumpangu*, or enclosure, in front of his house in Nkamba (Andersson 1958, 52). The *minyimbidi*, or singers, were located in a particular section of the *lumpangu*, as indicated in the account of Bahelele Nidimisina Jacques, a Kongo pastor trained in Swedish missionary churches in the Lower Congo. The *lumpangu* was divided into three sections and people entered through a door into the first section. "In the second part are found the prophet and his singers seated to his right and to his left and who sang when the prophet starts his work" (Vellut 2005, 61). The *minyimbidi* were crucial for the healing process. "The force and the pride of a prophet of that time depended above all on the manner of singing and the teaching of the word of God. When the singers did not come, the prophet did not work either. He waits until the singers arrive. They sing and the prophet starts his work" (Vellut 2005, 63). Bahelele also points out that the most popular song was number 462:

Zimpasi zingi vava nsi
Mayela tweti monanga
Masangaza madadanga
O wiza kutusadisa
O Mpeve, wiza, wiza
O wiza kutusakisa [sic]
C'est trop de souffrance ici sur la terre
Nous sommes malades
Les larmes coulent
Venez donc nous aider
O Esprit Saint, venez, venez
O venez nous secourir

There are many troubles here on earth
We are sick
Tears are flowing
Come help us
O Holy Spirit, come,
come
O come help us
　　　(Vellut 2005, 62–63, my translation of French)

In this song, the leaders and members of the *kingunza* movement are express-ing their desire for help from the Holy Spirit and their dissatisfaction with their lives. In the decades immediately preceding Kimbangu's movement, there were a number of developments specifically associated with the expan-sion of colonialism that may have been the cause of the "sickness" and tears that are described in the song: Kongo men forced to carry loads as porters; other forms of forced labor on colonial-era projects; the forced relocation of communities; violent raids from colonial military forces; increased food inse-curity due to the raids and forced labor regimes; depopulation of communi-ties as men went in search of work in urban areas; colonial administration and missionary attacks on community institutions and leaders such as ritual specialists and healers as well as local chiefs; and even actual physical sickness such as the global epidemic of Spanish influenza starting in 1918 and out-breaks of sleeping sickness, polio, and other diseases, which were often called "foreign diseases" or "colonial diseases" by the local population (Covington-Ward 2016, 78–80). The song seems to plead for the Holy Spirit to intercede as Kongo people face massive social transformations that ensure that their lives will never be the same again.

There were two types of hymns related to the movement: Protestant hymns taken from hymnals provided by Western missionaries, and inspired hymns that came to prophets and their followers and were taken up by the rest of the group. There are a number of hymns that were popular during the movement in 1921, according to archival documents and witness accounts. The first is "Onward Christian Soldiers":

> *Onward Christian Soldiers, marching as to war,*
> *With the cross of Jesus going on before.*
> *Christ the Royal Master, leads against the foe,*
> *Forward into Battle see His banners go!*[4]
> (Vellut 2010, 242, 299)

With terms like "war," "foe," "soldiers," and "battle," the hymn "Onward Christian Soldiers" used evangelical terminology that highlighted the con-flict between good and evil as a spiritual war or battle. Many of the Protestant hymns that were being used on Baptist and other Protestant missions in the Lower Congo incorporated similar terminology. Several of the existing first-hand accounts written by Protestant missionaries, both British and American

Baptist, point out that neither the Belgian colonial administration nor the Belgian Catholic missionaries were accustomed to evangelical terminology as used in the popular Protestant hymns of that time period, and they missed the possibility of a subversive double meaning. For example, Robert H. C. Graham, a British BMS missionary stationed in San Salvador nearby across the border in Angola, has this to say about the "Prophets Song": "The song contained nothing whatever against the Government, but was directed solely against the evil customs of the country. . . . [T]here is certainly nothing objectionable in the song from the political standpoint" (Vellut 2010, 92). Similarly, Peter H. J. Lerrigo, the foreign administrative secretary of the ABFMS, described one hymn for which Congolese men were arrested for singing as coming from missionary publications: "There is no doubt that some of the people have sung *ngunza* hymns. Indeed Mr. and Mrs. Moody have heard them sing one. It appeared in print in one of the Swedish mission publications. It is entirely innocuous" (Vellut 2010, 230). Some Protestant Baptist missionaries, then, viewed these hymns as either the same songs missionaries promoted or as songs that were aligned with Baptist hymns in theme in content. But, on the contrary, the colonial administration took references to war and battle and armor, which were really about spiritual warfare for Protestant Christians, literally.

Another notable hymn is what one missionary identified as the "Prophet's Song," which Belgian authorities came to see as "treasonable, so that anyone who sang it, or even hummed the tune, would be liable to arrest and imprisonment" (Vellut 2010, 91–92):

Chorus: In Heaven a Witness; On Earth a Witness; God knows altogether, Everything we do.
The chiefs of Congo perish, They are by drink enslaved; Ten chiefs of Congo perish, They are by drink enslaved:

Let us go and teach them, that so they may be saved.
The common people perish, In ignorance enslaved: (repeat two lines).
Let us go and teach them, That so they may be saved.
The market peoples perish, By fraud and tricks depraved: (repeat two lines).
Let us go and teach them, That so they may be saved.
And all the people perish, Through lack of faith unsaved: (repeat two lines).
Let us go and teach them, That so they may be saved.
   (Vellut 2010, 92)

While I am unable to verify that this song was in fact the most popular hymn, based on its content (references to Congo chiefs, market people, etc.) it does not seem to be a typical Baptist hymn imported by Baptist missionaries. The reference to Congo chiefs, in fact, may allude to the precolonial Kongo Kingdom, which existed in the lower Congo and northern Angola starting in about the fourteenth century. This hymn, then, can serve as evidence for the creation of hymns alongside the usage of pre-existing Baptist hymns. While I have not been able to discover the composer or writer for this hymn, it was unmistakably important in the *kingunza* movement.

Observers of the *kingunza* movement also recognized the immense importance of hymns for the leaders and followers of the movement itself. In his article in the *Congo Newsletter* about the impact of the *kingunza* movement on the Nsona Mbata district (spelled Sona Bata in his article), ABFMS missionary Peter A. MacDiarmid discussed hymn singing as one of several elements of the teachings of Kongo prophets, along with belief in the imminent coming of Christ, baptism, and the punishment of the wicked (*Congo Newsletter*, September 1922, 20–22). Moreover, he also acknowledged hymns as a source of potential antistate sentiment:

> The influence of hymns has been very great. Those who were ready for Christ's coming were filled with joy and much of this found vent in the singing of hymns. They began with Christian hymns but after a time there was added quite a number of prophet hymns set to the older tunes. After a time the State forbad [sic] the singing of these prophet hymns because it was claimed that they were anti-white, and particularly anti-State, containing germs of revolt. (*Congo Newsletter*, September 1922, 22)

MacDiarmid indicates here the place of hymns in the larger ideology of Kongo prophets, the evaluation of those hymns as a threat from the point of view of the Belgian colonial state, and the evolution of hymns from those taught by Western missionaries and included in printed hymnals to hymns authored by prophets themselves. Other sources also support his assessment of hymns in the *kingunza* movement. For instance, Thomas Moody, an ABFMS missionary heading the mission station at Nsona Mbata, recounted to Peter Lerrigo, the foreign administrative secretary for the ABFMS, the continued persecution of *ngunza* hymns even after Kimbangu's arrest. During a religious conference organized by the mission at Nsona Mbata on September 21, 1921, the state administrator camped out nearby with soldiers to keep an eye on the event. The administrator sent a list of nine Kongo men who supposedly were heard singing *ngunza* hymns on the way to the conference. "Moody replied that the hymn was entirely harmless and was a prayer for the coming of the spirit, to help in their struggle against evil. Adm. replied that other hymns had spoken of destroying white men. He turned over the nine men . . . for punishment" (Vellut 2010, 230). Clearly, when you are arrested for merely being suspected of singing hymns, the Belgian colonial administration viewed these spiritual songs as threats to their power.

The modern day Kimbanguist church currently emphasizes the evolution of hymns throughout the prophetic movement started by Simon Kimbangu. The Kimbanguist church currently has a belief in inspired songs and traces it back to the prophet Simon Kimbangu. According to oral history, when he sent helpers to purchase hymnbooks from missionaries, he was ridiculed for not having received "inspired hymns" and then was asked by another missionary to return some of the books he had. "Kimbangu was told by God that from then on he should never look to the missionaries for anything . . . there and then, in the presence of the missionary, a close colleague of Kimbangu . . . 'received' the first hymn: 'Soldiers of righteousness, put on your armour'" (Molyneux 1990, 153–54). The potential double meaning of Christian soldiers preparing for battle, and the struggle between Kimbangu and his followers and the missionaries and colonial administration, was probably not lost on the missionary who supposedly witnessed the instance of receipt of this inspired hymn. This oral history also shows how inspired songs are a way in which the spiritual authority of the church is established and maintained. When the colleague of Kimbangu received the inspired hymn, he also showed the missionary that Kimbangu and his followers had a direct line of communication with God and did not need the missionaries as mediators, interpreters, or gatekeepers. In regards to Christianity, Pope Gregory I is widely believed to have received the singing and melody for Gregorian chants from a dove perched on his shoulder channeling the Holy Spirit (Treitler 2009). Such beliefs align with already existing Kongo practices of continuous revelation in which the supernatural realm is believed to continuously interact with the world of the living (Thornton 1998, 235–271). In this sense, inspired hymns fit right in with other Christian and non-Christian Kongo beliefs and practices dating to the precolonial period.

Besides the double meaning possible in the songs as they were marshalled against government forces and missionaries alike, some of the participants in the *kingunza* movement also used the songs to impart moral lessons to their supposed European superiors. During the trial of Kimbangu and his disciples, the judge (Amédée de Rossi) asked one of the disciples about the meaning of the hymns: "When one of the prophets was asked what was meant by the militant phraseology used in hymns he replied 'we are warning against sin in the heart.' 'What do you mean by that?' the judge inquired. 'Oh' replied the prophet, against lying, adultery'—'that will do, that will do,' hastily broke in the judge" (Vellut 2010, 70–71). The judge apparently cut him off because his African concubine sat there in the courtroom, a fact Kimbangu and his followers knew very well (Vellut 2010, 70–71). Overall, the Belgian colonial administration, lacking familiarity with themes in Protestant evangelical hymns at the time, were threatened by the terminology used in the hymns.

THE BELGIAN COLONIAL ADMINISTRATION, MISSIONARIES, AND SEDITIOUS SONGS

Kimbangu and Morel

Hymns became a point of contention when Léon-Georges Morel, the administrator for the Cataracts territory, came to Nkamba to investigate Simon Kimbangu in May of 1921. Fortunately, there are at least two accounts of this encounter between Kimbangu and Morel, one written from the point of view of Kimbangu and his followers and the other from the perspective of Morel himself. Placing these two accounts in conversation with one another reveals both the importance of hymns in Kimbangu's movement, but also how hymns themselves were used to directly challenge state authority as well.

A manuscript confiscated from Nkamba by soldiers in June 1921 showed that two BisiKongo men, Nfinangani and Nzungu, were chronicling Kimbangu's story (Pemberton 1993). The document was typewritten in KiKongo and translated by the colonial administration after it was seized. Nfinangani was described as Kimbangu's secretary, while not much is known about Nzungu. One of the moments they include in their manuscript was Kimbangu's first encounter with Morel in Nkamba. Kimbangu met Morel on the road into Nkamba while Kimbangu and his disciples were experiencing spirit-induced trembling. Morel, accompanied by two soldiers, headed toward the village of Nkamba. According to the Kongo account, he chose to intentionally set up his tent near Kimbangu's house.

Once they arrived, the white man erected his tent near to the prophet's house. The prophet told him to move his tent from that spot because the singers passed that way. The white man said, "I, also, have come to see what is going on, but I have not come for a struggle". Immediately the prophet took the Old Testament, read it and said, "We are all, in respect of your arrival, gathered here in God's hands. God is the living God; everything else in which men put their trust is absolutely meaningless." (Pemberton 1993, 218)

The struggle for authority is demonstrable here as Kimbangu and Morel debate the placement of Morel's tent. Morel seems to be drawing on his position as a colonial administrator to bolster his ability to choose to set up his tent wherever he pleases. Kimbangu, however, draws on the spiritual authority inherent in the Bible to contest Morel's presence and his right to determine the use of the physical space at Nkamba.

In his own report, Morel describes his arrival in Nkamba in the following way: "The house of the prophet is located at the entrance of the village . . . it is surrounded by a large enclosure. . . . Upon my arrival the enclosure was occupied by forty people, singing Protestant hymns . . . in a more than vigorous manner. These songs continued until my departure" (Morel 1921).

The Kongo account of the encounter also mentions a slightly contentious exchange between the two of them. Right after, however, "straightaway the singers struck up with hymn 207: 'Onward Christian Soldiers, Marching as to War.' The singers sang at the top of their voices, with great joy, and could be heard everywhere." (Pemberton 1993, 219). Perhaps due to the battle imagery the songs invoked, or perhaps because of the loud singing of the hymns, Morel in his own report saw no joy in these hymns. Rather, he associated the singing and other practices at Nkamba with evil and insubordinate behavior:

They all retreat into the enclosure with the singers and then begin a diabolical bacchanal of screaming alternating with songs, dances, and readings of biblical texts. Around 10 oclock in the night, I asked the singers to stop the noise during the night, arguing that the crowd and the porters, having come from far, were in need of rest. One refuses categorically and openly. Coming to tell me: "that God had ordered that the songs continue without interruption for 10 consecutive days and nights. Since I only have a weak escort that does not allow me to make my views prevail without danger in the presence of a crowd so excited by religious fanaticism, I decide not to insist and the noise resumes, until morning the singers turning towards my tent to accentuate their echoes. (Morel 1921)

Notable in Morel's description here is his emphasis that his orders for the singing to stop were not only ignored, but directly challenged. He describes the reaction of one of the singers as "one refuses categorically and openly." The image here of an outspoken, truculent Congolese subject belies the stereotype of the pliant, childlike African seeking the guidance of Belgian paternalism. Rather, Morel is subjected to listening to the hymns all night, and Congolese are the ones controlling the space at Nkamba. This overall incident at Nkamba is a performative encounter because, through the open refusals to comply and stay in line with Belgian colonial expectations of Congolese behavior, Kimbangu and his followers used hymns to stake out a space of freedom for themselves, one in which colonial authority has no place. They subverted the prevailing status quo with their actions and songs, making Morel feel ill at ease and unsafe in the massive colony that Belgians were supposed to control. Moreover, Kimbangu and his followers redefined the space at Nkamba as governed by the rules and proscriptions of God and not the edicts of the Belgian colonial administration. This rendered Morel ineffective and weak and furthered the process of redefining the relationship between the Congolese and the Belgians, undoing the status quo and starting to formulate another set of norms in its place, one in which Congolese are decision makers deserving of the same respect as white men. No wonder then that in his report that he submitted to his superiors in the colonial administration after he left Nkamba, Morel recommended that Kimbangu be arrested and his movement stopped.

Kimbangu and Bowskill

Simon Kimbangu had been in hiding since June 6, 1921, after Léon-Georges Morel, the Belgian territorial administrator for the Southern Cataracts territory, had gone back to the town of Nkamba with many more soldiers to arrest him. When he arrived, Morel found a crowd of people singing loudly. His soldiers detained Kimbangu, but Kimbangu slipped away unexpectedly after the soldiers began to beat him and people in the crowd intervened (Mackay and Ntoni-Nzinga 1993, 239). A melee ensued between the assembled crowd and the small contingent of armed soldiers. Things escalated and the soldiers fired into the crowd, killing at least one child and wounding others. The entire district, including several other territories, was placed under martial law as government soldiers searched fruitlessly for Simon Kimbangu (Andersson 1958, 64). All the while, Kimbangu remained in a small village nearby, continuing to preach and heal, while his followers concealed his whereabouts. About three months later, he decided to emerge from hiding by openly returning to his hometown of Nkamba. He also chose to pay an unannounced visit to Ngombe Lutete (also known as Wathen, the British Baptist Missionary Society station where he was baptized). Joseph Sidney Bowskill, a BMS missionary posted there, described his visit and the events that followed in this way:

> Sept. 11th Sunday: Things were almost at their worst today. During morning service (only station children and a few workmen were there) the Prophet came along with a vast crowd of people and made a demonstration outside the chapel. They came singing their songs; children dancing. They then formed up in a mass and the Prophet shouted out "As the apostle Paul said, 'he that is not against us is on our part.' If you do not believe me, I shake off the dust of my feet to condemn you." Then reforming into a procession they slowly marched off . . . (Bowskill, Notes on the Prophet Movement, n.d., Wathen Station Minutes, in Vellut 2010, 30)

In a deposition that he gave several years later in 1925, Bowskill gave additional detail about the songs the crowd of Kimbangu's followers sang on that day:

> Kibangu [*sic*] was arrested in September two days after having passed here with a big crowd and having made a hostile demonstration against our mission . . . the followers of Kibangu [*sic*] then sang a long song; the final verse was that their leaders were imprisoned and that it was because of us missionaries, that we delivered them to the State. (Deposition of J. S. Bowskill, in Vellut 2010, 169–70)

Based on both of these descriptions of Kimbangu and his followers making an unannounced visit to the BMS mission station at Wathen, Joseph Bowskill clearly interpreted Kimbangu's words and the lyrics of the song as a warning or threat against the missionaries for working with the colonial government to suppress the *kingunza* movement. Kimbangu drew on the Bible to make a connection between a phrase from the past and the current events in regards to the prophetic movement in colonial Belgian Congo. The song, which seems to be a new creation of the movement rather than a Protestant hymn imported by Western missionaries, provided an undeniable public critique of missionaries' collusion with the colonial state. In a colonial context in which missionaries were often treated like paternalistic demigods, this public rebuke would have seemed quite shocking and out of the norm for a missionary like Joseph Bowskill.

Kimbangu and the March to Thysville

The power of hymns in collective singing was brought to the fore upon Simon Kimbangu's arrest and transport to Thysville, the seat of territorial colonial administration.[5] The British missionary Joseph Bowskill also commented on the use of hymns when Simon Kimbangu turned himself in to be arrested and crowds emerged to see him brought in:

> News got to Thysville that the Prophet had reappeared; men were sent to take him but he went to meet them and gave himself up. A great crowd of others joined him; they all sought arrest; begged for it. They got to Thysville, crowds came out to meet them; prophet hymns were sung and things became so serious that Martial Law was proclaimed and about 125 were put in prison. (Bowskill, Notes on the Prophet Movement, n.d., Wathen Station Minutes, in Vellut 2010, 30)

A popular Belgian colonial newspaper gave the following description of the same event: "The prisoners, all along the road, sing hymns. Black people come from everywhere, line along the road, sing with the prisoners. Simon Kimbangu exalts them" (Chome 1959, 52). Even more revealing, however, is the description of the same crowd provided by Amédée de Rossi, commander of the War Council, as shown in his letter to the governor of another province, dated September 13, 1921:

> You should have seen the arrival of the Prophet in Thysville. It was huge. An enormous crowd followed him, singing their famous song. He too sang with all the other prisoners. I went to the gathering and immediately stopped the singing. Right after, in the village Sanzele, a huge group of men, women, and children resumed singing. I took with me eight soldiers and with Mr. Dupuis we went to the village and proceeded to arrest many individuals. (Vellut 2010, 152–53)

And how did he get the larger group to stop singing? Apparently, de Rossi threatened to shoot them with a machine gun if they didn't stop singing "ngunza songs and the English national anthem" where "English national anthem" likely refers to "God Save the King" (Vellut 2010, 152, footnote 226;

156, footnote 229). But why exactly did the singing of songs provoke such an extreme reaction, from arrests to physical violence to death threats?

On the part of the Belgians, their overzealous responses to these subversive songs can be couched within larger worries about threats to their control over their colony, in particular concerns about the anticolonial movement of Marcus Garvey, whose literature was found among workers in the Congo (Mahaniah 1993; Kodi 1993). Moreover, they were already concerned about any non-Belgian presence, and they especially did not trust the British missionaries. Some of them were directly blamed for supposedly supporting the *kingunza* movement of Simon Kimbangu. The colonial administration was concerned that Kimbangu's movement might become an open insurrection, which would threaten their tenuous hold on their African colony, a colony that was more than seventy-six times the size of Belgium itself. A colonial magistrate wrote, "In Mayombe, the hatred for the whites was harshly manifested. In Kamba . . . they sang religious songs with a warlike manner, songs which they usually sang in the temple, but which became bad and hostile songs consequently in the presence of the white person in front of whom they sang" (Vellut 2010, 149). This demonstrates that the colonial administration began to see the movement as antiwhite in character and as a threat to their authority.

Both incidents of Kimbangu coming to Wathen station and the large crowds of people singing when Kimbangu was arrested can be seen as performative encounters. Both instances were public encounters, with varying audiences, from the children on the mission to the BMS missionary Joseph Bowskill to people in the town of Thysville. How might the idea of the status quo in colonial-era Congo start to shift in their minds when they watched this singing crowd face down a colonial administrator? Both incidents mark departures from normal relations between Western missionaries and administrators and an African populace in colonial settings. As previously indicated, herein lies the transformative potential in performative encounters, in the process of subverting the status quo, opening up new possibilities for interpersonal relationships and understandings of power and authority.

Another observation that can be made about Kimbangu's arrival into Thysville is that it has similarities to the arrival of Jesus Christ in Jerusalem on Palm Sunday. In the story of what has been called the triumphal entry noted in the four gospels, Jesus Christ arrives in Jerusalem riding on a donkey and "is acclaimed by crowds in messianic terms" (Coakley 1995, 1), including people putting palm fronds and branches on the ground in front of him.

In regards to Kimbangu, both colonial administrators and missionaries remarked on the massive crowd that came to meet Kimbangu and walked and sang with him as he went to turn himself in. Both are treated as messiahs and ultimately face terrible punishments: the crucifixion of Jesus Christ and the eventual sentencing to death of Simon Kimbangu, later commuted to life imprisonment. In this way the story of Kimbangu's arrest may be contextualized within a larger Christian narrative structure that remained compelling for Kongo Christians themselves in this colonial context, with hymns especially playing the role of subverting the colonial administration and white power structure that was normalized in this time period.

Hymns and Kimbangu's Trial

On October 3, 1921, Amédée de Rossi, the judge adjudicating the trial of Simon Kimbangu, rendered his verdict. Kimbangu and his followers were classified as a direct threat to the state and the hymns they sang were a part of this assessment:

> Whereas it remains established that through his acts, words, dealings, writings, songs, and his story dictated by himself, Simon Kibango [sic] has set himself up as a redemptor and savior of the black race in designating whites as the enemy, calling them the abominable enemy that it is true that the hostility against the authorities was manifested up to the present through seditious songs, insults, offences, and some isolated rebellions, it is however true that the progression of events could have inevitably led to a large revolt. (Chome 1959, 68, 70).

Here songs (hymns) were clearly identified as one of the practices the Belgian colonial administration deemed anticolonial and antistate within the context of the *kingunza* movement. That the judge called the songs "seditious" and clearly linked them with hostilities (real and imagined) against the colonial state reinforces the importance of these hymns for the *kingunza* movement overall. For these and other reasons, Simon Kimbangu was sentenced to death. As Harold Casebow (a BMS missionary) notes in his contemporaneous account, hymns played a direct role in the sentencing of some of Kimbangu's followers as well, such as two of whom received sentences of five years of penal servitude for "selling photographs of the 'prophet' and hymns, and the other, a lad, for writing a hymn" (Vellut 2010, 96). Hymns could shame, rebuke, and incite rebellion. Indeed, from the perspective of the colonial administration, hymns could break the grasp of Belgium's hold on the vast Congo colony.

THE RELEVANCE OF SANCTIFIED AND INSPIRED SONGS TODAY

Hymns, especially inspired hymns received through dreams and visions, continue to play an important role in many of the churches that emerged from Simon Kimbangu's prophetic movement. The Kimbanguist church, founded by Simon Kimbangu's sons, uses inspired hymns and chronicles the life and lessons of Simon Kimbangu in hymns as well (Simbandumwe 1992). In fact, inspired hymns are recognized as one of the three sources of Kimbanguist theology, along with the Bible and prophetic speeches of Kimbangu's youngest son and current leader of the Kimbanguist church, Joseph Diangienda (Mokoko Gampiot 2017, 83).

> In the Kimbanguist Church, sacred songs hold considerable importance, on a par with the Bible and the prophetic messages of the spiritual leader, which illuminate the meaning of the lyrics. As a body of oral tradition, these hymns are not just sung—they participate in a divine plan . . . these hymns are defined by Kimbanguists as "inspired hymns" or "songs of the angels." Due to their mystical character, they are distinguished from "profane" songs and even from the Christian music made by other Congolese churches. Because they are not the work of any composer, being attributed to God, these songs are seen as revealing what escapes the awareness of social actors. (Mokoko Gampiot 2017, 94–96)

For the Kimbanguist church, which was officially recognized in 1959, inspired hymns continue to play a highly significant role in the worship and belief systems for the leadership and followers. The Kimbanguist church continues the legacy of recognizing the influence of God on songs that are revealed through visions and dreams and are verified and recognized by the church's spiritual leaders. Mokoko Gampiot's research, where the author interviewed people who have received inspired songs, revealed that for some, the songs continued to come, with certain individuals receiving many songs over years and even decades (2017, 94–107). Receiving songs is viewed as a spiritual gift, one to be shared with the larger Kimbanguist religious community.

The DMNA Church (Dibundu dia Mpeve ya Nlongo mu Afelika, also known as the Church of the Holy Spirit in Africa [Église de Saint Esprit en Afrique, in French]) is one such church in Luozi Territory, DR Congo, that also draws on Kimbangu's legacy. The songs that are a part of the worship service of the DMNA church are also, for the most part, a feature that sets the church apart from the Evangelical Community of Congo (CEC) churches, the Protestant churches founded by Swedish missionaries in the nineteenth century. Although in all of the churches in Luozi the predominant language of the songs was KiKongo, there are differences in the composers of those songs. In the hymnbooks for one of the CEC churches for example, the vast majority of the songs were composed by European missionaries to the Congo rather than by Congolese themselves. On the other hand, a perusal of the hymnal of the DMNA church reveals that prophets, leaders, and members of the DMNA church itself composed the songs. Pastor Mpadi cited the hymnbook among the three sacred texts of the DMNA church. When asked why the hymnbook, titled *Nkunga mia Dibundu dia Mpeve ya Nlongo mu Afelika* (*Songs of the Church of the Holy Spirit in Africa*) and now composed of more than 278 songs by many different people, is considered to be sacred, he replied that the songs were "never composed, but received in visions and dreams" (Pastor Mpadi, interview, Luozi, November 14, 2005). All of the songs in the hymnal are inspired songs, which a group of elders evaluated for authenticity. Thus inspired songs are an important part of worship in the DMNA church, as stated in an interview:

> We take songs that remain sanctified, that remain really something of saints that must allow us to communicate with the divine. Then, when the piece is here, the sense of the music, in our vision it is that the angels sing with us, together. . . . In singing, all the songs are prayers! It's for that reason that I said that the songs [are] a substance that is transported by the music. (Pastor Mpadi, interview, Luozi, November 14, 2005)

Since the songs are inspired, when the congregation performs them, they are like melodic prayers to God. Moreover, like in the case of Kimbangu, they must be performed loudly; the singing and music are deafeningly loud to facilitate possession by the Holy Spirit.

The legacy of Kimbangu in the hymns of the DMNA church lies not only in their performance to bring on possession by the Holy Spirit, but also in how they stake a political claim eschewing the necessity of Western missionaries to compose hymns for Congolese consumption. Like Kimbangu and his followers, the leadership and membership of the DMNA church value an unmediated relationship with God, an approach that bolsters an independent church grounded in Kongo culture similar to the ideology of many churches that blossomed during the era of the *kingunza* movement. Hymns play a crucial role in establishing that independence.

CONCLUSION

The religious movement of Simon Kimbangu is not the only African movement that used songs to challenge colonial oppression and subjugation; in fact, songs were a form of anticolonial protest in a number of different contexts in Africa. For example, Chimurenga songs in Zimbabwe were more secular songs that explicitly addressed the devastating impact of the colonial state in everyday life (Chikowero 2015), while Christian hymns were repurposed to carry anticolonial messages during Kenya's movement for liberation from the British (Njogu 2007). In the broader diaspora historically, Negro spirituals became a form of coded protest against bondage for people of African descent enslaved in the United States. Nompumelelo Zondi's chapter in this volume also examines secular protest songs in contemporary South Africa. All these examples demonstrate the effectiveness of song for advocating for political and social change.

This chapter focuses a critical lens on the production, reception, and performance of hymns that drove Simon Kimbangu's Christian religious movement during its emergence in 1921. These hymns were a source of contention between those involved in the *kingunza* movement and the colonial administrators and Protestant and Catholic missionaries who encountered them. While their content drew on evangelical terminology, and Protestant missionaries largely saw the songs as benign, Belgian Catholic missionaries and local administrators were more threatened by their performance. These tensions reveal the fraught nature of colonial rule when faced with Kimbangu and other prophets directly and indirectly challenging white rule and supervision in their spiritual lives. The Belgians wanted to contain what they saw as a religious movement morphing into a political insurrection and doled out harsh punishments for even singing such hymns. Yet these hymns collectively represented a desire for independence and freedom on multiple levels, from the spiritual to the political. The nature of the relationship between the Congolese and European missionaries and colonial administrators would never be the same after Kimbangu, for the movement continued unabated for decades after his arrest, up to and even after independence in 1960. The collective performance of singing hymns played a crucial role in the unraveling of the status quo in the Belgian Congo.

NOTES

1. The Lower Congo, which in the context of the Democratic Republic of Congo includes the province known as Kongo Central (formerly Bas-Congo), is the westernmost province. The majority of the population here speaks KiKongo as a first or second language and identify as BaKongo or BisiKongo.

2. The Lower Congo is one of the few regions where many of the missionaries were Protestant rather than Catholic during most of the colonial period. Some of the missions active in the region included the BMS (Baptist Missionary Society, a British Protestant mission); the American Baptist Foreign Mission Society (ABFMS), an American mission operating mainly south of the Congo River; the Svenska Missions Förbundet (SMF), a Swedish Protestant mission particularly active north of the Congo River in Luozi Territory; and the Christian and Missionary Alliance (CMA), a North American mission with many established missions in the Mayombe area closer to the Atlantic ocean.

3. The Congo Free State was a colony run by King Leopold II of Belgium as his personal colony from 1885 to 1908. Based on a concessions system in which companies were given free rein, leading to massive human rights abuses and millions of deaths (especially of Africans being forced to collect rubber), the Congo Free State was annexed by the parliament of Belgium, which took over as the colonial power from 1908 to 1960.

4. "Onward Christian Soldiers" is a Protestant hymn written by Sabine Baring Gould, an English Anglican priest and composed by Sir Arthur Sullivan, an English composer. The song first appeared in the December 1871 issue of *The Musical Times*. It was soon after widely circulated in *The Hymnary*, a book of hymns published in 1872 (Bradley 2013, 66).

5. Thysville is a small city in the Kongo central province that is known today as Mbanza Ngungu.

WORKS CITED

Andersson, Efraim. 1958. *Messianic Popular Movements in the Lower Congo*. Uppsala, Sweden: Almqvist & Wiksells Boktryckeri AB.

Askew, Kelly M. 2002. *Performing the Nation: Swahili Music and Cultural Politics in Tanzania*. Chicago: University of Chicago Press.

Austin, J. L. 1962. *How to Do Things with Words*. Oxford: Clarendon Press.

Bradley, Ian. 2013. *Lost Chords and Christian Soldiers: The Sacred Music of Sir Arthur Sullivan*. London: SCM Press.

Butler, Judith. 2004. "Performative Acts and Gender Constitution." In *The Performance Studies Reader*, edited by Henry Bial, 154–66. New York: Routledge.

Chikowero, Mhoze. 2015. *African Music, Power, and Being in Colonial Zimbabwe.* Bloomington: Indiana University Press.

Chome, Jules. 1959. *La Passion de Simon Kimbangu, 1921–1951.* Brussels: Les Amis de Présence Africaine.

Coakley, J. F. "Jesus' Messianic Entry into Jerusalem (John 12:12–19 par.)." *Journal of Theological Studies* 46, no. 2 (1995): 461–82.

Covington-Ward, Yolanda. 2016. *Gesture and Power: Religion, Nationalism, and Everyday Performance in Congo.* Durham, NC: Duke University Press.

Frame, William Brown. 1921. *Congo Mission News*, October.

Goffman, Erving. 1959. *The Presentation of Self in Everyday Life.* Garden City, NY: Doubleday.

Goffman, Erving. 1961. *Encounters: Two Studies in the Sociology of Interaction.* Indianapolis, IN: Bobbs-Merrill.

Kodi, M. W. 1993. "The 1921 Pan-African Congress at Brussels: A Background to Belgian Pressures." In *Global Dimensions of the African Diaspora*, 2nd edition, edited by Joseph Harris, 263–88. Washington, DC: Howard University Press.

Mackay, Donald, and Daniel Ntoni-Nzinga. 1993. "Kimbangu's Interlocuter: Nyuvudi's "Nsamu Miangunza (The Story of the Prophets)." *Journal of Religion in Africa* 23, no. 3: 232–65.

Mahaniah, Kimpianga. 1993. "The Presence of Black Americans in the Lower Congo from 1878 to 1921." In *Global Dimensions of the African Diaspora*, 2nd edition, edited by Joseph Harris, 405–20. Washington, DC: Howard University Press.

Mokoko Gampiot, Aurélien. 2017. *Kimbanguism: An African Understanding of the Bible.* University Park: Pennsylvania State University Press.

Molyneux, Gordon. 1990. "The Place and Function of Hymns in the EJCSK (Eglise de Jésus-Christ sur terre par le Prophète Simon Kimbangu)." *Journal of Religion in Africa* 20, no. 2: 153–87.

Morel, Léon-Georges. 1921. Report, "Ministère des Affaires Étrangères (Archives Africaines), Brussels, Belgium." File 1634/9191b, unnumbered document.

Njogu, Kimani. 2007. "Religious Versification: From Depolitisation to Repolitisation." In *Songs and Politics in Eastern Africa*, edited by Kimani Njogu and Hervé Maupeu, 1–22. Dar es Salaam, Tanzania: Mkuki na Nyota Publishers Ltd.

Pemberton, Jeremy. 1993. "The History of Simon Kimbangu, Prophet by the Writers Nfinangani and Nzungu 1921: An Introduction and Annotated Translation." *Journal of Religion in Africa* 23, no. 3: 194–231.

Schechner, Richard. 1985. *Between Theatre and Anthropology.* Philadelphia: University of Pennsylvania Press.

Simbandumwe, Samuel. 1992. "Understanding the Role of a Modern Prophet in Kimbanguist Hymns." *History of Religion* 32, no. 2: 165–83.

Thornton, John. 1998. *Africa and Africans in the Making of the Atlantic World, 1400–1800*, 2nd edition. Cambridge: Cambridge University Press.

Thornton, John. 2001. "The Origins and Early History of the Kingdom of Kongo, c. 1350-1550." *International Journal of African Historical Studies* 34, no. 1 : 89-120.

Treitler, Leo. 2009. "Homer and Gregory: The Transmission of Epic Poetry and Plainchant." In *Oral and Written Transmission in Chant (Music in Medieval Europe)*, edited by Thomas Forrest Kelly, 115–54. Farnham, UK: Ashgate.

Vellut, Jean-Luc, ed. 2005. *Simon Kimbangu 1921: De la predication à la deportation; Les Sources. Vol. 1: Fonds missionaries protestants (1), Alliance missionaire suédoise (Svenska Missionsförbundet, smf)*. Brussels: Academie Royale des Sciences d'Outre Mer.

Vellut, Jean-Luc. 2010. *Simon Kimbangu 1921: De la predication à la deportation; Les Sources. Vol. 1: Fonds missionaries protestants (2), Missions Baptistes et autres traditions évangéliques*. Brussels: Academie Royale des Sciences d'Outre Mer.

Activist Operatic Spaces Depicting Reality

Puccini's *La Bohème* Becomes *Breathe Umphefumlo*

NAOMI ANDRÉ

Since the turn of the millennium postapartheid South Africa has been championed as an unlikely arena and vibrant space for new progressive directions in the international opera scene. This phenomenon has become visible (and audible) to opera audiences not only in Cape Town, Durban, and Johannesburg, but also across Europe and the United States. South African singers are winning international competitions and breaking into the upper strata of elite opera singers. As the calendars and schedules for only three star South African singers reveal (Pumeza Matshikiza, Musa Ngqungwana, and Pretty Yende), in the first half of the 2018–2019 season they performed at leading houses including La Scala, Covent Garden, English National Opera, Staatsoper Stuttgart, Bayerische Staatsoper Munich, Opera Bastille Paris, the Metropolitan Opera, Dallas Opera, Glimmerglass Opera Festival, Opera Philadelphia, Pittsburgh Opera, Utah Opera, Canadian Opera Company . . . the list goes on.[1]

The South African opera scene is exciting, for it encompasses a wide range of operatic activities. First-rate opera performances are being produced in South African opera houses; for example, at the Artscape and Baxter Theatres in Cape Town, you can see works by Mozart, Strauss, and other Western canonical opera composers in productions that reflect what is happening in Europe or the United States (the exception being there are now many more Black and Brown singers on stage in South Africa). Additionally, you can see Western operas presented in a South African adaptation so that the action is placed in a local township and the instrumentation is either the original Western orchestra (e.g., Bizet's 1875 *Carmen* into *U-Carmen eKhayelitsha* in 2005) or transformed into a township jazz or percussion ensemble (e.g., the Isango Ensemble's version of Mozart's 1791 *Magic Flute, Impempe Yomlingo,* in 2000). In such adaptations the language is translated into English and some of the vernacular indigenous languages (most frequently isiXhosa and isiZulu), and the music includes traditional South African melodies and rhythms superimposed on top of, or added in between, the original numbers. Moreover, the plots are set in the present time, with Black South African singers performing an adaption of the original story in new township settings. A third element, and perhaps most important as South Africa enters this golden era, is that we see that South African opera is not exclusively based on European and American works, as though borrowing from a foreign set of jewels. Instead, South Africans have become true participants and have rightfully claimed an original voice in the tradition. They are adding to and expanding the operatic repertoire and genre with newly composed works by Black South African composers collaborating in interracial artistic teams (e.g., *Princess Magogo ka Dinuzulu* by Mzilikazi Khumalo, 2002; *Winnie: The Opera* by Bongani Ndodana-Breen, 2011; *The Flower of Shembe* by Neo Muyanga, 2012; and the *Mandela Trilogy* by Mike Campbell and Peter Louis Van Dijk, revised 2012).[2]

   Breathe Umphefumlo, the South African film adaptation of Puccini's *La Bohème* directed by Mark Dornford-May, not only reveals a connection between the past and present, but also how the contemporaneous present for each production—what was real in 1896 and in 2015—reflects a truth for each original audience. The fraught term "verismo" has been used to outline how late nineteenth-century opera moved away from the aesthetics of Romanticism and melodrama and began to invoke a new lifelike reality combined with modernity.[3] My analysis of *La Bohème* and its transformation into *Breathe Umphefumlo* bolsters opera as an activist space where politics are performed through real-life situations that are given voice in opera.

   In 2004 Nelson Mandela and the Bill and Melinda Gates Foundation launched a campaign to treat HIV and tuberculosis (TB), to confront the deadliness of TB by "calling on the world to recognize that we can't fight AIDS unless we do much more to fight TB as well."[4] At the time of *Breathe Umphefumlo* (2015) and as this book goes to press (2021), the crisis has not abated. As reported by the World Health Organization (WHO) in September 2018, tuberculosis is one of the top ten causes of death worldwide. South Africa and Nigeria are the most affected countries on the African continent and have among the most concentrated occurrences in the world. Within this statistic, the Cape Town region (including Khayelitsha) is one of the districts with the highest incidents of TB in the world.[5] The WHO 2018 report stated that the rate of TB incidence is falling, but at only 2 percent a year; such a rate needs to accelerate to 4–5 percent a year to reach milestones of the "End TB Strategy." What makes this situation even more complex are the number of multidrug-resistant tuberculosis (MDR-TB) cases and the coexistence of people with HIV who have lowered immunity systems and are more susceptible to TB; not surprisingly, many who are HIV-positive also have TB, a situation especially prevalent in South Africa. This is the brutal reality reflected in *Breathe Umphefumlo*.[6]

Puccini's *La Bohème* tells the same story, but from a different historical and geographical perspective. Throughout most of the nineteenth century, consumption (as tuberculosis was then called) was thought to be a hereditary disease, and it was not until the late nineteenth century, right around the time of *La Bohème*, that scientific research revealed it was caused by bacteria and was contagious.[7] At that point, TB emerged as a disease associated with urban centers, poverty, and desperate living conditions. Despite the growing prevalence of the disease, throughout the nineteenth century consumption and TB were also associated with artists such as Anton Chekhov, Lord Byron, Frédéric Chopin, and many others who died of the disease. In French literature especially, popular novels and plays featured leading protagonists as consumptive heroes, as in Alexandre Dumas *fils La Dame aux Camélias* (1848), Victor Hugo's *Les Misérables* (1862), and Henri Murger's *Scènes de la vie de Bohème* (1851). Linda and Michael Hutcheon (1996) outline a thread of nineteenth-century consumptive opera heroines with Antonia in *Les Contes d'Hoffmann* (Offenbach, 1881), Violetta in *La Traviata* (Verdi, 1853), and Mimì in *La Bohème* (Puccini, 1896), these last two based on the Dumas and Murger novels just mentioned.[8]

A tragic fact in the midst of such high occurrences of tuberculosis is that with early detection and a strict drug regimen, today TB is considered to be curable. Even with drug-resistant strains, a combination of multiple TB drugs over a prolonged period in a careful treatment plan can usually cure the disease. Today many people in the West watch *La Bohème* and think that tuberculosis is a problem of the past. The updated version of Jonathan Larson's *Rent* (that premiered in 1996 before a workable treatment plan for HIV-positive people was discovered), where most of the characters are HIV-positive, felt like a plausible adaptation of the dire consequences and "life sentence" such a disease brought. In *Breathe Umphefumlo* (2015), Mimi is suffering from TB;

its current epidemic in Khayelitsha takes the urgency of tuberculosis from the nineteenth century back up to our present today.

Breathe Umphefumlo began as a stage version of *La Bohème Abanxaxhi* (*The Bohemian Transgressors*), which premiered in Cape Town in February 2012 and then had an impressive tour schedule that included the Hackney Empire Theatre in London (May 2012) and the Tokyo Metropolitan Theatre in Japan (December 2012). It was made into the film in 2015 by the Isango Ensemble, directed by Mark Dornford-May. The stage version took the ensemble's earlier engagement with contemporary social justice issues to a new level and was coproduced in partnership with the Global Fund to Fight AIDS, Tuberculosis, and Malaria. The opening of the film continued this commitment to keeping the production connected to the somber reality of the time by immediately presenting statistics that debunk the idea that tuberculosis is an old-fashioned disease that is no longer a problem. Right after the opening credits and within the first few minutes of the film, they project the statements: "Globally two million people died of TB in 2014. Khayelitsha is one of the worst affected areas in the world."

THE ISANGO ENSEMBLE AS A COMMUNITY-BASED SITE FOR NEW NARRATIVES

From an early point at the end of the 1990s, the Cape Town region has seen a few small, yet innovative, opera companies that have grown up through community organization with a mission to focus on the musical talent in the townships. The network of artists that has become the Isango Ensemble is now also one of the longest-running opera production companies in postapartheid South Africa. Their collaborative work covers the Cape Town region through a continuing relationship with the township of Khayelitsha. Their work has had a broad reach as they have traveled internationally (on multiple continents and most frequently to London and New York) and have made films of their works that have won prestigious film awards.[9] They describe themselves as creating "performance with a strong South African flavor by re-imagining Western Theatre classics within a South African or township setting and by creating new work reflecting South African heritage."[10] While they have adapted biblical parables and stories from Western and South African literature, an important part of their mission has been their work with opera, especially as they have helped reimagine the genre.

Their stage production of Bizet's *Carmen*, first performed when the company was known as Dimpho di Kopane, had its premiere as part of the Spier Festival in Stellenbosch and then traveled to London in 2001. This paved the way to their film version, *U-Carmen eKhayelitsha* in 2005. This first film helped them gain widespread international attention. I first heard about *U-Carmen eKhayelitsha* soon after it came out and was among those in the West who loved opera and was thrilled to learn of such an innovative and important new voice in the international opera world.[11]

The Isango Ensemble is not only a company that tours internationally, it also has produced four films (that are listed on their website and available for purchase). These films represent the range of their productions that focus on folk tellings of biblical stories and operatic adaptations. After their groundbreaking *U-Carmen eKahyelitsha* (2005), their second film, *Son of Man* (2006), presents the New Testament life of Christ in contemporary South Africa. *Unogumbe* (*The Deluge*, 2013) starts with Benjamin Britten's *Noye's Fludde* (1958), a biblical parable opera written for children, and moves the setting from England in the Middle Ages to present-day South Africa with the sung text translated into isiXhosa, the subtitles for the film in medieval English, and the orchestration rescored for African instruments. Ten years after *U-Carmen*, the Isango Ensemble produced another major opera film adaptation: *Breathe Umphefumlo* (a translation that could be *Breathe Breath* or *Breathe Soul*) in 2015 based on Giacomo Puccini's *La Bohème* (1896).

PUCCINI, *LA BOHÈME*, AESTHETICS, AND REALISM

Breathe Umphefumlo is a film adaptation that reimagines the plot and setting of Puccini's *La Bohème*. Puccini's opera was based on a French source, Henri Murger's *Scènes de la vie de Bohème*. These scenes were initially published separately in *Le Corsaire*, a Parisian literary journal, between March 1845 and 1849 in a total of nineteen stories. Murger was later joined by playwright Théodore Barrière to write a play based on these stories, which resulted in the coauthored *La Vie de la Bohème* that was staged at the Théâtre des Variétés in 1849. Murger added a few chapters and the collection was published as a novel, *Scènes de la vie de bohème*, in January 1851. Later that same year, Murger supplemented the collection with an additional chapter, and the second edition of the novel was published.

In terms of opera, Puccini composed the first, and most successful, setting of this story (*La Bohème*) with the aid of his librettists Luigi Illica and Giuseppe Giacosa in 1896. This version premiered in Turin at the Teatro Regio. The following year, in 1897, Ruggero Leoncavallo (best known for *I Pagliacci*, 1892) wrote his own *La Bohème*, which premiered at the Teatro La Fenice in Venice. Though Leoncavallo's *Bohème* did not become as popular as Puccini's setting (rarely is Leoncavallo's version staged today, though a few arias are excerpted and performed on recitals), Leoncavallo's position as a leading composer helped establish conventions and aesthetics that shaped opera of that time.

The aesthetics in the genesis of Puccini's *Bohème* provide an important legacy for *Breathe Umphefumlo*. No one goes to the opera admitting that they are looking for "real life." As a genre, opera is known for implausible plot lines, the fantastic, the tragic, and—sometimes—the preposterous. Early operas focused on mythological gods who might show up at the end as a *deus ex machina* to save the day. Tosca jumps off a building to express her despair, Azucena throws the "wrong" baby into the fire (as though there were ever a "right" baby to toss into a fire), and Brünnhilde flings a golden ring into the Rhine to restore world order. Besides the various stories and innumerous characters to keep track of, opera functions very well as an escape from our daily lives. And yet the focus on the depiction of reality is a trenchant theme that links both the Puccini *Bohème* and the Isango Ensemble adaptation *Breathe Umphefumlo*.

In contrast to its reputation as an elitist art that is a playground for the wealthy elite (and this is well-earned through its beginnings in courts and private aristocratic patronage), opera also excavates deeper meanings in the cultural life of its admirers. Two principal strengths are that it leads us into intensely felt emotions and that it connects us to others by reminding us that we all have a shared humanity. As a genre, opera has always been concerned with how it represented real life on stage. The artifice of opera relies upon the knowledge that the characters and story are fictional. Even if an opera is based on a real historical event, the telling of the story is made up. Yet from the earliest days of opera in the seventeenth and eighteenth centuries, the discourse of verisimilitude was a critical topic. This led to the ability to seem realistic and to reflect real experience by creating a world on stage that has elements that feel true-to-life. Even if we have never experienced the exact events of the opera (and, as suggested above, many plots are hyperexaggerated with extreme situations), the effectiveness of the drama is to have the audience pay attention, feel, and care about the plight of the characters on stage.

The late nineteenth century in Italian opera has frequently been linked to the artistic movement "verismo." Though debated in exact meaning, verismo was another articulation of how realism, coming out of the mid-century naturalism movement and also called truthism, became an aesthetic of late century opera.[12] Having roots in French and Italian literature (through writers such as Émile Zola and Giovanni Verga), the operatic version was connected to "*scene popolari*", scenes with local color that featured settings in southern Italy, folk songs, and an emphasis on regular people from the working and lower classes (as opposed to the stories about royalty and aristocracy that dominated earlier Italian opera). The larger verismo movement focused on a more personal moral system and code of honor that might not always fit with the law as it was upheld by the police or in courts of justice, especially if the latter were considered corrupt and disadvantageous to the common folk.[13]

The quintessential operas in the Italian verismo tradition are two short works that are frequently performed together as a double bill.[14] The first, *Cavalleria Rusticana*, was based on the "*scene popolari siciliane*" (a one-act play based on Sicilian themes) by Giovanni Verga (1884) and set by Pietro Mascagni to much acclaim in 1890. The second, *I Pagliacci*, was written by Ruggero Leoncavallo in 1892. Puccini is among the most popular composers today who has multiple works that are considered to fit strongly in the verismo tradition through melodramatic situations infused with brutal violence: *Tosca* (1900), *Madama Butterfly* (1904), *La fanciulla del West* (1910), and *Il tabarro* (1918; the first part of *Il Trittico*).[15]

On the other hand, Puccini's *La Bohème* is not generally seen to highlight verismo characteristics. Instead, *Bohème* is considered to be of a more sentimental nature. The opera focuses on young artists who live on the margins of Europe's respectable society in Paris's Latin Quarter in the 1830s. As they struggle to stay warm in the winter the central themes of falling in love, sustaining their relationships, and figuring out how to move into responsible adulthood shape their stories. This is an ensemble opera where the men are artists (Rodolfo is a poet, Marcello is a painter, Schaunard is a musician, and Colline is a philosopher) and the women are artistic with their crafts and skills (Mimì is a seamstress and Musetta teaches voice lessons). Though they deal with "real life" issues—paying rent, buying food, needing medicine, and fighting illness—there is also a jocularity to the presentation of their stories. The guys playfully banter in the beginning of act 1 about freezing and in act 4 about their broken hearts. While they all need jobs, they are able to cleverly get out of paying rent to their landlord Benoit by getting him a little drunk

and then pushing him out of their apartment as the young bohemians pretend to be offended by the older and married Benoit's flirtatious fantasies
with women other than his wife.

They all need money, but none of them seems to spend time looking for
a job or coming up with a regular source of income. In acts 1 and 2 money
seems to haphazardly appear as Schaunard gets a job playing music until a
parrot dies and the friends successfully trick Musetta's older protector Alcin-
doro into picking up their dinner bill at Café Momus on Christmas Eve. In act
3 Musetta and Marcello are working at a tavern and inn as a singing teacher
and painter, but this is a temporary situation. Later in the act, even when
Mimì and Rodolfo fight and decide to separate, they agree to stay together
until spring because it is hard to be alone in the winter. Continuing long-term
commitments are not a part of their vision for the future. In their nineteenth-
century insulated world, consequences and responsibility can be delayed.

The final act begins just as the first act opened: with Rodolfo and Marcello,
later joined by Schaunard and Colline, horsing around in their garret room.
It is not until the women arrive and Mimì's imminent death is apparent that
there is an abrupt shift in the tone; they suddenly realize that they must act
more maturely and take responsibility for their friend. Colline sells his coat
and Musetta sells her earrings to send for a doctor and to buy medicine and a
hand muff for Mimì. Musetta prays and the friends rally together. Schaunard
and Colline barely have time to react as her death comes so quickly before
the end. Rodolfo cries out Mimì's name before the curtain falls. Marcello and
Musetta come together, and we sense their relationship will be more serious
this time and might possibly even last. Mimì's death can be seen as a sacrifice
that begins to bring sobriety and a new, more mature stage of adulthood to
their lives.

In a stylized prose that was loosely based on his own life and those of
his friends, Murger's *Scenes from the Bohemian Life* were a glimpse into the
lives of young people living in Paris against the backdrop of post-Napoleonic
political instability and revolutionary outbreaks.[16] The story is set in the Latin
Quarter, on the Left Bank in the Fifth Arrondissement that is especially well
known for its prestigious educational institutions (Grandes écoles) with the
Sorbonne, the École normale supérieure, the Collège de France, and several
others. Yet neither Murger nor Puccini portray these young bohemians as
students, nor as active agents engaged with the political protests of the time.
Puccini's opera allows them to live in a heightened time politically and be
a part of the alternative world of the universities and Left Bank, yet not be

further defined than struggling artists who are trying to get by. Unlike the larger themes in earlier Romantic operas (such as those by Verdi or Meyerbeer) that juxtaposed politics or religion against the personal dramas of the protagonists, the ensemble cast of Puccini's opera lives in an insular world that is embellished with the local color of the Latin Quarter in the 1830s, yet the action is not directly affected or shaped by the setting.[17]

Instead, what makes the characters feel modern in today's terms is the atmosphere and texture of this point in their lives: they are young people who are in the process of becoming adults. They are no longer children, yet not fully matured into members of society who are balancing a domestic sphere that includes a family alongside a professional public persona that includes a productive job and career. By today's standards, they belong to an in-between, late adolescent and early twenties group that is infused with a romanticized vision of youth, love, and trying to "make it" as artists.

In continuing the modern correlation, it is as though some of the characters have come from wealthy families who can help bail them out when they get tired of "slumming" it in bohemia. In fact, in *La Vie de la Bohème*, the coauthored play by Murger and Barrière, Rodolphe (Rodolfo) has a wealthy uncle who is trying to marry him to a rich young widow, and Rodolphe's access to wealth is quite achievable if he were to give up his bohemian lifestyle. Puccini's opera only hints at this possibility once.[18] Throughout the different versions of the French novel and play, the patriarchal codes of the nineteenth century in France work better for the young men as they seem to have higher educational levels than the women, and the men share the services of Baptiste, the butler, even when they are not able to pay him regularly. In the play, the men (Rodolphe, Schaunard, and Colline) are creative artists and thinkers; their activities could lead into respectable careers. The two women who get adapted into the opera (Mimì and Musette) list no description or title. By the end of the novel, the men become respectable middle-class gentlemen.

In the play Mimì is an orphan, and in the novel and opera Mimì does not have any family besides her friends. Her death at the end can be staged as either a wake-up call to the others that they need to change their ways or as a sign of impending doom that might overtake them all. Puccini's opera ends immediately with her death and Rodolfo's pained crying out of her name. Though we might hope for the best for Rodolfo in his writing career, for Marcello and Musetta to make a lasting commitment to each other, and for Schaunard and Colline to establish themselves as a musician and a philosopher, we do not get to see what happens afterwards. They have not yet been recognized for their talents and they have not exhibited a great motivation or drive. As we saw in the opening of act 4, the men were in the same position they were in at the beginning of act 1. In the audience, we have little indication of what the next steps for them might actually be.

SETTING THE SCENE IN *BREATHE UMPHEFUMLO*

The world in *Breathe Umphefumlo* is quite different from Puccini's Latin Quarter. The setting is defined in the first few minutes after the opening credits, as the film takes us from the first scenes in the township of Khayelitsha to the short commute to the university. Though the nineteenth-century sources (Murger's novel and Puccini's opera) are set in the educational environment of Paris's Fifth Arrondissement, the university was not featured in those stories. Here we quickly learn that our protagonists are university students and they are connected to the local political environment. The film opens on Youth Day, June 16 (winter in South Africa), and we are introduced to each of the main members of the ensemble cast through their university major and their aspirations after graduation.[19] But before we even meet the main characters, we are given an introduction to the trenchant themes in their world: politics, economics, and education.

After the opening credits, the establishing shot shows a wide view of a large sprawling township: rows of small rectangular shantytown homes made of corrugated metal, a vast array of electrical wires across the network of households, and the far-off view of Table Mountain in the distance. "Umphefumlo" (translated from isiXhosa as "Breath," "Breathe," and "Soul") comes up on the screen as the diegetic sounds of wind and passing cars sweep across the soundscape. Immediately, in a smaller font, the words "An adaptation of Puccini's La Boheme." [*sic*] appear. Next the words change and we see "Khayelitsha. Cape Town, South Africa." The frame transitions to a close-up of laundry blowing in the wind and the word "Winter" is shown. In addition to the wind, we hear the diegetic sounds of the township community with low voices in the background and a child crying.

The scene shifts to a driving white van in motion, and when it passes, we are at the side of a road in front of a concrete building with two low windows. We see a little girl in a pale pink dress with a purple burgundy hat sitting on a wooden chair. She is looking at a little boy, smartly dressed in leopard leggings and a patterned shirt; he is carrying some flowers and brings his wooden chair to sit next to her at the side of the road. They both look to be around six years old and seem like small bystanders in this winter day. They watch a woman walk along the road in front of them and they watch a car go by. The little girl gets up and leaves suddenly. As the little boy gets up and looks after her, the words appear on the bottom of the screen: "Globally two million people died of TB in 2014." The little girl comes back, takes his hand, and leads the boy off screen; we are given another fact: "Khayelitsha is one of the worst affected areas in the world." The two children are off-screen and we see their two empty chairs, haunted images of their absence. We hear deep panting, like someone struggling, and then we see a young woman with labored breathing walking along the street.

During this opening scene, in less than ninety seconds, we are introduced to several things at once. The stark landscape of Khayelitsha in the winter, the depressing (and, to many, surprising) statistics of the 2014 situation of tuberculosis in Khayelitsha, and the disconcerting presence of the little girl and boy—unattended, adorable, and precious—waiting at the side of the road. They are both observers and witnesses to the quickly moving cars and people passing by. With the cold weather and the threatening health crisis, they come to represent innocence and vulnerability in the midst of impending danger. Puccini's opera features lively children in the second act chorus on Christmas Eve outside in the busy Latin Quarter where they beg their mothers to buy them a toy from Parpignol, the toy maker. The Parisian children are presented as tiny consumers with energy and entitlement. The young girl and boy in Khayelitsha are silent, somber, and alone, bystanders as they take care of themselves.

We do not see the little girl and boy again, at least not exactly. Instead, we see them—or others who could have once been them—transformed from primary-school-age children to young adults at university. The scene shifts to a young man playing with a soccer ball. It is still winter in Khayelitsha and could be moments later from the scene with the two little children. The young man with the soccer ball runs from the background into the foreground, chases, and then boards a *kombi* (minibus) taxi. The radio in the taxi lays out the scene by telling us that it is a typical winter day, though the electricity cuts are still a major problem and especially bad around the university. We are told to enjoy the holiday, Youth Day, but not to forget those who died. The announcer further explains, educating those listening who might be too young to remember, as well as those of us watching the film who might not know, what Youth Day is. He refers to "the schoolchildren of Soweto who on this day in 1976 gave their lives to protest against the apartheid educational system. Children who were cruelly gunned down by police while peacefully protesting. We will never forget your sacrifice all those years ago." At this point, less than three minutes into the film, we are introduced to another major theme as children are linked to the protest movement during apartheid through the Soweto Uprising on June 16, 1976. These children—those who participated in the Soweto Uprising, the little boy and girl in the opening of the film thirty-nine years later in 2015, and the young university students we are about to meet—all seem to be on the front lines of a major crisis, from protests to health epidemics. We see that the difficult realities of growing up during the struggle have continued, in altered forms, decades later. Youth are not safe and are confronted with danger; disease lurks around them and a protest from the past becomes relevant for the present.

We find out that the young man with the soccer ball we have been watching is a university student; when he gets out of the *kombi* taxi he is no longer in Khayelitsha, but rather at the dorm for his school (unidentified in the film, but the credits reveal these shots were filmed at Stellenbosch University). The "story" of the film proper seems to begin here, and we are introduced to each of the major characters as we see the adaptation of Puccini's opera *La Bohème* brought into the world of Mark Dornford-May's *Breathe Umphefumlo*. Both works are ensemble-based, with six main characters who form a group of friends in their late teens and early twenties. As the details of the plot are broadly concerned with love, jealousy, and Mimi's eventual death at the end, these South African bohemians are presented in true-to-life ways that are deeply intertwined with the economic and political landscapes of their daily lives.

Table 1. Names of Principal Characters in *La Bohème* and *Breathe Umphefumlo*

La Bohème	Breathe Umphefumlo	Actor/Singer
Rodolfo, poet	Lungelo Silwana	Mhlekazi (Wha Wha) Mosiea
Mimi, seamstress	Lusanda "Mimi" Ndlazi	Busisiwe Ngejane
Marcello, painter	Mandisi Dingaan	Sifiso Lupuzi
Musetta, singer	Zoleka	Pauline Malefane
Schaunard, musician	Sizwe Peter	Zebulon (Katlego) Mmusi
Colline, philosopher	Xolile	Luvo Rasemeni
Alcindoro, Musetta's boyfriend	Ayanda	Zamile Gantana

THE HIGH STAKES OF SOUTH AFRICAN BOHEMIAN LIFE

Puccini's opera *La Bohème* is infused with a verismo realism that, in comparison to the nineteenth-century Romantic grand operas of Verdi, Meyerbeer, and Wagner, follows different expectations. The annoying details of everyday life—freezing in the cold, not having money to pay the rent—become signifiers of much larger themes that cover up the characters' anxieties and insecurities. Rather than admitting his fear that Mimì is dying and he does not have the money or resources to help her, Rodolfo pretends to be jealous and angry at her for flirting with other men. Instead of recognizing the seriousness of her incessant coughing, Mimì would rather pretend that she is fine, that she will not succumb to a fatal disease, and that she does not need to depend on Rodolfo or their friends. While honor, love, and jealousy are presented in obvious bold strokes in mid-nineteenth-century Romanticism, the modernity of *Bohème* is that the characters retain a likeability while also lacking a full sense of self-awareness. Their naivete is an immaturity that is compellingly masked as youthful innocence.

The main characters in *Breathe Umphefumlo* are less protected from the brutal reality in which they live. Unlike the opera with settings in the garret apartment framing the story (acts 1 and 4) and then two outdoor acts filled with local color—Christmas Eve in Paris at Café Momus in act 2 and the snowy tavern scene in act 3—the story of the film progresses in a more linear narrative with an unfolding plot line. In the first half of the film that is set around the university, five of the six main characters are students enrolled at the university. They do not have classes due to the national holiday (Youth Day) and they are struggling with electric power outages; hence, like the 1830s bohemians who are too poor for firewood, these South African students are cold due to the lack of heat; both groups are using candles. As he is running down the stairs of his dorm during a fire alarm (the elevator is out) Lungelo (our Rodolfo), who is studying for a BA in journalism and who aspires to be a poet and soccer star, sees Lusanda drawing flowers in her room. She is a botany major (who aspires to be a Nobel Prize winner) and goes by the name of "Mimi." They sing their magical duet where they fall in love as the darkness descends while lighting their candles. Their voices soar, and the orchestral accompaniment, reduced primarily to pitched percussion (xylophones, marimbas, and steel drums), provides a rapturous sonic net to support their voices without getting in the way. Though Mimi coughs at this first meeting, it is a small point that is not emphasized. We also saw her cough earlier in the film and watched her take medicine; Mimi is aware and is taking care of her illness.

In the fresh bloom of love, Mimi and Lungelo leave the dorm and head to the outdoor market with the Youth Day concert featuring Zoleka, a former music student, turned jazz diva.[20] The electricity has come back on and the mood is festive. The chorus around them sings about South African leaders— Nelson Mandela, Walter Sisulu, Chris Hani, Hector Pieterson, Lillian Ngoyi— and chants "Free Africa." Zoleka's current boyfriend (Ayanda) is a wealthy yet unethical politician, and the crowd taunts him: "he's corrupt, a cheat, a selfish ox full of greed." They continue in a more political vein: "We want funding and student grants. We want to educate ourselves." Sizwe (the Schaunard role), whose character is gay in this adaptation, says about Ayanda, "And he's a total anti-gay pig!" The expected jealousy and confrontation between Zole-ka's current boyfriend and her former one, Mandisi (Marcello from *Bohème*), ensues as Zoleka wins back Mandisi and sends Ayanda away.

The film takes a different turn in the next scene as the students have gotten in trouble (presumably for the rowdiness at the Youth Day concert, though this is not fully explained). In an unexpected move, they find out that they have all been expelled from the university. At that moment, the lighthearted atmosphere of the first part is cut short. The safety net of being students with a promising future ahead of them is yanked away and the reality of their hardship moves from the sidelines into center stage.

The next scene, signaled with the subtitle "2 months later," is back in Khayelitsha. Mimi has been living with Lungelo and Mandisi, away from the university. While we see them together relaxing in the sun near the water, it is clear that Mimi's coughing has gotten worse. Rather than running away and fighting about it (as in the equivalent point of *La Bohème*, act 3), they go to the clinic. In a scene that juxtaposes Mimi and the doctor inside a treatment room and Lungelo with Mandisi in the waiting room, the conflict of the situation rises to the surface. The doctor tells Mimi that she has been good about taking her medicine, but that the TB has advanced and they need to do more tests. Mimi realizes that this is a turning point as she begins to accept the asperity of the situation. She sings, "The truth is hard to bear when you know the ending. I did everything right, but it's not worked." Out in the waiting room, Lungelo laments, "I can't nourish her with my love alone," as he realizes that he is not able to save her.

OPERA TODAY AND STARK REALITIES

Mimi and Lungelo are born into a world where many areas have nearly eradicated TB, but they do not have access to the cure. This realization, despite their best efforts and intentions, is the stark reality that Puccini's opera never reaches. In *Bohème* act 3, the lovers fight as they deny what is happening and no real conclusion is reached. We see their fear and insecurities, but we do not see them do anything as a couple together to confront Mimi's sickness or Rodolfo's anxiety. They decide to stay together until springtime, not because they have a plan, but because they admit that it is hard to be alone in the winter. In the film, Mimi and Lungelo make a plan to stay together and try to earn extra money. We see them picking lilies that grow wild naturally by the side of the road; with Mandisi they wrap up the flowers in small bunches and try to sell them on the street. When this does not yield much, Mimi realizes she is draining their income and she decides to leave and tells them she is going back to live with her family.

In the final portion of the film, we see the subtitle "Spring" with flashbacks to happier times in the past. The film moves to Mandisi and Lungelo, washing a car outside under a highway underpass. The guys have set up a little business washing cars. They have a podium with their handwritten sign, "Ex-Unt Car Wash," with the following eye-catching options:

Colour Wash with an Artist
Pimp it with Poss
Get Clean with the Queens

Soon the other two guys—Sizwe and Xolile (also expelled from the university)—arrive with a modest dinner. After a quick scene that shows Mimi's deteriorated condition as she coughs up blood, we see Zoleka pull up in her little green car to the guys' underpass car wash and help Mimi hobble to a makeshift sitting area made up of abandoned, discarded chairs. They give Mimi the fanciest one, a ragged recliner, and she sinks in, barely able to walk another step. Off to the side, Zoleka says to Mandisi that it turns out that Mimi does not have any family; they are all she has. Mimi had called her, said she was having trouble breathing, knew she was dying, and wanted to be near Lungelo. Mimi and Lungelo sing their final duet, as in the opera, but with the reduced orchestration that has become the sonic signature of the film with pitched percussion and choral voices in the background. Zoleka says a prayer for Mimi and when Mimi dies, Lungelo very softly and painfully says Mimi's name twice. The ending feels quieter than expected. The camera pulls up to the highway above and you see the sun setting over Khayelitsha. The film closes with the diegetic sounds of cars driving by.

Mimi's death is not brought on by neglect or by the fact that she and her friends did not try to take care of themselves. Throughout the film we saw Mimi taking her medication for TB and she (along with Lungelo and Mandisi) visited the health clinic to assess her situation. They do this even though they have been expelled and no longer have access to the university health system. The ending is devastating because in the beginning of the film we have so much hope for this first postapartheid born-free generation moving from the townships to the universities. Mimi dies within a larger postcolony system that has failed her.[21] This setting of Bohème feels especially rooted in its time as the vestigial entanglements of the apartheid regime seem simultaneously close and far away. Apartheid is already a few decades in the past and the promise of belonging to a new generation that has such embedded potential gives us hope; so much seemed to be within their grasp at the beginning of the film. The opportunity to get a university education, pursue one's dreams in the arts and—as was the case with Mimi—science and her love of botany and flowers. Love, happiness, and success should have been accessible.

Instead, the health crisis of tuberculosis provides an eerie connection to the past, both recent and into the nineteenth century. As we learned in the opening moments of the film, TB has become a dangerous threat; "globally two million people died of it in 2014," and "Khayelitsha is one of the worst affected areas." The film's credits thank the Global Fund to Fight AIDS, Tuberculosis, and Malaria and provide a reminder that in addition to TB, South Africa has had a terrible time with the HIV/AIDS epidemic.

This film was released in 2015, during the height of the #RhodesMustFall and #FeesMustFall protests. Across South Africa, student protests erupted on university campuses demanding that schools provide more economic opportunities, not raise school fees, and adapt a decolonized curriculum that wrote their experiences into syllabi and did not erase Black people from history. Though these issues are not overtly addressed in Breathe Umphefumlo, the film holds its own in a climate where the university system is not working for a large group of its students. The arbitrary and ambiguous reasons for their expulsion and the lack of resources for them once they leave the university present a seemingly impossible situation. These brave and vulnerable Black students do not have a lot of guidance on how to navigate academic institutions. They are coming of age in a time when the government systems do not provide viable opportunities for them to make a livelihood. These young adults seem to have fallen in between the cracks of broken assurances and the lack of safety nets for their basic well-being.

On the forefront of engaging opera in South Africa since the new millennium, the Isango Ensemble has been an important voice in the first postapartheid generation of opera. It has a vision that sees township life as a critical artery for telling everyday life stories operatically. Through the use of isiXhosa with English subtitles, they have written the undulations, clicks, and vowel-driven language into an international operatic canon. By filming much of their work in Khayelitsha, they have animated this township as a world stage for real life and as a fantastical arena for allowing a global audience to deeply feel and share love, anger, jealousy, triumph, and defeat. Unlike the fiery blaze of their first film production, *U-Carmen eKhayelitsha*, *Breathe Umphefumlo* takes the intimate and private moments of Puccini's *Bohème* and weaves them together into a story that shows how a hopeful generation of young people are flailing against the odds and confronting the brutal legacy of apartheid in a country that has not yet lived up to its promises.

NOTES

Many thanks to Bongani Ndodana-Breen, Kunio Hara, and Mia Pistorius for their excellent suggestions and comments in the preparation of this chapter.

1. These houses represent the posted schedule for only three South African singers in the first part of the 2018–2019 season: Pumeza Matshikiza (http://pumezamatshikiza.com/), Musa Ngqungwana (http://www.musangqungwana.com/schedule.html), and Pretty Yende (http://prettyyende.com/schedule/). It is not possible to give a full picture of the 2019–2020 season given the global COVID-19 pandemic that closed opera houses and theaters worldwide by mid-March 2020 through the rest of the season and the following 2020-2021 season in most places worldwide.

2. The *Mandela Trilogy* started as *African Songbook: A Tribute to the Life of Nelson Mandela* and was first performed on June 17, 2010, by Cape Town Opera at the Artscape Opera House, in Cape Town in celebration of Mandela's ninety-second birthday and to serve as a cultural showpiece concurrent with the 2010 World Cup Soccer tournament in South Africa (http://capetownopera.co.za/touring-production/mandela-trilogy/).

3. A short, helpful bibliography on the vexed understanding of the "verismo" includes Giger 2007 and Bentley 2019.

4. Check 2004. Mandela himself had TB while he was imprisoned at Robben Island. Fortunately, he was successfully treated.

5. Information on the global situation of TB, specifically in South Africa, has

been gleaned from the World Health Organization (especially helpful sites: https://www.who.int/news-room/fact-sheets/detail/tuberculosis and https://extranet.who.int/sree/Reports?op=Replet&name=%2FWHO_HQ_Reports%2FG2%2FPROD%2FEX-T%2FTBCountryProfile&ISO2=ZA&LAN=EN&outtype=html), "TB Statistics South Africa (http://www.tbfacts.org/tb-statistics-south-africa/) and the Treatment Action Campaign ("Together We Can Kick TB out of Khayelitsha," March 24, 2010, https://tac.org.za/news/together-we-can-kick-tb-out-of-khayelitsha/).

6. As this book goes to press, we are confronted with the new deadly pandemic, COVID-19, which will most likely compound the lethal crises as it interacts with TB and HIV/AIDS.

7. German scientist and doctor Robert Koch is generally credited for introducing the modern ideas of TB in his famous lecture March 24, 1882, that announced the discovery of *Mycobacterium tuberculosis* and gave a medical basis for thinking about TB.

8. Hutcheon 1996, 29–50.

9. For more information about the Isango Ensemble see their website http://isango-ensemble.co.za/. I have also written about this group and their production of *U-Carmen eKhayelitsha* (stage and film) in André 2018, 155–56.

10. From the Isango Ensemble website, "About Us—Our History," http://isangoen-semble.co.za/.

11. I have written about *U-Carmen eKhayelitsha* in André 2018 and André 2016, chap. 5.

12. See Giger 2007, note 2; and Bentley 2019.

13. Sansone 2001; Dibbern 2000, 237–310.

14. *Cavalleria Rusticana* is in one act. *I Pagliacci* has a prologue and two acts, but works well as the second half of an evening with the two operas presented with one intermission between the two.

15. "Giacomo Puccini," *The New Grove Masters of Italian Opera*, 331, calls these the verismo operas of Puccini.

16. For a more detailed discussion of the revolutions in Paris between 1830 and 1848 see Pinkney 1972, 512–20.

17. Verdi's *Don Carlos* (1867) brings into play the politics surrounding King Philip II's court during the Spanish Inquisition; *Aida* (1871) focuses on the orientalist view of the politics between ancient Egypt and Ethiopia with a strong religious dogma of the Egyptian priests that is represented by Western contrapuntal harmony. Meyerbeer's *Les Huguenots* (1836) takes place during the St. Bartholomew's Day Massacre in 1572 when the French Catholics attacked the French Protestants (Huguenots). *Le Prophète* (1849) also involves historical religious conflict, based on the life of John of Leiden, an Anabaptist leader in sixteenth-century Münster, North Rhine-Westphalia Germany.

18. In Murger's novel (*Scenes from the Bohemian Life*) there are several chapters that refer to wealthy relatives of the struggling artists (e.g., Chapter 4, "Ali-Rodolphe; or, the Turk perforce" with his uncle Monetti, a stove-maker, chimney-doctor, and sergeant of the National Guard who helps out Rodolphe a little). In the opera there is one quick

reference in act 2 when Rodolfo and Mimì buy the little hat. When she looks at a coral necklace, Rodolfo says, "Ho uno zio millionario." ["I have a millionaire uncle."]. Oddly, this is never referred to again, even when they all need money. Though Murger's Rodolphe does have a wealthy uncle, it is not clear in the opera if it is true or a wished-for dream. Or, even, an empty boast to impress Mimì (whom, we remember, he has only just met and is no doubt hoping to sweep off her feet by any means possible).

19. In the film, this is accomplished a bit awkwardly with a freeze-frame and a jump scene to an imagined graduation where they hold up a large placard that has their degree on one side and an accomplishment on the other. Mimì's card, for instance, says "BSc Botany" on one side and "Nobel Prize Winner" on the other.

20. Zoleka (the Musetta character) is portrayed by Pauline Malefane, one of the original members and the codirector of the ensemble with her husband Mark Dornford-May.

21. I am referring to Achille Mbembe's construction of the postcolony, a way to address specifically the postapartheid/postcolonial situation in South Africa.

BIBLIOGRAPHY

Abbate, Carolyn, and Roger Parker. 2012. "Realism and Clamour." In *A History of Opera*, 397–424. New York: W. W. Norton & Company.

André, Naomi. 2018. *Black Opera: History, Power, Engagement*. Urbana-Champaign: University of Illinois Press.

André, Naomi. 2016. "*Carmen* in Africa: French Legacies and Global Citizenship." *Opera Quarterly* 32, no. 1 (Winter): 54–76.

Barrière, Theodore, and Henri Murger. 2014. *The Bohemian Life: A Play in Five Acts*. Translation and adaptation by Harris M. Worchel of *La Vie de Bohème: Pièce en cinq actes* (1849).

Bentley, Charlotte. 2019. "Beyond *Verismo*: Massenet's *La Navarraise* and 'Realism' in *Fin-di-siècle* Paris." *Journal of the Royal Musical Association* 144, no. 1: 29–54.

Budden, Julian. 1994. "The Musical World of the Young Puccini." In *The Puccini Companion*, edited by William Weaver and Simonetta Puccini, 39–60. New York: W. W. Norton & Company.

Carter, Tim. 2015. "Giuseppe Giacosa, Luigi Illica, and Giacomo Puccini, *La Bohème* (Turin 1896)." In *Understanding Italian Opera*, 197–241. Oxford: Oxford University Press.

Check, Erika. 2004. "Mandela Launches Fight Against HIV and TB." *Nature*, July 15.

Dahlhaus, Carl. 1989. "Melodrama and Verismo." In *Nineteenth-Century Music*, translated by J. Bradford Robinson, 351–59. Berkeley: University of California Press.

Dibbern, Mary. 2000. "Introduction to the Literary Sources." In *Carmen: A Performance Guide*, 237–310. Hillsdale, NY: Pendragon Press.

Giger, Andreas. 2007. "Verismo: Origin, Corruption, and Redemption of an Operatic Term." *Journal of the American Musicological Society* 60, no. 2 (Summer): 271–315.

Giradi, Michele. 2000. *Puccini: His International Art*. Translated by Laura Basini. Chicago: University of Chicago Press.

Gobbato, Angelo. 2018. *A Passion for Opera*. Aukland Park, South Africa: Staging Post.

Greenwald, Helen. 2012. "*Ars moriendi*: Reflections on the Death of Mimì." In *The Arts of the Prima Donna in the Long Nineteenth Century*, edited by Rachel Cowgill and Hilary Poriss, 167–85. Oxford: Oxford University Press.

Groos, Arthur, and Roger Parker. 1986. *Giacomo Puccini: La Bohème*. Cambridge: Cambridge University Press.

Hutcheon, Linda, and Michael Hutcheon. 1996. *Opera: Desire, Disease, Death*. Lincoln: University of Nebraska Press.

Murger, Henri. 1984 [1905]. *The Bohemians of the Latin Quarter*. First published by Sociétè des beaux-arts, Paris. Reprint, New York: Howard Fertig, Inc.

Murray, John. F. 2004. "A Century of Tuberculosis." *American Journal of Respiratory and Critical Care Medicine* 169: 1181–86.

Phillips-Matz, Mary Jane. 2002. *Puccini: A Biography*. Boston: Northeastern University Press.

Pinkney, David H. 1972. "The Revolutionary Crowd in Paris in the 1830s." *Journal of Social History* 5, no. 4 (Summer): 512–20.

Sansone, Matteo. 1994. "Giordano's *Mala vita*: A 'Verismo Opera Too True to Be Good,'" *Music and Letters* 75, no. 3: 381–400.

Sansone, Matteo. 2001. "Verismo (opera)." *Grove Music Online*. Accessed February 4, 2019. http://www.oxfordmusiconline.com.proxy.lib.umich.edu/grovemusic/view/10.1093/gmo/9781561592630.001.0001/omo-9781561592630-e-0000029210.

Schwartz, Arman. 2016. *Puccini's Soundscapes: Realism and Modernity in Italian Opera*. Florence: Leo S. Olschki.

Verbaan, Aly, and Siyavuya Mzantsi. 2015. "Tutu Holding Out Hope amid TB's Devastating Effect on Country." *Cape Times* (South Africa), March 15, regional news, p. 3.

Walsh, Richard, Jeffrey L. Staley, and Adele Reinhartz, eds. 2013. *Son of Man: An African Jesus Film*. Sheffield, UK: Sheffield Phoenix Press.

Wilson, Alexandra. 2007. "*La Bohème*: Organicism, Progress and the Press." In *The Puccini Problem: Opera, Nationalism, and Modernity*, 40–68. Cambridge: Cambridge University Press.

FILM REVIEWS OF *BREATHE UMPHEFUMLO*

Cronje, Jan. 2014. "'La Boheme' Adaptation and a Cry for Understanding." *The Weekend Argus* (South Africa), August 23, regional news, p. 7.

Duma, Mnqobi. 2015. "Review: *Breathe (Umphefumlo)* When You Don't Have Enough to Breathe." Durban International Film Festival. reel-times-blog. July. https://durbanfilmfest.co.za/news/reel-times-blog/item/1837-review-breathe-umphefumlo-when-you-don-t-have-enough-to-breathe.html.

Lodge, Guy. 2015. "Berlin Film Review: *Breathe Umphefumlo*." *Variety*, February 9.

https://variety.com/2015/film/festivals/berlin-film-review-breathe-umphefumlo
-1201427629/.

Mitchell, Wendy. 2015. "Breathe Team Sings with Beggar's Opera." *Screen International* (February 7).

Romney, Jonathan. 2015. "*Breathe Umphefumlo.*" *Screen Daily*, February 9.

Rooney, David. 2015. "*Breathe Umphefumlo*: Berlin Review." *Hollywood Reporter*, August 2. https://www.hollywoodreporter.com/review/breathe-umphefumlo-berlin-revi ew-771070.

Rosser, Michael. 2014. "La Boheme Update Wraps Shoot." *Screen International* (October 9).

Shackleton, Liz. 2015. "Fortissimo Picks Up Dornford-May's Breathe." *Screen International* (January 27).

Vourlias, Christopher. 2015. "U-Carmen Team Parses Puccini." *Variety*, February 3, p. 123.

The Intrinsic Power of Songs Sung During Protests at South African Institutions of Higher Learning

NOMPUMELELO ZONDI

INTRODUCTION AND BACKGROUND

In South Africa, songs have been used in numerous social and political activities to give voice, unity, and power to the people. They fulfill the role of providing collective vocal expression, as was witnessed in the time of apartheid, and they have utility and meaning in contemporary times. In keeping up with age-old warrior traditions of the ancient founders of the country, struggle songs continue to be viewed as a fundamental part of South Africa's past, present, and future (Nkoala 2013). This chapter demonstrates, and is a tribute to, the power of the old battle or mocking songs. These songs were once signatures for action in past struggles.

The #FeesMustFall movement (2015–2016) succeeded in harnessing and rendering the old in innovative forms that brought about a new gravitas that captured the present era. In essence, the songs mentioned in this chapter reflect their contribution to the uneasy calm that prevailed in the South African higher learning sector nationally. By interrogating the fundamental and intrinsic power of songs during student protests, the views of the students who participated in the #FeesMustFall demonstrations reveal that these songs serve a variety of functions in different historical epochs. One such view pertains to song as a voice of the underprivileged in the postapartheid era. By "owning" such songs and seizing the opportunity to make their experiences in the higher education environment the focus of the songs, read in conjunction with the narratives that accompany them, the holistic meanings of the songs are revealed as they relate to current issues affecting higher education.

The context for this analysis of struggle songs goes back to the apartheid state as a form of Afrikaner nationalism. Apartheid, a word meaning "apartness" and whose legacy will live for generations in South Africa, was official national policy between 1948 and 1994, beginning with the National Party. Their political leader, Hendrik Verwoerd, is credited with being the chief architect of apartheid. Separation or apartness according to race existed in every aspect of daily life; Black Africans became aliens in their homeland. In practice, apartheid was especially brutal because economic interdependences between Blacks and whites made it largely impossible to keep the races apart. Apartheid laws forced millions of Blacks to live in impoverished areas in the townships and in the rural areas where they were denied basic human rights. The basic and higher education systems of South Africa were also not exempted from racial divides, and this is a key point for understanding the background of the #FeesMustFall movement. Under the scrutiny of world powers, some of which intervened by applying economic sanctions, the apartheid system eventually fell, as South Africa underwent a severe period of international isolation and intense pressure to change (Barnes, 2008).

When South Africa achieved democracy in 1994, the postapartheid higher education sector required fundamental transformation. Akoojee and Nkomo (2007) argued for creative approaches to engage issues of redress in, access to, and transformation of higher education. Malabou (2008, 5) argues that transformation, by its very nature, implies constant remodeling, modification, and restructuring. Songs that emerged from within the Black South African communities afflicted by apartheid became a tool that served a different purpose than it had during apartheid. These songs kept students zealous as they worked together to achieve their educational demands, regardless of their racial and social class. Even though the fluidity of songs knows no boundaries, their new meaning in different contexts illustrates how performance, art, and politics can come together, even when supporting different causes.

The governing African National Congress (ANC) and its alliance partners, the Congress of South African Trade Unions (COSATU) and the South African Communist Party (SACP), continue to have the monopoly on the use of struggle songs (Nkoala 2013). My chapter here supports Nkoala's observations, but it also reveals that students have utilized struggle songs to address new higher education challenges. In the same way Black artists resorted to music to help society remain sane amidst the devastation of apartheid, concerned scholars found a voice in poetry as a way of frustrating the ruling class while championing the cause of the oppressed. In his protest poetry Benedict Wallet Vilakazi, writing between the 1930s and 1940s, indicated how "human beings need to be treated with dignity regardless of race and class" (Zondi and Canonici 2005, 84–85). His poetry reveals that "the basic human principle was grossly trampled upon by colonial and capitalist system that had befallen the Black population of Africa" (ibid.). Exploring his poem "Ngoba . . . Sewuthi" ("Because . . . You Now Say"), Zondi and Canonici (ibid.) highlight Vilakazi's contribution to the fight against Black people's sufferings under the injustices inflicted by the colonial government. They argue that such a government represented the interests of white capitalists who aimed at personal enrichment without caring about the social development of the Black population that was deprived of all human rights and was living in a state of servitude on its own land. In the examination of another of Vilakazi's famous protest poems, "Ezinkomponi" ("In the Mine Compounds"), I found Vilakazi expressing the voice of the disenfranchised miners in their struggle with mine magnates and machinery to authenticate their respective roles in the conflict (Zondi 2011). This famous protest poem remains a cry for help in the face of destructive industrial advancement that pits the values of gold and money against human values that are worth living for.

In a similar vein, between the 1950s and 1980s, musicians composed and produced many powerful protest and freedom songs. These motivated, inspired, and encouraged the oppressed never to give up. In that sense, for Black people, song was one of the powerful means of communicating their feelings to those who oppressed them. In contemporary times, the tradition of criticism and protest has found various methods of expression. In a societal context like that of South Africa, protest is often directed against the injustices of the government. In most cases, people take to the streets and demonstrate their protest through mass action. The demonstrations are usually an articulation of interests designed to publicize the demonstrators' feelings of injustice and to attract the attention of leaders. Protest has become a channel of accessing those who wield political power. In this regard, protest and demonstration are methods used by people who are not the elite; they have become the tactic of society's powerless, those who do not have access and cannot influence decision makers.

Struggle songs are characteristic South African instruments of social power that are reminiscent of the pre-1994 struggles. While most of them have been modified to fit contemporary contexts, their essence continues to advance the struggle. During the protests that took place at institutions of higher learning in mid-October 2015 through 2016, in a chain of events that happened over a period of eighteen months at all universities country-wide, the same songs that were sung during apartheid played a central role during the student-led protest movement #FeesMustFall. Even though the name of the movement suggests that it was about the demands to abolish university fees, additional concerns were raised: stricter consequences for sexual harassment and assault (protesting the growing number of rapes on campuses) and the decolonization of education. Between October 2015 and December 2016 there was an increase in vicious incidents accompanying these demonstrations. It is exactly during these periods that students supported a newly named philosophy called "Afro-radicalism" and advocated for turning back the clock to 1994. They argued that the transition in 1994 out of apartheid was a failure. They demanded to go back to that critical time to create a truly democratic South Africa where their concerns and well-being would be woven into the fabric of the new state. These students and their supporters also called for decentering the Eurocentric supremacy embedded in the academic disciplines and replacing it with an educational system that embraced knowledge about Africa and the Global South. Additionally, the protesters demanded the deceleration of student fees and increasing government funding for universities.

Chapter 2, subsection 29(1)(b) of the Constitution of South Africa (1996) states that "[E]veryone has a right to higher education which the state, through reasonable measures, must make progressively available and accessible." The provision, however, does not spell out that the state is obligated to provide free higher education. Prior to 2015, students from poorer institutions with almost all Black enrollment had regularly been objecting to mounting fees and the cost of higher education since 1994. The #FeesMustFall demonstrations underscored the predicament of nonaffordability of higher institution tuition fees for students coming from needy and middle-class homes. The goal was to provoke higher education bureaucrats into devising alternative funding mechanisms to address the problem. The rationale was that since education is a public good that has significant positive influences on society, all stakeholders ought to contribute to meeting the costs of providing higher education. Beneficiaries of these positive influences, such as the government and private sector, must join the students and institutions of higher learning to contribute to the solution. The year 2015 marked the first time since democracy that students from tertiary institutions flexed their muscles under the #FeesMustFall banner to steer the wheel of transformation regarding access to higher education for marginalized groups. Remarkably, these protests brought together students from both historically advantaged and historically disadvantaged universities. Additionally, these demonstrations attracted wide media coverage that generated solidarity protests in London and New York. Prior to 2015, institutions that catered mainly to disadvantaged Black students had experienced protests and unrest as students made a number of demands, including concerns about escalating university fees. These earlier appeals, however, went under the mainstream radar and were largely ignored. The involvement of other racial groups meant that the financial crisis that had been affecting Black students from poverty-stricken communities for more than two decades was finally being taken seriously.

This current chapter is informed by research I conducted between 2004 and 2007 in the rural community of Zwelibomvu in KwaZulu-Natal, South Africa (Zondi 2008). After observing how steeped in song the residents of Zwelibomvu were, I set out to investigate the role of songs in this community. What had prompted me to conduct such a study was that within a variety of ceremonies, there was almost no occasion that took place in this community where song was absent. In my study I confined myself to the songs sung by the women of this region. The fascination with that study left an ineffaceable passion for studying songs in various contexts. It is against this backdrop that when the #FeesMustFall movement emerged, with songs being central to it, I seized the opportunity to find out if there were new meanings attached to the struggle songs that were already known but which were now primarily being sung by the "born frees" (born after 1994) during the movement.

THEORETICAL FRAMEWORK

Protest songs of any nature are shaped by the specific contingencies that create each context. Abdullah Ibrahim (in Mbhele and Walker 2017), in writing about the documentary film *Amandla! A Revolution in Four Part Harmony*, argues that there has seldom been a protest movement that has not, at some stage, made use of song as a device to keep up the morale during protests. My study here focuses on data that was collected from four universities in the KwaZulu-Natal province. In line with Ibrahim's assertion, my research brings an in-depth representation of the protesting students who were steeped in song. The focus had to be on the meanings and interpretations the current students attached to the songs, not on previously held general notions about these songs. To conduct this study, it was necessary to have a clear grasp of these songs and to understand the background of South Africa's apartheid regime and the encoded meanings that were a part of a specific song repertoire.

#FeesMustFall songs are embedded in historical memory and function as tools to persuade the authorities that change is inevitable. As Pring-Mill has observed, the significance of struggle songs lies in that they present historical actions documented with a passion that not only represent an individual singer's personal response, but also the perspective that comes from a mutual understanding of events from a larger collective (Pring-Mill 1987, 179). In this sense, the drive that motivates protesters ensures that speaking in one voice unites and motivates them to maintain resilience amidst opposing forces. Perkins asserts that "inspiration play[ed] an important role in mobilizing the hearts and energies of people to strike back at forces which appear[ed] to be insurmountable (Perkins 1976, 226).

The songs examined in this chapter were used by freedom fighters during political struggle in South Africa; they became famous among Black South Africans and they became part of the legacy of apartheid. This study examines what the songs sung during #FeesMustFall meant to the protesters in the face of oppression and neglect Thus the study moves beyond my previous research (Zondi and Canonici 2005) and focuses on the contemporary function of songs as engaged by young people trying to prove that democracy belongs to all, specifically in the context of higher education.

METHODOLOGY

Holloway and Wheeler (2002, 51) hold that in qualitative research "the processes and the social and cultural contexts which underlie various behavioural patterns . . . [are] mostly concerned with exploring the 'why' question of research." Taking this point forward, Mouton (2001, 148) maintains that qualitative studies provide "the life worlds of the actors being studied and produce insider perspectives of the actors and their practices." In line with these assertions, my study makes use of qualitative research methods to examine students' protest songs during the #FeesMustFall campaign in 2015–2016 that erupted on campuses all over South Africa and became a national movement. The goals of this research were to analyze why and how students found songs central to their demonstrations. This study chose four universities in the province of KwaZulu-Natal, South Africa, that provided a representative sample of what was happening in the universities nationally; this chapter also presents the students' own views on this subject. Institutions that participated in the study were University of KwaZulu-Natal (Pietermaritzburg Campus), University of Zululand, Durban University of Technology, and Mangosuthu University of Technology. These were selected based on their location in the province of KwaZulu-Natal, the province in which I, as the researcher, resided. Given the financial crises around higher education throughout the country, these four institutions well represented the lack of funding for poorer students.

A BRIEF BACKGROUND OF THE PARTICIPATING INSTITUTIONS

The following section provides a brief background and context of the institutions informing the study. These short histories help situate these institutions in the time of apartheid and after any changes, such as the consolidation and combination of universities, after apartheid was dismantled in 1994.

The University of KwaZulu-Natal (UKZN as it is known) became a reality after the merger of the University of Natal and the University of Durban-Westville on January 1, 2004 (https://www.ukzn.ac.za>about-ukzn>history). Prior to that, the University of Natal included the campus in Pietermaritzburg. In fact, when founded in 1910 as the Natal University College, the campus was in Pietermaritzburg. In 1931, it expanded to include a campus in Durban. All the while, the entity catered to whites only. Both staff and students were against government imposed racial segregation and they actively fought for a nonracial education. In 1947, a medical school for nonwhites was opened in Durban. In time, other campuses emerged and with them a nonsectarian ethos. The University of Durban-Westville was established in the 1960s as the College for Indians on Salisbury Island in Durban Bay (https:// ukzn. ac.za/about-ukzn/history/). Without disbanding any of the campuses, more campuses were created after the merger, with the focus on the reorganization of the program offerings in various campuses. Presently, the University of KwaZulu-Natal is one of the most transformed universities nationally. In its transformation charter, it categorically states that its notion of transformation is "deeper and broader than a narrow categorization based on race and gender representation," but that it means "changing the identity and culture of the university in every respect of its mission" (https://www.ukzn.ac.za docs). For this reason, Pietermaritzburg adds an important profile for inclusion in this study.

The University of Zululand (Unizulu) was established in 1960 as the university college of Zululand. Perceived as the epitome of apartheid South Africa as it applied to racially and ethnically segregated education, it is situated in Empangeni under the Mkhwanazi Traditional Authority. In the beginning, it was affiliated with the University of South Africa (Unisa) and catered to Zulu and Swazi groups (https:// www.unizulu.ac.za/about-uni-zulu/historical-milestones/). Currently, the University of Zululand is the only comprehensive tertiary educational institution north of the Tugela River in KwaZulu-Natal, South Africa. Positioned in the rural community, Unizulu continues to cater mainly to historically underprivileged students. If this institution were excluded from this study, the study would not present a holistic picture of the songs studied.

Durban University of Technology (DUT) came about in 2002 as a result of the merger of Technikon Natal and ML Sultan Technikon. The previous Natal Technikon was founded by Dr. Samuel George Campbell in 1907 and mainly catered to white students. On the other hand, ML Sultan was founded by an unschooled philanthropist, Hajee ML Sultan, in 1946. It catered to Indian students. This was ML Sultan's way "to expose the racist logic of Verwoerd" (https:// www.mlsultan.com/ml-sultan-technikon.html). The institution now has three campuses in Durban and two in Pietermaritzburg, and it focuses on practical education. From this brief description, it is easy to understand the racial history of South Africa especially with reference to higher education. The history provided here takes a similar trajectory as the University of KwaZulu-Natal.

Mangosuthu University of Technology (MUT) was formerly known as Mangosuthu Technikon. The idea of establishing a tertiary educational institution specializing in technical subjects was put forward by Mangosuthu Buthelezi, a leader of the long-standing Inkatha Freedom Party (IFP) in KwaZulu-Natal. The driving force behind its establishment was "benevolence and empowerment of the disenfranchised" (https://www.mut.ac.zahistorical-background). While the institution catered to Black population groups, because it was situated in KwaZulu-Natal, Zulu ethnic groups were the main beneficiaries. The institution also held the views of the Inkatha Freedom Party in the past, but today it represents students from all political organizations in South Africa.

DATA COLLECTION

Data for this study came strictly from students who had physically participated in the #FeesMustFall demonstrations at these four institutions. The questionnaires written in English provided a brief background of the study. The first page of the questionnaire guidelines explained how the questionnaires were to be returned; information about time frames and how responses were going to be treated was also provided. Participation was voluntary. In order to maintain uniformity and since responses were expected back two weeks after the questionnaires had been distributed, colleagues from participating institutions recruited and provided one reliable student to serve as a research assistant in the distribution and collection of the questionnaires. Thus while I had initially designated e-mail as a way to return completed questionnaires, the plan swiftly changed when research assistants pointed out challenges that some of the students might experience. The most pertinent hitch was students not being able to access free Wi-Fi after hours (and in some cases even during the day while on campus), as not all institutions were adequately equipped. Thus, in order to maintain uniformity we decided that all questionnaires would be left with the research assistant at each participating institution.

Given that all participating institutions were in the province of KwaZulu-Natal, we chose Monday, February 13, 2017, between 8:00 a.m. and 6:00 p.m. to deliver the two hundred copies at participating institutions. Each package contained two hundred questionnaires, which were individually stamped with the name of a participating institution and marked with numbers 1–200.[1] In each case, student research assistants received them. It was agreed that these would be distributed on February 15 between 12:00 noon and 4:00 p.m. and that research assistants would stand near the student center of their institutions to distribute them to willing students. At one university the research assistant reported that questionnaires were finished within the first two hours of their distribution, while at the other three institutions, the last copies were distributed closer to the deadline, 4:00 p.m. Students were expected to return their responses two weeks later by placing them in a box marked for that purpose and which would be placed at a specific office next to the student center (at each participating institution). The due date for completed questionnaires was Thursday, March 2, 2017.

Besides the participants' biographical details, which appeared on the questionnaire and which respondents were not obliged to provide, three compulsory questions appeared on the questionnaire. They were:

- Are you a student at the campus where you found this questionnaire? **(YES/NO)**. If the answer is **NO**, please do not proceed with this questionnaire. However, if the answer is **YES**, please provide the name of the institution and proceed to the second question.
- Did you participate in the recent students "#FeesMustFall" movement? **(YES/NO)**. If your answer is **NO**, then please do not proceed with this questionnaire. However, if the answer is **YES**, then proceed to the next and last question
- In your opinion, what role did songs have in "#FeesMustFall" movement? Kindly elucidate on your response and provide at least one song that mainly spoke to you.

In total, eight hundred questionnaires were distributed. Not all of them, however, were returned. The following table reflects the exact figures per participating institution: In total, 416 completed questionnaires were received; receiving more than half the original questionnaires is a fair sample. The next process was to select ten responses from each campus randomly to ensure that data sample reflected fair representation of participating campuses. Thus, a total of fifty responses were studied and coded from HISR-01-HISR-50. Songs presented in this study are those that participants referred to in the questionnaire. They thus form part of the data for the study.

The next stage was to go through the responses of the fifty participants from which again only ten respondents were randomly chosen to give a sense of what students thought to be the role of songs during the #FeesMustFall movement. The rationale behind this selection was that they represented general themes that emerged from the rest of the data. Since it would not have been possible to present all fifty responses, ten were selected alongside narratives that accompanied them. For anonymity, names were not used even in cases where participants gave their names. Rather, pseudonyms and codes allocated during data categorization were used.

As requested in the questionnaire, most students quoted at least one song as part of their response to the third question, which expedited the choice of songs to draw from in this study. For ease of navigation, all songs will be presented immediately followed by their corresponding participants' views on what they meant to them in the context in which they were performed. At the end, a personal reflection will guide a discussion, providing some trends that emerge from the data. Participants were free to provide their views in their mother tongue, but those presented here have been translated into English.

Similarly, songs as texts have been presented in the original indigenous language in which they were sung (which was either isiZulu or isiXhosa), with their close English equivalent translations. It is vital to describe methodically the translation process that went into the songs as well as participants' opinions about them, as this is fundamental in the understanding of the workings of African indigenous languages. In so doing, a number of considerations informing translation practices and phenomena have been taken into account. These point to developments that have influenced translation studies over time. In this study, drawing on five approaches, I have adopted an eclectic approach as the models work better when viewed in this more holistic light. While there are positive aspects in each of the approaches, none of them fully encompassed the meanings. As a native speaker of these languages, I was able to bring these various approaches together to provide a more comprehensive meaning. The models and approaches I used include the word-for-word (literal) versus sense-for-sense (free) translation process (in Munday 2016), the equivalence-based approach (Kruger and Wallmach 1997; Naude 2011), the functional approach (Reiss 1989), the polysystem approach (Even-Zohar 1990), and the Descriptive Translation Studies approach (Toury 1995; Hermans 1999).

In order to show how the synergies in the approaches mentioned above work, I offer a few highlights of each model. In word-for-word translation, translations are literal, while sense-for-sense translation incorporates sense or intended meaning of the source text with the corresponding meaning in the target language. The equivalence-based approach propagates the view that for the target text to be considered a good translation it has to be the mirror image of the source text. The functional approach shifts the focus on source text as the only determining factor of how the translation process should be carried out by considering the culture within which the translation activity occurs. The polysystem approach postulates that when literatures of minor languages are translated into literatures of more powerful and dominant languages, they tend to assume the norms and conventions of those influential languages. Lastly, Descriptive Translation Studies emphasize cultural context while admitting that translations cannot be the exact equivalents of the source text. By trying to move away from any of the normative and prescriptive lines of thought (inherent in each approach), I have adopted a heterogeneous approach that takes into account positive and helpful aspects from each of the models presented. Thus I believe my translations to be as reliable as they can possibly be. The participants' positions on the role of songs are presented in English, as it is the language in which all participants responded.

SONG ANALYSIS

In this study, I demonstrate how remarkable song has been in shaping new radical student community informed by political narrative. While some of the participants mentioned more than one song, in this study only one of the songs voluntarily cited (by each participant in the sample) will be studied. The following **five** songs are presented in the order of popularity as illustrated by the highest number of participants in the study sample who mentioned that song. The message in the song becomes clear when studied against the views held by students about the song. Thus I also include student perspectives (labeled as HISR for each completed questionnaire) for each song.

The first song to be explored was cited by forty-seven of the fifty samples, or 94 percent. In this study, the leader or the soloist sings the parts labeled as "Call" to which the refrain or the chorus respond, which is termed "Response." The discussion around two sets of songs will be handled simultaneously due to the theme that runs through them, while the last one will be discussed separately. I must point out from the onset that narratives that accompany these songs reflect the respondents' views. I have tried to respect my participants by not trying to intercept their responses to suit anticipated or preferred interpretations.

Song 1: Senzeni na? (What have we done?)

Call:	Senzeni na?
	(What have we done)
Response:	Senzeni na? Senzeni na?
	Senzeni na? Senzeni na?
	Senzeni na? Senzeni na?
	Senzeni na? Senzeni na?
Call:	Sono sethu
	(Our sin)
Response:	Sono sethu ubumnyama
	(Our sin is being Black) (sung eight times)
Call:	Vuka Shaka
	(Rise up Shaka)
Response:	Vuka Shaka, sibagwaze
	(Rise up Shaka, let us stab them) (sung eight times)

HISR-03 PERSPECTIVE

Although new songs have been composed over the years in response to current struggles, some of them have remained unchanged. One such song is **Senzeni na?** This song spurs us on during our protests, as it reminds us of what apartheid did to our nation. We, born frees, want to put a total end to discrimination of any kind, especially where access to education is concerned. We do not want our children to go through the kinds of injustices that still surround us more than twenty years after democracy. This song fuels us with vitality as we celebrate complete participation of our peers, regardless of race, social class, and gender. It is remarkable that even the parts of the song "Sono sethu, ubumnyama" (Our sin is being Black) and "Vuka Shaka, sibagwaze" (Rise up Shaka, let us stab them) do not create any tensions among students. We all sing with one voice even though this would have been absurd in the past.

HISR-44 PERSPECTIVE

The voices and body movements become immensely powerful communication tools during our protests. Bound by a common goal, to shake off the burden of fees that prevent us from focusing on our studies, the songs play a great role in the chemical composition of our systems, which compels us never to give up on the good work we have begun. In particular, **Senzeni na?** kind of put us in the shoes of those struggle icons who had to face the evils of apartheid head-on. As a group, we feel connected as if by an umbilical cord. This song motivates us to walk long distances to present our grievances at the government headquarters without any fatigue.

DISCUSSION OF SONG 1

The students' perspectives on the songs above raise important issues about apartheid in South Africa. Almost every adult South African knows song 1 as well as the story around the persecution of Solomon Mahlangu, who was hanged in 1979 for fighting the apartheid state. There is no province in South Africa that has no township or road named after this hero. In the language of

Aristotle, the first song can be understood as rhetoric, which refers to the use of language in such a way as to impress the listener and influence them for or against a certain course of action (Freese 1992, vii).

Highly esteemed by the Greeks, rhetoric is as old as language itself and the beginnings of social and political life (ibid.). Three modes of persuasion characteristic of rhetoric and furnished by the spoken word emerge in the song above. These are the speaker/orator, the audience, and the speech itself. As far as this song is concerned, it was sung for the authorities of apartheid during the struggle. Thus the speaker/orator was understood in the plural as singers sang as a group to achieve a common goal: fighting against apartheid. The audience was the oppressor and the speech was the message carried through the lyrics of the song. Group dynamics made the song an effective tool in the fight against the political system. The dynamic nature of struggle songs enable them to be removed from their initial place to any environment to which they can speak, hence the notion of mobility of song genres (Borthwick and Moy 2004). In the context of the students' protests, the speaker/orator remains part of the group. The audience is both the institutions' management as well as the law enforcement agents who always seem to be in alliance against the "oppressed" masses. The lyrics are only alive through the performances, which give them the power that causes some reaction in those to whom they are directed.

When the root of the verb *-enza* (to do) and its suffix *–eni* (what have we done) are used together with *na?* (an emphatic form of the question form structure in the isiZulu language), this can only mean urgency of issues under consideration. In the case of this song, the singers are emphasizing that they are ill-treated even though they have not done anything wrong. Sung at funerals and rallies during apartheid, this protest song brings memories of sadness, as its tempo and rhythm are reminiscent of the sufferings of Black people in the past dispensation. Surface repetition as well as deep structural repetition in the song (signified by *na?*) display emotions of despair and melancholy.

The song with the second highest number of citations, forty, or 80 percent of the sample, is "Solomoni."

Song 2: Solomoni (Solomon)

Call:	Solomoni!
Response:	iYho Solomoni (three times)
	(O yes, Solomon)
Call:	Wayelisoja

	(He was a soldier)
Response:	iSoja loMkhonto weSizwe
	(A soldier for Mkhonto weSizwe)
Call:	Elabulawa
	(Who was killed)
Response:	Ngamabhul'eAfrika
	(By the Boers in Africa)

HISR-17 PERSPECTIVE

The protest songs we sang during the #FeesMustFall movement empowered me in many ways. I felt that just as I was learning the history of my country I was also becoming part of the history we were making. The song "Solomoni!" for example, made me identify with the street name of the township, Ashdown in Pietermaritzburg, from which my roommate comes. Being a white young South African woman who knew nothing about Solomoni Mahlangu, I learned a touching story of a young MK soldier who died a disgraceful death when he was hanged by the apartheid government in 1979. This is a very recent history of my own country, yet I did not know it. This iconic figure died at a tender age of twenty-three, which instilled feelings of shame about the apartheid government from which I benefited. The songs invoke feelings of sadness and the last words by Solomon, "My blood will nourish the tree that will bear the fruits of freedom. Tell my people that I love them. They must continue the fight," can only reinforce my intentions never to have a hand in the persecution of my fellow citizens.

HISR-23 PERSPECTIVE

The song "Solomoni" encourages me to be selfless. It conjures patriotism in me when I think that a young man, Solomon, did not spare his life. He showed that his country came before all else. I remember the last time we sang that song, many of us were in tears, especially when the police used tear gas to disperse us without listening to our story.

DISCUSSION OF SONG 2

The song "Solomon," just as the two participants mentioned, is a narrative of a young martyr who died for what he believed in: justice for all mankind. Serving as a repertoire and archive, the song evokes feelings of patriotism in the youth of South Africa as seen in the solidarity the #FeesMustFall movement displayed. Fayoyin and Nieuwoudt (2017) support these ideas when they maintain that songs "promote group cohesion and facilitate emotional bonding" (Fayoyin and Nieuwoudt 2017, 1–2). They further assert that music can be seen as a tool to advocate for awareness toward messages conveyed through songs (ibid.). These positions are apt when one considers what the participants said.

The third song was mentioned by the respondents thirty-eight times, or 76 percent of the sample.

Song 3: Ilizwe loo-khokho bethu (Land of our great grandparent)

Call:	Sizabalaz'elilizwe loo-khokho bethu
	(We are fighting for this land of our great–grandparents)
Response:	Sizabalaz'elilizwe
	(We are fighting for this land)
Call:	Sizabalaz'elilizwe labant'abamnyama
	(We are fighting for this land of the Blacks)
Response:	Sizabalaz'elilizwe
	(We are fighting for this land)
Call:	Elilizwe loo-khokho bethu
	(This land of our great-grandparents)
Response:	Sizabalaz'elilizwe
	(We are fighting for this land)
Call:	Elilizwe labant'abamnyama
	(This land of our great-grandparents)
Response:	Sizabalaz'elilizwe
	(We are fighting for this land)

HISR-12 PERSPECTIVE

For me, whenever we sing these songs, I am energized. They serve as a mobilizing tool, an invitation to be part of the new history by our generation. It feels right to come together with my fellow students in the fight for justice.

One of the songs about Black people's land appropriation, "Ilizwe loo-khokho bethu," which we sang during picketing, evokes feelings of melancholy, as I feel disgusted about the unfairness of the apartheid era. The struggle icons such as Nelson Mandela should rejoice wherever they see young people trying hard to eradicate discrimination. Their blood and sweat was not in vain.

HISR-39 PERSPECTIVE

As an isiXhosa young man who relies on the wages of a single parent (who works as a domestic servant), tremendous anger saturates my entire being as I ask myself why being born Black should be a curse. Singing and dancing for "Ilizwe loo-khokho bethu" lets out, and allows me to dispel, the feelings of anger that consume me. I always feel my white counterpart has had an easy life while mine has been full of burdens. After letting out all that negative energy through song and dance I feel calm and a sense of forgiveness takes over, especially as we engage in this campaign with our fellow white brothers and sisters. The songs sung during the #FeesMustFall campaign charged me with a strong will power to be in solidarity with those who held similar beliefs to mine. No higher order of authority could silence me.

DISCUSSION OF SONG 3

The third song mainly addresses the sensitive issues of land reallocation. The 1913 Natives Land Act allocated only 7 percent of arable land to Africans while giving the rest of the fertile land to the whites. According to the Restitution of Land Rights Act 22 of 1994, land that had been seized from communities after 1913 due to racial discrimination had to be returned to them. Alternatively, such communities had to be fairly compensated for it (see Restitution of Land Rights Act 22 of 1994). Political parties debate this issue on a regular basis more than ever before. The Economic Freedom Fighters (EFF), under the leadership of Julius Malema, they say that the time for restitution (without compensation) is now. Songs such as "Ilizwe loo-khokho bethu" highlight contemporary matters, among them land, as viewed by young people in the present.

The fourth song was mentioned by thirty-six respondents, or 72 percent of the sample.

Song 4: Thina sizwe (We, the Nation)

Call:	Thina sizwe
	(We the nation)
Response:	Thina sizwe, esimnyama
	(We the nation of Blacks)
Call:	Sikhalela
	(We are crying for)
Response:	Sikhalela, izwe lethu
	(We are crying for our land)
Call:	Elathathwa
	(That was taken)
Response:	Elathathwa ngamaburu
	(That was taken by the Boers)
Call:	Mababethwe
	(They should be hit)
Response:	Mababethwe bazoyek'umhlaba wethu
	(They should be hit so that they leave our land alone)
Call:	Mababethwe
	(They should be hit)
Response:	Mababethwe bazoyek'umhlaba wethu
	(They should be hit so that they leave our land alone)

HISR-15 PERSPECTIVE

The song, "Thina sizwe" was, in most cases, sung mainly at the end of the day's picketing activities. For me at this time we would be very tired and most of the time some of the students would have been taken by the police for disturbing public peace. Nevertheless, those of us that were lucky enough to escape would gather and sing this song as a prayer. Even though we were exhausted, the song relayed the message that we were not going to give up.

HISR- 45 PERSPECTIVE

"Thina sizwe," a song sung very softly at any given time always brought a somber mood to those of us that had survived the events of the day. For me songs like this one represent emotion that cannot be spoken or written. Through song I feel like I am connected to everyone who supports our effort to make things right. This is not only for us, but we are continuing the legacy left by our forebears. I found it remarkable that there was no point at which anyone displayed an intention to quit. Exhausted as we would be, we did not surrender.

DISCUSSION OF SONG 4

The song has been widely sung by various people in South Africa. It commemorates part of the anticolonial struggle. Recently, the political party Freedom Front Plus wanted it censored, saying that it has a harmful effect on minority groups. This song, like most of the struggle songs, has a way of triggering memories that take us back in time and space. We were not there during the struggle but through songs such as this one our imaginations are sparked and we are building memories that link protest and the power of these songs.

The fifth popular song in the sample was "Asiphelelanga," which respondents mentioned thirty-five times, or 70 percent of the sample.

Song 5: Asiphelelanga (Some people are missing)

Call:	Asiphelelanga
	(Some people are missing)
Response:	Asiphelelanga
Call:	U. . . . .
	(So and so)
Response:	Akekho la
	(is not here) (this gets repeated three times)
Call:	Asiphelelanga
Response:	Asiphelelanga
(More names of missing individuals mentioned)	

HISR-09 PERSPECTIVE

Songs have a special way of igniting a spirit of unity among protestors. Whenever the song "Asiphelelanga" was sung it served as a tool to update us and let us to know who the police had taken into custody or the management suspended from the university. Hearing their names made our sense of purpose real and we fought tooth and nail to have their suspension uplifted or their release from jail a reality.

HISR-26 PERSPECTIVE

I was always vigilant during mass action. I did not want my name to be among those that would be called out during the late hours before we retire to our residences. I was, however, one of those who provided feedback to the main activists about who I saw taken into the police van.

DISCUSSION OF SONG 5

The fixed formulaic phrase "Asiphelelanga," accompanied by the leader mentioning the name of the missing persons, indicates that the song is a community affair. It is performed for an audience. The audience in this case is both the singers and those to whom the songs are directed. Everyone becomes attentive as the leader mentions the names. This is an example of a song that has crossed boundaries since the time of apartheid. Its fluidity is visible in that during the apartheid era it was sung to name and shame those who had collaborated with the oppressors while pretending to be allies with the struggle icons. In the #FeesMustFall context, naming was a way of alerting everyone about those who had become victims of the group effort to right the wrongs of the institution of learning. In both the apartheid era and the #FeesMustFall movement, the witnessing of naming names is a communal event. The meaning behind these names changed, however, as the song that had been used a tool to name and shame dissenters was now, in 2015–2016, a means to name victims who needed rescue.

CONCLUSION

During apartheid, the oppressed adopted several ways to address their situation. While some were violent, others were nonconfrontational. Among the latter, song became a tool to illustrate the broken souls that characterized Blacks in South Africa during apartheid. Songs accompanied the gains of having more Black students in college after apartheid and the challenges that came with it. Songs conveyed the need to open up the curriculum to all by offering financial aid to a larger number of students and by including the experiences and accomplishments of Black South Africans and the Global South in the educational narrative. Decoloniality was no longer an option; it had become a necessity to reflect newer methods of decolonizing the curriculum and university classrooms.

The study revealed that through song manipulation, various effects were produced. For instance, repetition (of parts in each song) served a purpose of emphasizing a point while keeping the singers in solidarity. The study also demonstrated how songs can be recontextualized when they move from one music genre to another even while maintaining the same words (songs 1–4). The element of substitution (modeled through song 5) illustrates that the same song can be used over and over again with different intentions. In song 5, for example, naming could be used as a tool to exalt individuals, such as when they had been locked up for a good cause, as well as to shame them when they had done the contrary. Songs further allow reflection for the performers as they protest through long demonstrations. In this way, the dynamic nature of songs allows them to be used to address various situations; they can transcend their initial environment and have multiple coded meanings.

Songs sung during the #FeesMustFall movement contributed to an awakening of conscience in a new generation as they appealed to students from all backgrounds to direct their minds toward attaining justice for all. Thus, even though South Africa is still far from embracing what a democratic country should look like, there is hope that future generations will reap the harvest from the seeds sown by the present cohort. From this study, I am convinced that struggle songs will continue to live on in the memories of people. Not even the recent agreement (Magome 2012) entered into by ANC members and AfriForum about how the struggle songs should be sung with restraint given their hurtful impact on minority groups will stop these songs from being part of the demonstrations that decry discrimination of any kind.

As is clear from the words of the "born free" students during the #FeesMustFall protests, the power of these songs transcends local situations; this was seen in the struggles during apartheid as well as in the early years of democracy. These songs retain their power as they bring people together through melody, harmony, repetition, and communal singing. United in their goals for greater access to a more equitable education, increased financial support, and a representative curriculum of the history and experiences of Black South Africans, the protests created interracial and interethnic community among the nation's rising generations in their efforts to hold their government accountable for a true democracy.

NOTES

1. See the Appendix.

REFERENCES

Akoojee, S., and Nkomo, M. 2007. "Access and Quality in South African Higher Education: The Twin Challenges of Transformation." *SAJHE* 21, no. 3: 385–99.

Barnes, C. 2008. "Incentive and Sanctions in Peace Processes and Conditionality." *Accord*, issue 19: 36–39.

Borthwick, S., and Moy, R. 2004. *Popular Music Genres: An Introduction*. Edinburgh: Edinburgh University Press.

Even-Zohar, I. 1990. "The Position of Translated Literature within the Literary Polysystem." *Poetics Today* 11, no. 1: 45–51.

Fayoyin, A., and Nieuwoudt, S. 2017. "The Power of Song in the Struggle for Health and Development Outcomes in Africa: Lessons for Social and Behaviour Change Programmes." *Intellectual Property Rights: Open Access* 5, no. 2: 189 doi:104172/2375-4516.1000189.

Freese, J. H. 1992. *Aristotle. The 'Art' of Rhetoric*. London: William Heinemann.

Hermans, T. 1999. *Translation in Systems: Descriptive and Systemic Approaches Explained*. Manchester: St Jerome Publishing.

Holloway, I., and Wheeler, S. 2002. *Qualitative Research for Nurses*. Oxford: Blackwell Scientific Publication.

Kruger A., and Wallmach, K. 1997. "Research Methodology for the Description of a Source Text and its Translation(s)—a South African Perspective." *South African Journal of African Languages* 17, no. 4: 119–26.

Mbhele, M., and Walker, G. R. 2017. "Struggle Songs Let Us Be Heard." *Guardian*, October 13, 2017, Arts and Culture. https://mg.co.zaarticle/2017-10-13. Accessed March 15, 2018.

Malabou, C. 2008. *What Should We Do With Our Brain?* New York: Fordham University Press.

Nkoala, S. M. Sisanda. 2013. "Songs That Shaped the Struggle: A Rhetorical Analysis of South African Struggle Songs." *African Yearbook of Rhetoric* 4, no. 1, 2013, online. ISSN 2305–7785.

Mouton, J. 2001. *How to Succeed in Your Masters and Doctoral Studies: A South African Guide and Resource Book*. Pretoria: Van Schaik.

Munday, J. 2016. *Introducing Translation Studies: Theories and Applications*. London: Routledge.

Naude, J. A. 2011. "From Submissive to Agency: An Overview of Developments in Translation Studies and Some Implications for Language Practice in Africa." *Southern African Linguistics and Applied Languages Studies* 29, no. 3: 223–41.

Perkins, Eugene. 1976. "Literature of Combat: Poetry of African Liberation Movements." *Journal of Black Studies 7*, no. 2: 226: http://www.jstor.org/stable/2783968. Accessed March 5, 2018.

Pring-Mill, R. 1987. "The Roles of Revolutionary Song—a Nicaraguan Assessment in Popular Music." *Popular Music* 6, no. 2: 183. http://www.jstor.org/stable/853420. Accessed March 5, 2018.

Reiss, K. 1989. "Text Types, Translation Types and Translation Assessment." Translated by A. Chesterman. In *Readings in Translation Theory*, edited by A. Chesterman. Helsinki: Finn Lecura, 105–15.

Toury, Gideon. 1995. *Descriptive Translation Studies and Beyond*. Amsterdam: John Benjamin.

Zondi, N. B. 2008. "Bahlabelelelani—Why do they sing? Gender and Power in Contemporary Women's Songs." PhD dissertation, University of KwaZulu-Natal.

Zondi, N. B. 2011. "Three Protagonists in B. W. Vilakazi's Ezinkomponi (On the Mine Compounds)." *Literator* 32, no. 2: 173–87.

Zondi, N., and Canonici, N. 2005. "Protest against Social Inequalities in B. W. Vilakazi's poem, 'Ngoba . . . sewuthi' (Because . . . you now say)." *Literator* 26, no. 1: 83–99.

WEBSITES

Call and response (music). https://en.m.wikipedia.org. Accessed November 18, 2018.

Chapter 2, subsection 29(1)(b) of the Constitution. https://mg.co.za.

#FeesMustFall: History of South African student protests reflects inequality's grip. https://mg.co.za. Accessed September 21, 2018.

Magome, Momogotsi. 2012. "Struggle songs will be sung 'with restraint,' ANC Tau SA agree." https://www.iol.co.za.

Music in the movement against apartheid. www.htps://en.m.wikipedia.org. Accessed May 25, 2018.

Natives Land Act of 1913. www.sahistroy.org.za/topic/native-land-act-1913. Accessed May 30, 2018.

Restitution of Land Rights Act 22 of 1994. www.justice.gov.za/lcc/doc/1994–022.pdf. Accessed May 29, 2018.

Zama, Zanele. 2018. "Thina Sizwe'—the Song the Freedom Front Plus Want Censored." http://www.702.co.za/articles/312297/listen-thina-sizwe-the-song-the-freedom-front-plus-want-censored. Accessed March 25, 2021.

https://www.gov.za/sites/default/files/images/a108-96.pdf. Accessed October 27, 2018.

https://ukzn.ac.za/about-ukzn/history/. Accessed on 25 March 2021.

https://www.ukzn.ac.za>about-ukzn>history. Accessed August 24, 2019.

https://www.ukzn.ac.za/docs. Accessed August 24, 2019.

https://www.mut.ac.zahistorical-background. Accessed August 24, 2019.

https://en.wikipedia.org>wiki>university_of_zululand. Accessed August 24, 2019.

https://en.m.wikipedia.org>wiki>ML_Sultan_Technikon. Accessed August 24, 2019.

APPENDIX TO THE INTRINSIC POWER OF SONGS SUNG DURING PROTESTS AT SOUTH AFRICAN INSTITUTIONS OF HIGHER LEARNING

Questionnaire sample showing participating institutions

Dear Participant

I am Nompumelelo Zondi. I am conducting a survey on the study entitled 'Intrinsic Power of Songs Sung During Protests at Institutions of Higher Learning (South Africa): Students' Perspectives'

Your institution has been selected to participate in this study whose ethical clearance was obtained from my previous institution at the time of the conception of the study. Please note that participation is voluntary.

The questionnaire will be distributed by my research assistant in your institution between 12:00 noon and 04:00 pm on 15 February 2017. He/she will be stationed at the proximity of your student center. You are asked to return your questionnaire to the same research assistant between 10:00am and 03:00pm on Thursday 2 March 2017. He/she will stand with a box marked #FEESMUSTFALLSONGS at the same venue the questionnaire was distributed.

Even though it is not compulsory to provide your biographical details, please go carefully through the 3 questions on the questionnaire.
Please note that this document is made up of two pages (including this page). The first page will bear a unique number written on the top right hand side to identify it. The second page will have a stamp of a shortened version of the name of your institution at the bottom of the page. If these two identifiers are absent, the form will not be valid.

Name and surname of participant..
Name of the Institution ....

1. Are you a student at the campus where this questionnaire was distributed? **YES/ NO (Circle the correct response).**

   If your answer to the above question is **NO**, please do not proceed with this questionnaire. You may destroy your questionnaire in any way you deem fit. However, if your answer is **YES**, proceed to the second question.

2. Did you participate in the recent students "#FeesMustFall" movement? **YES/ NO (Circle the correct response).** If your answer is **NO**, then please do not proceed with this questionnaire. You may destroy your questionnaire in any way you deem fit. However, if your answer is **YES**, then please proceed to the next and final question.

3. In your opinion, what **role did songs** play in the "#FeesMustFall" movement? Kindly elucidate on your response by providing at least **one song** that mainly spoke to you during these protests **(Please feel free to also write at the back of this page should you need to)**

....
....
....
....
....
....
....
....
....
....
....
....
....
....
....
....
....
....
....
....
....
....
....
....
....
....

Thank you for your participation

CONTRIBUTORS

Naomi André is professor of Afroamerican and African Studies, Women's Studies, and the Residential College at the University of Michigan. Her books include *Black Opera: History, Power, Engagement* (2018), which examines race, gender, sexuality, and nation in opera in the United States and South Africa. She is the inaugural Scholar in Residence at the Seattle Opera.

Yolanda Covington-Ward is department chair and associate professor in the Department of Africana Studies (secondary appointment in anthropology) at the University of Pittsburgh. Her book *Gesture and Power: Religion, Nationalism, and Everyday Performance in Congo* (Duke University Press, 2016) won both the Amaury Talbot and Elliott P. Skinner Book Awards. She is currently president of the Association of Africanist Anthropology.

Frieda Ekotto is Lorna Goodison Collegiate Professor of Afroamerican and African Studies and Comparative Literature at the University of Michigan. Her early work involves an interdisciplinary exploration of interactions among philosophy, law, literature, and African cinema. She is currently working on LGBTQI+ in sub-Saharan Africa and holds an Honorary Degree from Colorado College. She is the second vice president of Modern Language Association and incoming president in 2023.

Anita Gonzalez is professor of African American Studies and Performing Arts at Georgetown University and a co-founder of the Racial Justice Institute. She is the coeditor of *Black Performance Theory* and is the author of *Afro-Mexico: Dancing Between Myth and Reality* (2010) and *Jarocho's Soul* (2004). She is also a series editor for the *Dance in Dialogue Series* at Bloomsbury Press.

Jendele Hungbo is associate professor of Communication and Media Studies at Bowen University, Iwo, Nigeria. He previously taught at North-West University, Mafikeng, South Africa. His research work on media and cultural studies in Africa has appeared in leading academic journals.

Judith T. Irvine is Edward Sapir Distinguished University Professor of Linguistic Anthropology Emerita at the University of Michigan. Her research focuses on language and communication in social, cultural, and historical contexts. She has conducted ethnographic, linguistic, and sociolinguistic fieldwork in Africa (mainly Senegal); research on the colonial history of African linguistics; and theoretical work on ideologies of language.

Marthe Djilo Kamga is an artist who works in multiple media (as a performer, film director, author, photographer). The questions that run through her work concern the reappropriation of imaginary and real spaces, the silence in the interactions between oppressed and oppressors, and the transmission and archiving of stories by and for the invisible people.

David Kerr is a research associate at the University of Johannesburg. He has published in the fields of African Studies, cultural and social anthropology, cultural studies and media studies. His current research explores the everyday and often ephemeral forms of street performance which occur in the Dar es Salaam's informal settlements. Alongside his academic work he is involved in an initiative which seeks to form equitable and ethical collaborations with musicians in Dar es Salaam.

Innocentia J. Mhlambi is associate professor in the Department of African Languages at the University of the Witwatersrand. She teaches African-language literatures, Black film studies, oral literature and popular culture, and visual culture. She is the author of *African-Language Literatures: Perspectives on isiZulu Fiction and Popular Black Television Series (2012)* and co-editor of *Mintiro ya Vuulavula: Arts, National Identities and Democracy* (2021). She is currently researching Black opera in post-1994 South Africa.

Thomas M. Pooley is associate professor of musicology and Chair of the Department of Art and Music at the University of South Africa, and coeditor of *Muziki: Journal of Music Research in Africa*. He conducts research on music, language, and cognition in isiZulu performances and tone systems in Southern Africa.

Nikolas Sweet is assistant professor of anthropology at Grinnell College. His research on language and social interaction in West Africa engages with questions of verbal creativity, ethnicity, and mobility.

Nompumelelo ('Mpume') Zondi is professor and head of the African Languages Department at the University of Pretoria, South Africa. Her research is predominantly rooted in gender issues. She has published broadly locally and internationally in accredited journals focusing on traditional songs. Her first monograph, *Bahlabelelelani-Why do they sing? Gender and Power in Contemporary Women's Songs* was published in 2020.

Pages in italics indicate figures and tables.